SIN OFFERING: FREEDOM FROM SIN

Bible quotations are from the King James Version of the Bible.

First Edition published in 2008
Second Edition translated by Yeong Kook Park and Joseph Park / 2013
Published by Good News Mission
300 Nassau Rd, Huntington NY 11743

Translation Copyright © 2015 by Good News Mission
All Rights Reserved. No Portion of this book may be reproduced
in any form without the written permission of the Publisher.

ISBN 978-0-692-40297-9

Printed in U.S.A.

Sin Offering
Freedom from Sin

PASTOR OCK SOO PARK

PREFACE

While the Israelites were waiting for Moses to come down from Mt. Sinai, they made the golden calf and committed the sin of idolatry. Because they did not know how to take care of this sin, 3,000 of them had to die. Had they at that time given a sin offering and received the forgiveness of sin, they would not have to have died.

In addition, the children of Israel murmured against God, resulting in a plague that killed 14,700. The plague ended when Aaron made an atonement for the people.

Today as well, people who do not have to die are dying, and people who do not have to be cursed are cursed because they do not know about the forgiveness of sin. A countless number of people have fallen into sin and are heading towards destruction.

This book is a compilation of sermons from a Bible Seminar held for the citizens of Seoul in 2007 titled, "Sin Offering: Freedom from Sin." At the time, many citizens of Seoul came to the seminar, listened to the words of the Bible Seminar and received the forgiveness of sin in their hearts. At the time, I preached about the sin offering from the book of Leviticus in the Old Testament, the four gospels of the New Testament, and Hebrews.

The offerings shown in Leviticus in the Old Testament are images of the offerings of the true Tabernacle in heaven. Through searching these images closely, we can clearly see Jesus in the New Testament who fulfilled the prophecies of the Old Testament. Furthermore, Hebrews allows us to understand the sin offering that was given in the true Tabernacle in heaven. When such words were preached, many people, who had suffered in sin despite attending churches, realized the secret of redemption which was finished once and for all and were filled with joy.

We become free from sin when we come to precisely know the sin offering that Jesus, who is our high priest, accomplished for us. We come to gain the assurance of being born again, become freed from destruction, and gain eternal life. I am wishing that many will gain this in their lives. With this wish, *Sin Offering: Freedom from Sin*, has been written. I glorify God who has led me to publish this book.

I hope that through this collection of sermons many who were suffering in sin will gain the assurance of the forgiveness of sin. I hope that they will live a joyful spiritual life.

Ock Soo Park

April 25, 2008
Ock Soo Park,
Pastor, Good News Gangnam Church

Sin Offering
Freedom from Sin

CONTENTS

4	Preface
9	1. While He Doeth Somewhat Against Any of the Commandments of the Lord
34	2. If His Sin Which He Hath Sinned Come to His Knowledge
56	3. Bring a Kid of the Goats, a Female Without Blemish
76	4. And He Shall Lay His Hands on the Head of the Sin Offering
97	5. Shall Take the Blood Thereof With His Finger, Put It Upon the Horns of the Altar
119	6. It Shall Be Forgiven Him
143	7. People Who Were Destroyed Because They Did Not Have the Sin Offering
160	8. The Power of the Sin Offering Which Has Finished the Judgment
184	9. The Eternal Sin Offering Given at the Temple of Heaven
209	10. For the Law Maketh Men High Priests, Which Have Infirmity
235	11. The Completed Offering

CHAPTER 1
While He Doeth Somewhat Against Any of the Commandments of the Lord

When people commit sin, such as adultery, theft, telling a lie, or hating somebody, for the most part they will think, "I should not commit sin, I should never do such a thing again." This is the first stage of thought. But, thinking like this is a completely wrong way to live spiritual life. God made man to be in pain when he is sick, so that through his symptoms the cause of his disease can be treated. In the same way, through the act of committing adultery, one must see that, "Ah, inside of me, I have a heart that is different from the heart of God," and come to the realization that he has an adulterous heart.

Hello, everyone. I am so thankful that I can see you again here at the Olympic Stadium and share the precious Word of God with you. I would like to speak about the sin offering during this one week. People vaguely know that Jesus died on the cross and that sins are forgiven. But I'd like to take this one week and talk with you about how our sins are forgiven through the sin offering, how we can take care of the traits of sin that arise within us, how we can be freed from sin, and how we can have freedom. I'm hoping that this would not end with you simply studying this from the Bible. But, by the time this conference is over, I hope that through the sin offering, you will all be freed from sin. I hope that you will be able to sing, "Happy day, happy day, when Jesus washed my sins away!" I hope that you will sing that song as you live a joyful spiritual life.

This is our first session and I would like to talk to you about the aspect, *while he doeth somewhat against any other commandments of the Lord concerning things which ought not to be done and be guilty.*

And if any one of the common people sin through ignorance, while he doeth somewhat against any of the commandments of the Lord concerning things which ought not to be done, and be guilty; Or if his sin, which he hath sinned, come to his knowledge: then he shall bring his offering, a kid of the goats, a female without blemish, for his sin which he hath sinned. And he shall lay his hand upon the head of the sin offering, and slay the sin offering in the place of the burnt offering. And the priest shall take of the blood thereof with his finger, and put it upon the horns of the altar of burnt offering, and shall pour out all the blood thereof at the bottom of the altar. And he shall take away all the fat thereof, as the fat is taken away from off the sacrifice of peace offerings; and the priest shall burn it upon the altar for a sweet savour unto the Lord; and the priest shall make an atonement for him, and it shall be forgiven him. (Leviticus 4:27-31)

Our Lives Follow the Exact Path of the Prodigal Son

The Bible tells us about our lives. Genesis chapter one talks about the creation of the heaven and the earth. In chapter three, it talks about how man commits sin. Afterwards, man lives wallowing inside of the pain, sadness, suffering, despair, and hopelessness that comes through sin. But He forgave our sins by crucifying Jesus on the cross. After that truth comes into our hearts by faith, we receive the forgiveness of sins and we can rejoice. Then in the book of Revelation it talks about how we enter into the new heaven. This is what comprises the 66 books of the Bible. Leviticus chapter 4 verses 27 through 31, which we read tonight, has condensed all

While He Doeth Somewhat Against Any of the Commandments of the Lord

of this in a very simple way. It starts with committing sin, and through committing that sin the curse falls upon the sinner. The goat must be put to death for this sinner and the blood from the lamb is sprinkled. It begins with the process of sin and proceeds until it reaches, "It shall be forgiven him." Our whole life mirrors this plotline.

When we look at the stories in the Bible, although they may seem different, but it's so interesting that they all flow the same way. In the story of the prodigal son, in Luke chapter 15, we see the younger son departing from the father. Afterwards, he lives riotously, spends time with the harlots, falls into sin, and becomes very pitiful. Then he realizes this and returns to the father. The father puts the cleanest and best robe on him. This represents the washing away of sins. Then it talks about how he eats, drinks, and enjoys himself at the father's house. So go all the stories of the 66 books of the Bible. Then, I want to ask all of you here this evening, where are you? Are you inside of the story? Your life is contained in the story of the prodigal son. Your life is also inside of the words of the Bible. Just like the prodigal son, you too, are walking through life.

People trust themselves, become high-hearted, arrogant, and commit sin. This is how our lives begin. Do you know the first thing we learn to do when we are born? We learn to speak and we learn how to live. But even before this occurs, Satan begins to work as soon as we are born, to lead us to depart from God and live arrogantly. So when we are young and we are told, "You're pretty, you're great, you're smart," these words become etched in our minds.

When I was a student, I did not do so well in my studies. But somehow, when I was in the third grade of elementary school, I finished third place in my class. It was my first time doing so well. This was at a school in the countryside, immediately after the Korean War. There were buildings burnt down, and we were pretty much studying underneath the trees. I brought my report card to my father. He was so happy and he took me to my grandfather. My father said, "Father, Ock Soo recently placed third in his class."

My grandfather heard this and was so happy. He said, "Wow, that kid. Wow."

It was the third grade, so I was about 10 years old. So it happened 55 years ago.

What my grandfather said at that time, "Wow, that kid, wow," I still cannot forget those words. It's not because I'm so smart that I am able to remember those words from when I did well.

The good that you do for others, the time you prayed all night long, how you fasted for several days and prayed, or how you helped others, all of these things are etched in your memory. It's not because you are smart that you remember these things. Satan has you to remember them. No matter how poor someone may be, he retains the memories of the great things he has done. Go ahead and try to put down the most detesable people around you. They will say, "Yeah, right. Still, at least I did this!" and will have that kind of a heart. Satan has exalted the hearts of man. When you think that you are smart, or that you did something well, your heart becomes higher and higher. The problem with your heart becoming exalted is that you become unable to hear in your heart what others are saying. We can easily test whether you are high-hearted or not.

When you open the Bible and read about the people with high-hearts, you can see that the Scriptures have not entered into their hearts. Even after going to church for 10 or 20 years, people barely have a heart that comes from receiving the Scriptures. It is because their hearts are high, so that the Word does not enter them.

How do people live without having the Word enter into them? Just outwardly, they go to church and they say, "Today, I went to service, I gave offering, and I prayed." They say these things but they go on living with the heart of believing in themselves more and more.

Spiritual life can only be accomplished in the heart. However, there are many people who pray and read the Bible but walk in their own world of Spiritual life, which has nothing to do with God. The younger son in Luke chapter 15 was unable to listen to anyone. The father would say, "Do you think doing business is easy?"

The younger son continues to request for the wealth, saying, "Father, give me money."

So the younger son took the money. Then what happened to him? He riotously spent all of the money.

We might think, "If he had taken about 1 million dollars from his father, he could have spent 7 to 8 hundred thousand dollars on himself and then he would have 2 to 3 hundred thousand dollars remaining. If that were the case would he have to starve? He spent all of the money with the harlots, like a fool. He should have saved some." It's easy to say these things as we sit here. But once you fall into the harlots, you are unable to control yourself. You think that it's because the younger son was a fool that he turned out that way. But it is because you have not fallen into the younger son's situation yet. If you had, you would have also turned out the same way. Now, the younger son had lost everything and he went into the pigpen and was hungry. He ate the husks that the swine ate. At that point, do you think he will be regretful or not? Once you're in that kind of a situation, no matter how foolish you are, you're bound to become regretful.

Once he realized his sin and he returned to the father, he was received by the father, who washed him clean, and put good clothes on him. This represents the washing away of sins. Secondly, the father put a ring on the hand of the younger son. This symbolizes that he has now become the son of the father. The father put shoes on the younger son's feet, they ate the fatted calf and were merry.

All of this is connected with the story of our lives. Our lives flow through this kind of process. But we don't live a thousand or ten thousand years in this life. Typically we live about 70 to 80 years. But for some people, that's too long and they die at 60. Even that's too long and some die at 40. There are also people who die at 30. Of those people, there are some people whose lives end while they're in the midst of believing in their own greatness. Some people's lives end while they trust themselves, become arrogant, and live riotously. There are some people who have failed in everything, they live in suffering and in hunger, and then they die. Some people realize all of this and they end their lives in that state. Some people turn around and they end their lives back at the father's house. That's how life is bound to be. If life ends before receiving the forgiveness of sins, before returning to the father's house, it would be a pitiful end.

The words of the Bible that you will hear during this one week will take you quickly through that life, which would normally take you 70 or 80 years. Even without becoming a drunk, becoming riotous, or frequenting brothels, you can go through the process of these things in your heart. We will learn about these things and learn how to return to the father during this one week.

I sincerely would like to tell you one more time, not just in theory, but by the day this conference is over, I hope you will have shed your sin and will be there at that glorious seat; that holy seat; that righteous seat; like the younger son at his father's house. I hope that you will become one with the father God and will be people who live together with Him eternally. That is my sincere hope.

The Pastor's Wife a Long Time Ago

A long time ago, there was a pastor who lived in Pyeonyang. He was tall and he was very handsome. With a very gentle heart, he dealt with his church members. He was a very precious pastor. When this pastor would give a sermon, the church members received great grace in their hearts. However, the wife of this great pastor, we cannot express how ugly she was. Not only was her face ugly, but she was always so envious and so jealous. She would throw a fit even when the pastor would only say, "Hello," to a female church member. A long time ago, you would wear coats and on that coat they would attach these white collars around the neck of the coat.

But this pastor's collar was always dirty and black. If his coat had a hole in it, it should be patched up with the same fabric as the coat. But the pastor's wife would patch up his black coats with yellow fabric, and she would patch up his white coats with blue fabric. Even when it came to the rubber shoes, she would always buy these black rubber shoes that were an inch or two bigger than the pastor's feet. The pastor would always be dragging his shoes around.

So, according to this pastor's wife, "If he's good looking, girls are going to follow him around. If his shoes fit well, he's going to walk around with those girls." That's why she would not allow those things. When the pastor would come home from visiting his church members, the pastor's wife would go around yelling and throwing a fit, saying "Which girl were you hanging out with today?" This pastor would always carry around two coins in his coat pocket. So whenever his wife would say these things, he would shake the coins in front of her and say, "Be quiet. I'll buy some candy for you." In this way, he spoke kindly to his wife.

While He Doeth Somewhat Against Any of the Commandments of the Lord

The church members thought, "How in the world can this be? Is there no other woman in the world, that a great pastor like him married a woman like her?"

Once, in the middle of Sunday Service there was a loud noise outside so an elder quickly stepped outside. There was a candy vendor, and he was slapping on his metal rods saying that the pastor's wife had taken candy from him on credit. She had told him that he would get paid for the candy on Sunday because that's when the offering comes in. The elder felt so embarrassed, so he quickly paid off the candy vendor, returned to the chapel, and thought, "How could the pastor's wife be this way?"

As more and more time passed, the church members became more and more irritated with the pastor's wife. They even began to think, "I wish the pastor's wife were dead." And maybe it was because of that, not long after, the pastor's wife fell ill and passed away. The pastor wept bitterly. The church members acted as if they were crying, but inside, they were glad that this happened.

Not long after the funeral of the pastor's wife, the elders of the church approached the pastor.

"Pastor, we want to discuss something with you."

"Please, go ahead."

"Pastor, you need to now re-marry. Because your new wife would be the mother of our church, we would like to select her for you. Pastor, please just wait."

"Sure. Go ahead and do that."

From that point on, the elders contacted and searched the neighboring churches, and looked for a beautiful woman. A long time ago, being able to cook and knit well was very important. They then brought in this widow who was excellent at making food and knitting, and brought her in to be the pastor's new wife.

After getting re-married, the pastor's appearance completely changed. His coat was always clean, and his face was very bright and well. And he wore rubber shoes that were always as white and as shiny as jade. The pastor's wife treated the church members so well. The church members would say, "That's our pastor's wife!" and they liked her so much.

The pastor loved his new wife as well. When the pastor returned home from being out his wife would say, "Honey you must be thirsty," and serve him rice punch. After breakfast, she would cut up some fruit for him. The pastor was so happy to be sitting with his wife and talking with her. In this way, one year, two years passed. As the pastor would enjoy being together with his wife and talking with her, he would realize, "Oh, the appointment time for the home visit has already passed! Alright, I won't go on that visit today." Even when he would make plans to pray, the time to pray would also pass him by while he was spending time with his wife. Before, this pastor would not spare any time to spend with his wife, and he would always be reading the Bible, praying, and going on home visits. Now his time spent going to home visits, reading the Bible, and praying grew shorter and shorter while the time that he would spend with his wife grew longer and longer.

Three years passed. More and more people would doze off and fall asleep during the pastor's sermons. There was no more power in the pastor's sermons. Then about the fifth year, the members of the church began to say, "The previous pastor's wife was good. We miss the pastor's wife from back then. I want to see our old pastor who used to wear the black coat, patched up with the yellow fabric. I want to see our pastor again, dragging around those oversized rubber shoes." Only then, the church members realized the value of the pastor's previous wife.

There's the first level of thought and the second level of thought for every person. When facing a certain situation or a certain task, if you put aside the first level of thought that arises immediately, and move on to the second level of thought, often times you will realize that the first level of thought was wrong. That's why people who's hearts are humble and wise do not make decisions at the first level of thought. They think through the second level, the third level, and the fourth level of thought. Even when playing chess, the novice players who think at the first level of thought only think about offensive moves. But a good chess player thinks, "Why is the knight attacking me? Why is the knight moving forward? Should I take out the rook? Oh, then that's going to force him to move his bishop. Oops, I almost lost my rook!" Similarly, they think to the second and to the third level of thought.

Our students go to Africa to preach the Gospel, and from time to time they get sick. Although they go to the hospital, many hospitals in Africa are very shabby. If you say that your stomach hurts, they give you medicine for stomachaches. If you have a fever, they give you medicine to reduce the fever. And if you have a headache, they give you headache medicine. Instead of examining why the stomach hurts, why the patient has a fever, whether he has malaria or typhoid and then treating the cause, they just give you medicine. Such doctors are unworthy. A true doctor is one who searches out the reason why someone is sick and treats the cause.

This is also true with the world of spiritual life. When you do not know the Bible deeply, you make decisions on everything at the first level of thought. "Ah, I told a lie. I'd better stop lying. Oh, I didn't go to church on Sunday. I'd better keep Sundays. Oh, these days, I do not pray. I'd better pray. Ah, I stole! I'd better not steal." These are people who stop at the first level of thought.

But when we read the Bible, God reveals to us the cause, and He shows us the path to get it treated.

Did He Say to Ask for Forgiveness When You Commit Sin?

The words of Leviticus chapter four, that we read today, tells us in detail the process by which a person can be freed from sin once he commits sin. Leviticus chapter four describes the sin offering.

We can see that it is divided into four parts: when a priest commits sin, when the congregation commits sin, when the tribe's ruler commits sin, and when a common person commits sin.

To discuss all four of these aspects, the scope would be too large to cover in one week. So I would like to discuss with you the last part, about the sin offering given when a common person has committed sin.

First, we will all read together chapter 4 verse 27.

And if any one of the common people sin through ignorance, while he doeth somewhat against any of the commandments of the Lord concerning things which ought not to be done, and be guilty;

And then verse 28.

Or if his sin, which he hath sinned, come to his knowledge: then he shall bring his offering, a kid of the goats, a female without blemish, for his sin which he hath sinned.

Everyone, we say, "Oh, I told a lie. I stole. I committed adultery. I committed murder." We call these kinds of things sin. You may be saying in your heart, "Yeah, pastor, I know that already. Everybody knows that stealing is a sin. Everybody knows." You feel that way in your heart, right? Yes, I know that too. Then, what do people do when they commit sin?

"God, I lied today. Please forgive me. I know I shouldn't do that, but that woman was so pretty. So I mindlessly followed her and ended up committing adultery. Lord, please forgive this sin. Lord, somehow and for some reason, I ended up committing such and such a sin."

That is what people say. But, we must ask, is that what God told us to do when we commit sin?

"Hey, what do you mean? I know that if we commit sin we should repent and turn around. Are you telling me that even though we may sin, we do not need to be remorseful; we do not need to turn around? Is that okay?" Is this how you feel in your heart?

I don't know about you, but I was already going to church by the time I was grown up. My mother, long ago, learned the Bible from missionaries and attended church. My mother did not have any brothers or sisters, and her parents loved her very much. Back then, it was forbidden that people go to church. However, even though my grandmother knew, she permitted her to go. My grandfather also knew, but he held his peace and allowed her to go.

But, my mother married into our family, the Park family, and at that time it didn't make sense for a newlywed woman to be attending church. So, she was unable to go to church. You know, when I was young my mother would be knitting or doing some work, and she would always sing praises.

The song that she often sang was,
In rapture when Christ comes again
For us to Him belonging.
I vividly remember how my mother used to sing that hymn.

As we were growing up, Mother would send us to church, so I began attending church from a young age.

We were taught by the church that we needed to repent. And that repentance was to confess all of the sins that you've committed and to beg for God's forgiveness. I thought that was what repentance was and that was what I did. Repentance means to turn around. However, I would commit sins and beg for forgiveness and turn around, but I would find myself sinning again. I would repent and sin again, repent and sin again, repent and sin again. That life repeated itself. Although I was young, I felt I was going to go to hell because of sin. I told many lies. I stole many things. I was terribly tormented. Even though I repented, sin was not resolved.

Every early morning I would go to the chapel, and even before the pastor would come out I would go and kneel on the wooden floor and confess all the sins that I'd committed and begged for forgiveness. I was always the first one to go to the church and I was in charge of ringing the church bell. And the pastor's home didn't have an alarm clock, so I would go and wake him up.

"Pastor! Pastor! It's time for early morning service!"

"Oh! Mr. Park, is it already time for early morning service?"

After the early morning service I would remain by myself and again confess my sins. I repeated this life over and over again for such a long time, but since I was not doing true repentance, there was no change in me. It was just another life of repenting and sinning, repenting and sinning again. I thought that if I became more determined, more strong willed, and tried harder, that it would work out. So I was determined to not sin and I tried to be strong-willed. I am aware now, but when I look back, I didn't know anything then. Can my determination overcome temptation? Can my efforts overcome sin and set me free from sin? I continued to live a life of trying to turn around, becoming determined, and strong-willed every day. But if the repentance I was doing was accurate and right, and Jesus had helped me, then my life of sin would have ended. Instead, my life of sin just continued.

It was at the age of nineteen when the day came that I can never forget. I realized what true repentance was according to the Bible. I became free from sin. Afterwards, I never once was determined to be free from sin, but Jesus entered into my life and my life changed so much. Back then, every evening I would gather with my friends, play poker, and do bad things. "I shouldn't go there anymore, if I go there I'm going to commit sins. If I go today, I might steal other people's apples and peanuts and dig up other people's sweet potatoes and eat them. I shouldn't go." But even though I would say those things, I could not hold back, and I would end up going.

What a wonderful change in my life has been wrought
Since Jesus came into my heart

Like this hymn, changing our lives is not through our will, effort, or determination. It's up to the power of Jesus Christ. Before, I struggled to overcome sin without Jesus, and I struggled to not commit sins, by being strong willed and determined. But after Jesus entered into my heart, even though I didn't try to avoid committing sins, I became distant from sin. I began to seek the Word, and I began to read the Bible. Once, there was something I needed to take care of and I looked at the clock and I had about one hour left. I thought to myself, "I'm just going to read the Bible until then," and I started to read the Bible. But when I stood up after reading the Bible, the sun was already setting. Without even knowing it I had forgotten about my appointment to meet a friend and I had just fallen into the Scriptures. As the Word entered into my heart, it amazingly changed my life. My eyes towards the Bible began to change. Often, I would feel in my heart, "This is not my heart. This is the heart of Jesus."

The Source of Sin Must be Treated, Not the Symptoms of Sin

Everyone, when we commit sins such as adultery, theft, lying, or when we commit the sin of hating someone, we usually begin to think from the first level of thought, "Oh, I'd better not sin. I should never do such a thing again." But living your spiritual life that way is completely wrong. Why do we commit adultery, steal, tell lies, or commit murder? The answer is very simple. You feel pain inside your body if you have an ulcer. Without the pain, you may not even know that you're suffering from the ulcer. So the pain in your body is to let you know that you're sick. When you go somewhere and you fall and bang your elbows, it's painful and it hurts right? It means that if you just leave it like that, the wound is going to get bigger, so you should quickly get it treated. That's the reason why God has given us nerves and pain. He did not give it to us for us to simply suffer and be in pain.

In the same way, when you commit adultery, it is not that you should say, "Oh God, somehow I ended up committing adultery. I was terribly wrong to do so. Please forgive me." Through seeing that you committed adultery you come to the realization that, "the heart inside of me is different from the heart of God," and you know that there is a lustful heart inside of you.

For a long time I was a member of the education committee at the Suwon prison and the Daejeon prison. I educated the inmates there. At that time, many of the inmates received salvation and some of them became pastors. Many of them became workers for God. When I first went to the prisons I didn't know the heart of the prisoners very well. But as I went there often, I came to know the inmates' hearts. The inmates are quite interesting. For example, if there is an inmate that came to prison for stealing, do you know what they think about while they're in prison?

"Ah, during that incident, if I had worn gloves I wouldn't have left fingerprints behind. Then I wouldn't have gotten caught. I did not wear gloves, that's why I got caught!"

But that is not the end of their thoughts. They have the heart that, "The next time I go to steal, if I wear gloves, surely I will not get caught." When their thoughts flow in that direction, they want to quickly put on gloves, and go out, and try again. It's really true. In the heart of the inmates that are in prison, the heart of wanting to commit sin arises in them. When they imagine how they will wear the gloves, commit theft and not get caught, they feel this sense of excitement. But do they say that? No, of course not. They just keep it in their hearts, and on the outside nobody knows. Once he finishes his sentence, he gets released from the prison. "Prison guards, please take care! I'll see you next time!"

"Let's not see each other next time. Stop coming back here!"

After that person leaves, the prison guards talk amongst themselves. "How long do you think it will take for that guy to be back? Do you think he'll last one month?"

"Nah, he's not going to last one month. I think he'll be back in ten days."

The prison guards know that, among the inmates, a good portion of them will commit crimes again and come back to the prison. Why? Because they are not able to bear it without committing the crimes that they had been imagining and planning out. But in the prisons, they are unable to, and they keep still. But once they're released, they go and try it again. That's why some people end up back in prison in one month. Some people are back in prison in twenty days. Some people come back in ten days. And some people leave in the morning and return in the evening.

Let me ask you. While that person was in prison do you think that person had the heart to commit sin or not? He did. Of course not all prisoners are that way, but many of them are. But because they're unable to sin in the prison, that heart is not revealed to the outside. But once they're released and people see they have committed theft again, what do they say? "Oh that person had the heart to steal again." You come to realize that fact. It's just like when you have the cold, your nose runs, you cough, and you have a fever. Likewise, when you have malaria, you feel dizzy and you have much pain. When you have typhoid, you get a fever and have diarrhea. Likewise, what is in our hearts is revealed on the outside.

God allowed people with sickness to be in pain, so that through the symptoms, they can get the source of their diseases treated. For example, if I have a cold, but I say, "Oh, I better stop having a runny nose. Lord, please stop my nose from running. I believe!" and if I say, "Fever, come down! Let this fever go away!" and I forcefully close my mouth to keep myself from coughing, imagine how ridiculous that would be. If I have a runny nose, a fever, and a cough, then I have to realize that it's because of a cold and I would get my cold treated.

Everyone, if you steal or commit adultery or lie, what does that mean? There is no adultery in the heart of Jesus. There is no hatred, there is no theft. So what does this mean? In this world there are two hearts. There is the heart of God and there is the heart of Satan. So, by seeing the sin that you commit, you come to see, "Ah, my heart is not the heart of Jesus. If I continue this, then I will be destroyed. This heart needs to be changed to the heart of Jesus." This is what we need to realize. Without coming to that realization, we are left to commit sins. Everyone, can you say amen to that? Yes, that's right.

After committing theft, I would say, "Oh I'd better not commit theft," and I would pray, "Lord, please do not let me steal, I believe in you." I've done that so many times. I opened up my notebook and wrote down the sins that I've committed one by one, every one of them. I wrote several pages. Then I looked at them and I prayed, "God these are the sins that

I've committed. Forgive me. I've committed these sins. Please forgive me." The next day, I would commit the same sins again. That is not repentance. To repent means to turn around. If you turn from sin and then sin again, then how is that turning around? The reason why churches in Korea today are unable to have faith is because they are practicing the wrong kind of repentance. When I talk about true repentance, there are lots of people who say, "Pastor Ock Soo Park teaches that it's okay to not repent." But the important thing is, what does the Bible say?

A Life That Could Only Be Led by Sin

When you commit sin, and realize that you've committed sin, what should you do? Let's look at Leviticus chapter 4. Please listen closely to what I am reading.

And if any one of the common people sin through ignorance, while he doeth somewhat against any of the commandments of the LORD concerning things which ought not to be done, and be guilty; Or if his sin, which he hath sinned, come to his knowledge…, then he shall come to the early morning service and zealously confess his sins, beg for forgiveness, and be determined, and labor to not commit sins. Is that what the Bible says? But, do many Christians live this way or not? If so, is that according to the Bible or not according to the Bible? Everyone, try being determined a thousand, or ten thousand times to not commit sin. Let's see if that works. It does not work. It's all too clear. Apostle Paul clearly said in Romans chapter 7:

For the good that I would I do not: but the evil which I would not, that I do. Now if I do that I would not, it is no more I that do it, but sin that dwelleth in me. I find then a law, that, when I would do good, evil is present with me. For I delight in the law of God after the inward man: But I see another law in my members, warring against the law of my mind, and bringing me into captivity to the law of sin which is in my members. O wretched man that I am! who shall deliver me from the body of this death? (Romans 7:19-24)

Apostle Paul tried to not commit sin and tried to do good deeds, but he ended up committing sin. That's who we are. If you could refrain from sinning by simply trying not to, then you wouldn't be human, you would be God. If you could just say, "I'm not going to commit adultery, I'm not going to commit theft, I'm not going to lie," and be that way just by saying so, then you're not human. Why is this so? It is because Satan is stronger than we are, and the power of sin is stronger than we are. Who is dragged around because he wants to be dragged around? People are dragged around because they are weak.

Everyone, do you know how people end up committing adultery? Take me, Pastor Ock Soo Park, for example. One day the devil puts a lustful heart inside of me, and I am tormented. "I have a wife and I'm a pastor. Is it okay to commit adultery? Oh, no I shouldn't! I should not commit adultery! I should not!" This is the kind of heart that all people have.

When the lustful heart enters into them, their faces turn red. They start to think, "Why am I having these thoughts?" There's nobody who says, "Alright! This is great! I have the heart to commit adultery inside of me! Let's go commit adultery! Whoever wants to commit adultery, come forward!" Nobody says that.

When a lustful heart enters, people think, "Why am I having these thoughts? I'm a pastor. I have a wife. How can I have this kind of a heart? I shouldn't have this kind of a heart," and they try to fight against that heart. That's what happens when Satan only puts a small heart of lust in you. Suppose he puts in a great big dose of lust. What happens then? No matter what a gentleman you may be, you too, will fall.

A few years ago, my voice was bad and I was examined in New York. The doctor said that I had three small lumps, as small as beans, on my vocal cord, and that they had to be removed. The day of the operation came, and in the operating room were the anesthesiologist, the surgeon, and an elder that I knew, who was a doctor. The three of them were there. The anesthesiologist said to me, "Pastor when I say breathe, take a deep breath."

"Okay."

Soon after the anesthesiologist said to me, "Pastor, take a deep breath." I took a deep breath, and he said the surgery was over. The anesthesiologist, while I was lying down, said to me, "Pastor, take a deep breath," while he administered liquid anesthesia through the IV.

I don't remember what happened after that.

No matter who the person is, once the anesthesia enters the body, he becomes unconscious. This is also the same thing with committing sin. Only when a small lustful heart enters into you, you may be able to withstand it. But if a large heart enters in, you too, have no chance. Everyone will commit adultery. The only person on this earth who can fight sin and defeat it is Jesus. That's why, when the devil places a lustful heart inside of you, the heart to say, "I'm not going to, I'm not going to," collapses quickly.

When the lustful heart defeats you, what happens to you? You become dragged around by the lustful heart. Then it's no longer you walking around, but it's the lustful heart that's dragging you around. Then you end up having no choice but to commit adultery.

That's why it's not about trying to avoid committing adultery. When Jesus Christ, who can overcome the lustful heart, enters into you, then you can live a holy life. Your determination, your will, your effort - all these things only add more pain to you. Many Christians today don't know about this simple truth. When I occasionally go to the prayer houses in the mountains, from various valleys here and there you can hear the people crying out, "Lord, forgive me of my sin!"

For I Was Conceived in Sin

Today, the foolish thing about Christians in Korea is that many of them think, without reading the Bible, "All I have to do is pray. All I have to do is go to church on Sundays. All I have to do is keep the Ten Commandments and not sin." And they think that's all there is to it. If that were the case, why would the Bible be this thick? The Bible tells us about the world of the heart. That you committed theft, adultery, that you lied, that you hated others. Through those things God is teaching you the state of your heart. "Right now I have a heart that is not of God. I have the heart of Satan. I have to change that heart."

That's why repentance is not about repenting of theft. You need to realize beyond the theft that you committed and turn from it. You must turn from the evil heart that leads you to committing theft. To deliver this sermon to you, I must open the Bible, I must concentrate, and I must search through it.

Does the Bible talk about the kind of repentance that the Christians in Korea practice today? The one where they say, "I stole, I committed adultery, I lied." There was one person who did do that kind of repentance. It was Judas Iscariot. Judas Iscariot repented like many Christians do today.

I have sinned, in that I have betrayed innocent blood. He threw the silver he received from betraying Jesus into the temple. He was tormented, sorrowful, and in pain for the sin that he had committed.

But he was cursed, and he was not saved.

In the Bible, it talks about the salvation that apostle Paul received. There's a story of how Cornelius gets saved, and how the eunuch of Ethiopia gets saved. In the Old Testament, it talks about how David receives the forgiveness of sins after committing adultery with Uriah's wife.

I asked many people, "Sir, do you know the story of how David committed adultery with Uriah's wife?"

"Yes, I do. I know that story."

"Pastor, do you know the story of how David committed adultery with Uriah's wife?"

"Oh yes, I do."

"Deacon, do you know the story of how David committed adultery with Uriah's wife?"

"Yes, I know that story."

"Elder, do you know the story of David committing adultery with Uriah's wife?"

"Yes, I do. I've known that story for a long time."

And I would ask them again, "Why did the Bible record such things? The Bible is written through the inspiration of the Holy Spirit of God. Why did the Holy Spirit have them record these kinds of things?"

Then people are unable to answer. You see, these stories are recorded in the Bible to teach us how to have our sins forgiven. Because if we were taught just how to have our sins forgiven, we wouldn't understand. To make it easier for us to understand the whole process, beginning with how sin was committed, these words were written.

And it came to pass in an eveningtide, that David arose from off his bed, and walked upon the roof of the king's house: and from the roof he saw a woman washing herself; and the woman was very beautiful to look upon. (2 Samuel 11:2)

According to the words recorded in 2 Samuel, the process of committing sin is precisely described. David went and committed sin with Uriah's wife, and Uriah's wife conceived. Then, it also precisely describes the detail of how he ended up committing another sin. David called in Uriah, who was out in the battlefield. "You've put in so much hard work at the war, so why don't you go home and get some rest?"

"I will not."

"Go!"

"I will not."

"Go!"

"I will not."

"Go!"

David had him drink a lot of wine, so that while he was drunk he would have him go home and sleep with his wife. He wanted Uriah to believe that when the child was born, it was his own child. But Uriah did not go home. So David had Uriah killed in the battlefield. Afterwards, Prophet Nathan appeared and rebuked David. Then it talks about how David received the forgiveness of sin. Psalms 51 is a poem written after David committed adultery with Uriah's wife, and within it says this:

Behold, I was shapen in iniquity; and in sin did my mother conceive me. (Psalms 51:5)

Everyone, if this was done according to the way of modern churches, David would have said this:

"God, you know I did not remember you, and I got drunk and I slept late and I woke up late in the morning and I was walking on the rooftop of the palace. There was this woman bathing and she was so pretty. I was out of my mind, I was crazy. I committed adultery. God please forgive this sin."

David did not confess his sin of adultery and ask for that to be forgiven. He did not bring forth the result of the sin that he committed, but rather he brought forth the cause, the source. Shall we search the Scriptures? Psalms 51:5.

Behold, I was shapen in iniquity; and in sin did my mother conceive me.

What was in David's heart? The fact that he committed adultery tells us that his heart was filled with lust. David, by committing adultery with Uriah's wife, realized that he was nothing but sin. For David to confess, *Behold, I was shapen in iniquity; and in sin did my mother conceive me,* he is saying that, "I am nothing but sinfulness."

You Must Be Changed to the Heart of Jesus Christ

At church I often talk about true repentance. True repentance is realizing that the core of your heart is filthy and dirty, recognizing that you belong to Satan, and turning from that. You cannot do good by just trying to do good. Nor are you unable to do good because you do not try.

It is because you belong to the devil, you belong inside of sinfulness, and that is why you cannot help but to commit sins. Satan continually strikes up an evil heart inside of you. But God is telling us that it is not about trying to keep ourselves from sinning or laboring to become good. He is telling us that our hearts are filthy and dirty, and that He cannot accept our hearts. But people keep trying to become good.

When a person gambles and loses money, he feels like next time he will win money.

So, he goes again and loses again. The next time he feels like he's going to win again, but he ends up losing, yet again.

That's how Christians in Korea live today; they sin, but this time it seems like they will be better, yet they sin again. They are being deceived. When we read the Bible, we can see that because we are evil by nature, we cannot become good. Simply put, suppose a person who likes soccer turned on a videotape of a soccer match, but instead of showing soccer it only showed golf. "Where's the soccer match? Why is it showing golf? Is the soccer match on soon? Maybe it's after this program?" He continues to watch asking himself the same questions, even though it's continually showing nothing but golf. "Ah, this was a golf videotape!" When he ejects it, he realizes it was a golf videotape. Then he goes and searches, "where is that soccer videotape?" He finds the tape of the World Cup soccer match. Then he puts it into the VCR and it shows soccer. When you put in a boxing tape, it will show boxing. When you put in a soccer tape it will show soccer. When you put in a golf tape, it will show golf. In the same way, because we are the descendants of sin, no matter how determined and hard we try to do good, we cannot. That is why we must be born again. Your heart must be changed to the heart of Jesus Christ.

Did you commit adultery? Did you steal? Did you murder? Did you lie? Did you commit sin everyone? What must you do? Even though you realize that you've committed sin, and you try to be determined about not sinning, a thousand or ten thousand times, you will still fail.

A long time ago, someone gambled away his whole wealth. He lost the title to his land, to his house, and he came home, having lost everything. He was so bitter. His wife was at home trimming the green onions. The green onions weren't even that big. These were just ugly little green onions that didn't even look edible. When he saw his wife picking them, it drove him crazy. "If I had not gambled, I could have bought a truckload of those green onions." He was so tormented as he thought to himself, "Alright, this cannot continue. My fingers are the problem." So one day, he put his hand in the paper cutter and snipped off his fingers, in order to keep himself from gambling again. After cutting his fingers off, his wife was shocked to see his hands covered with blood.

"Honey! Just stop gambling! It's not your fingers' fault!"

"It's because of these fingers that I gambled!"

The wife cried and she was so grieved thinking, "Why did you do that?"

Afterwards, he stopped gambling, and they lived on happily. Maybe about a month passed, and the husband was nowhere to be found.

"Where did he go?" the wife thought as she looked for him. Then in the wife's heart she thought, "Did he go gambling, maybe? No, that can't be. He even cut his own fingers off, there's no way he could be gambling. He must not be." She looked for him, but still, he was nowhere to be found. Again she thought, "What if? Oh no, I shouldn't think this way about my husband. My husband wouldn't do that." With that she comforted herself. But then again, she thought, "What if?" She got up, and went to the casino where people gamble. She opened the door, and how could it be? Her husband was sitting there with the poker cards between his toes, and he was there gambling.

It may sound funny, but it's not that he lacked determination. If he cut his own fingers off, how tremendous was his own determination and will? But that determination and will was powerless in front of sin. Everyone, we are descendants of sin. That's why, when we commit sin, no matter how long we tell ourselves, for a hundred days or a thousand days, "I'm going to be good, I'm going to be honest," in the end it's all useless. It is because we already have a lustful heart, a dirty heart, a deceitful heart, an evil heart, and an ambitious heart. Unless that heart is changed, even if we decide in our hearts a thousand or even tens of thousands of times, it's all useless.

I formed an organization called the International Youth Fellowship, and I am leading many college students through this organization. Many college students have changed, and they go to South America, Africa, and Southeast Asia as short-term missionaries. I don't tell those students to not steal, or to not commit adultery. I teach them how they can change their hearts and how they can have their sins forgiven. And I teach them how to have Jesus enter into their hearts and to cast out the sins inside of them. When students come in front of Jesus and receive the forgiveness of sins, and after Jesus enters into their hearts, whether it be 10 students or 100 students, I can see all of them changing.

A Work Not Done by Me, but by Jesus

A friend of mine is here at this place tonight. After receiving salvation, I lived without having time to check up on my friends. But recently, as my name has been in the newspapers and also on TV, a few of my friends have contacted me on an individual basis, and I've had a chance to see them. It's so good to have friends from my youth that I used to play with when I was young. A few days ago, a friend of mine called me, "Come to the Surak-san Station. Let's have some dinner together." I met my friends at the Surak-san Station. We talked about the old days. My friend said that he would buy dinner so we ate together. The raw gizzards they were selling on the street were so cheap, so I bought some with my friend and we ate together. Not from the restaurant, but this raw gizzard we ate from the side of the street was so delicious. Nowadays, when I'm walking down the street I often look around thinking, "Is there anybody around here selling gizzards?" But in Gangnam, where I live, there weren't any places that sold gizzards, so I haven't had a chance to eat them around where I live.

After dinner, we went to the home of another one of our friends. The friend said to me, "Hey, Pastor Park, you're in my home, so why don't you pray for me." Before I prayed, I preached the Gospel to him. Another friend who was there together with me so sweetly listened to the Word. As I was preparing to leave after the prayer, there was a book that I had with me, so I gave it to my friend. That friend came to this conference tonight and I met him earlier today. That friend so sincerely said to me, "Pastor Park, I read your book and quit drinking through it. Until that moment, I had such a big drinking problem. But after reading that book, whenever I wanted to have a drink I would think of the times I got drunk in the past and all of the problems that I created. So from that day on I never drank again." Everyone, it's not because Pastor Ock Soo Park has some special power. That friend didn't just read a book, but he read the heart of God that was inside of that book. Once the Word settles inside of the heart, and once the light enters into the heart, the darkness departs. Whether it is quitting drinking, or cigarettes, or drugs, that is how all of this comes about.

Once I went to a city named Vladikavkaz in Russia. One of our missionaries is based in Moscow. One day, he met a young man in the street and preached the Gospel to him, and that young man got saved. The young man said to the missionary, "Missionary let's go to my hometown," and bugged him continually to go. Vladikavkaz is a four hour flight from Moscow, and they went there together. In Russian, "Vladi" means to conquer. "Vladivostok" means to conquer the east. "Vladikavkaz" means to conquer the mountain. Vladikavkaz is completely in a mountain area, and it's a city where the old Soviet Union used to produce Vodka. The old Soviet Union had clear policies: a region for manufactured goods, a region for Vodka, a region for agriculture, a region for nuclear weapons. In this way they were able to divide up regions and have them produce goods, and then distribute them throughout the whole nation. But after the Soviet Union disintegrated, in regions where they had nothing but nuclear weapons, you would hear sometimes that they would sell nuclear weapons. Vladikavkaz was a place where they made Vodka. The people of the old Soviet Union enjoyed drinking Vodka because the weather there is cold. Because of that, the Vodka sold well and the people in Vladikavkaz lived very abundantly. But as the Soviet Union disassembled, they were no longer able to sell Vodka. The Vodka factories closed their doors one by one, and many young men became unemployed and just wandered the streets. That's when the mafia came and introduced drugs into that city. Many of the young people in Vladikavkaz ended up becoming drug addicts. As they would do drugs, they would get addicted. Once addicted they would get spasms, their faces would turn blue, and one by one they would die. To treat these drug addicts, the government built drug rehab schools, and people caught doing drugs would be sent there for three years. For three years they don't do drugs and they would receive education and training. But the moment they are released, on their way out they go to buy drugs.

The treatment was not effective. Parents would see their kids dying from the drugs and would be so sad. The missionary preached the Gospel in Vladikavkaz. People there received the forgiveness of sins and Jesus entered into their hearts.

Now, they are able to quit drugs. A church was established in Vladikavkaz. When I went there, somebody invited me to a meal. He was a person who did not believe in Jesus. I could not forget it.

It was a meal in the exact same manner that the kings of Russia would eat. When I went in, there was a maid holding a basin of water standing next to me. I asked, "Am I supposed to drink this?" She told me to wash my hands. I washed my hands, and another person brought a towel and wiped my hands for me.

Then that person said to me, "Pastor Park, I don't believe in Jesus. But you sent a missionary here, and it is reviving many young people in Vladikavkaz. Pastor, I was thankful to you so I wanted to treat you to this meal." Everyone, this is not something I did, but it is something that Jesus did.

I saw many drug addicts, many game addicts, many drunkards, and many gambling addicts, and also many murderers in prison. And even though these people seemed impossible, I saw so many of them change.

They did not try to change themselves. If you try to change yourself, it does not work out. Instead, you have to realize that it cannot be done through your strength.

People who are short in thought don't know that they are unable and they just continue to try harder. But people who can think a little bit will realize, "Ah, it cannot be done through my efforts." When people realize that, they can forsake their own ways and receive the forgiveness of sins. That's why, when Jesus Christ enters into the heart, no matter who the person is, that person will change just as I, who was once a dirty human, also changed. As long as he's not some animal, he will change. As long as he's not a robot, but a human, when the Word of God enters into his heart and he receives the forgiveness of sins, he will certainly change through Jesus Christ.

Last week I had a conference in Daejeon. A college professor came to see me. "Pastor my daughter had so many problems as a child. But she changed after meeting the IYF. Right now, she's in South America as a short-term missionary. I really like the IYF. That's why I brought some of my students and we attended your conference, Pastor. Please, Pastor, recruit my students into the IYF and send them out as short-term missionaries." This is not something Pastor Ock Soo Park did. Jesus Christ did this.

Everyone, today we talked about Leviticus chapter four, about the sin offering and how sin is committed. We commit sins because of the sin that's inside of us. It is not that you must know the end result of the sin that you committed. You must know the source of your sin. It is not that you should see the end result and say, "Oh, I'd better not commit theft." You have to know that at the core you are a sinner. If you receive forgiveness for that sin and Jesus enters into your heart, then you will all change, and you will rejoice. You will be happy. The heavens and the world will appear different to you. Love will arise, and the heart to love your family will arise. You'll be completely changed. That change is not a result of your effort or your zeal, but it is through Jesus Christ.

We'll continue tomorrow on the topic of the sin offering. What I explained to you tonight is that it does not work when we try to shed our sin. But we can change when we receive the forgiveness of sins, and Jesus Christ enters inside of us.

CHAPTER 2
If His Sin Which He Hath Sinned Come to His Knowledge

Peter has yet to find out who he really is. He only knows of the good things that he has done; how he left behind his boat and fishing net to follow the Lord. But he hasn't discovered yet who he really is. Peter cannot achieve this on his own. That is why the Lord wanted to lead Peter to realize what kind of a person he truly is.

Before the cock crows tonight you will deny me three times.

"Lord, is that all you think of me? I'm so disappointed. Even if I die, I will never deny you Lord!" To that very moment, because of all the good things that he had done, Peter was unable to see himself.

Hello, everyone. Today is our second session. We will begin by reading from Leviticus chapter 4 verse 27.

And if any one of the common people sin through ignorance, while he doeth somewhat against any of the commandments of the Lord concerning things which ought not to be done, and be guilty; Or if his sin, which he hath sinned, come to his knowledge: then he shall bring his offering, a kid of the goats, a female without blemish, for his sin which he hath sinned. And he shall lay his hand upon the head of the sin offering, and slay the sin offering in the place of the burnt offering. And the priest shall take of the blood thereof with his finger, and put it upon the horns of the altar of burnt offering, and shall pour out all the blood thereof at the bottom of the altar. And he shall take away all the fat thereof, as the fat is taken away from off the sacrifice of peace offerings; and the priest shall burn it upon the altar for a sweet savour unto the Lord; and the priest shall make an atonement for him, and it shall be forgiven him. (Leviticus 4:27-31)

Because They Did Not Learn Spiritual Life

The Gracias Choir sings hymns before I preach the Word. The stage is divided into two sections, and the choir sings from the lower part of the stage. When the music ends, the stage crew cleans up the chairs and microphones. It is our brothers who do this, and in my eyes, it's so amazing how quickly they can put everything away. Whether it be the violin, the cello, or the oboe, each instrument has its own microphone and chair. The crew is so good at putting everything away. Last week, we had a Bible conference in Daejeon. At the time, the crew that was responsible for putting away the microphones would drop them and even step on them. People just simply think, "Anyone can clean up the microphones and put away the chairs." Here on the stage, it's marked where the first violin's chair and mic should be, where the second violin's mic and chair should be, all of these things are marked. So, it may seem that anyone can do a good job of this.

But when they actually do it, sometimes the microphones cables become tangled, or the chairs and the music stands end up on the wrong side. Sometimes they misplace the microphones. Such things can happen. The brothers who do this, practice many, many times. Although it seems to be a simple task, in reality it is not so easy. It may seem like something that anyone can do, but it's not something everyone can do.

There are also reasons why spiritual life does not work out. However, in truth, spiritual life is easy and fun. Even when I'm sleepy and dozing off, if I'm told to give a sermon, I wake up immediately and get excited. Spiritual life is very easy but people fall into difficulties because they don't know certain truths. It's so much fun for me to teach about these things.

Even if you don't labor to live a good spiritual life, but realize, "Oh, that's what it is, that is how we're supposed to live spiritual life," through listening to the Word of God, spiritual life becomes so easy. If you think a little bit, read the Bible, and realize what it is about, spiritual life is very easy. But people don't do that. People so easily say, "What? All we have to do is just place the mics there, what's so hard about that?" Likewise, people simply think, "What? All you have to do is pray, keep the law, go to church on Sundays, tithe, and just not commit sins." But those who think of it in general terms like that can never live a spiritual life.

Do you know why Korean churches today are so spoiled and corrupted that Christians in society can't get any recognition? It's because they did not learn spiritual life. It is because they simply think, "All I have to do is just try hard." Everyone, during this week, I hope you will learn spiritual life step by step. It will be so much fun.

I went to Paraguay not too long ago. In Paraguay, we have our mission retreat center on a lot the size of 200 acres. The brothers who manage that retreat center ride on horses to care for it. I've never ridden a horse before. So I wanted to try it one time. I said, "Bring a horse here. I want to try riding one." The brothers then said something to one another and brought the most tame horse of all the horses. They say that the wild, rugged, and ferocious horses are very dangerous.

As soon as I got on the horse, the brothers held the reigns and walked the horse.

I felt like a knight in shining armor. The brothers were worried that I would fall off the horse and get hurt. But I wanted to ride the horse without anyone holding onto the reigns. So I told the brothers to let go. Although the brothers let go of the reigns, they stayed nearby. Then, I gave the horse a kick and the horse started running. Although it was not smooth, it was a lot of fun. Right then the brothers said, "Pastor, it's time for your flight. We must go quickly." I could not ride any longer, and we had to go to the airport. I got to ride that horse one time and it was a lot of fun. When you pull on the reigns, the horse stops. You tug the reign to the right when you want to go to the right. When you want to go the left, you tug to the left.

When you give the horse a kick, it begins to run.

Even now, I sometimes think, "When I go to Paraguay, I'm going to ride the horse again."

If you learn spiritual life, it's so much more fun than horseback riding. You can't even compare the two. When certain things begin to happen, and you can recognize it saying, "Ah, this is just like the situation in John chapter 7," it is so much fun. Even when you meet people and give them spiritual counseling, when you listen to that person's story and realize, "Ah. This person's situation is just like John chapter 5. Then, if I tell him about this...." With that, when you tell them the words of the Bible, you can see it resonate with them and fit them well. When I explain these words to them and see the words coming upon them by faith, preaching feels so much fun. That's why, even when I am dozing off and feeling sleepy, when it comes time to talk about these kinds of things, my eyes become wide open.

However, many people today live spiritual life in a very difficult way.

They do it agonizingly. Rather than living spiritual life because it's fun and joyful, they suffer and go through pain. Perhaps you may be saying right now, "It's fun for Pastor Park. But what's so fun about spiritual life?" But as you learn about the sin offering step by step, you will begin to have the heart, "Wow, it is a lot of fun. I want to hear more. I want to learn more." That heart will arise within you.

God said that He does not make our spiritual life difficult, but rather that He lightens our load.

All He Did Was Try To Kill The Fly

Today's the second session. Regarding the sin offering, I want to talk about, *Or if his sin which he hath sinned come to his knowledge.*

A long time ago, a certain man went into the mountains to gather some wood. There he found a baby bear. Maybe the mother bear was dead and this baby bear was lost, struggling in the woods. So the man held the baby bear and brought it home. He gave the bear food and milk. The baby bear for several days was very sad and without energy. But as he became accustomed to his new home, he began to liven up.

As he lived there for one year, two years, three years, he grew very much.

He became a true member of the family. He would eat with them, wrestle and play with them.

One summer day, the man was lying down on his porch in the middle of the day. But the flies kept landing on his face and would wake him up from his sleep. You wouldn't know if you have not been to the jungles of Africa. But in the jungle, the bugs can distinguish very well between the locals and the foreigners. If you wear thin clothes and sweat and enter the jungle, all kinds of bugs come and land on your back. But the bugs do not land on the backs of the locals at all. It is because the bugs don't eat sweat. Even when the locals sweat, it's only water. But in the sweat of the foreigners, there's salt. So the bugs are attracted to the foreigners. When a person is taking a nap, why does a fly land on that person's face? The flies are craving for salt. Because there's salt in the sweat that flows on a person's face, it is so tempting for the flies to land on the person's face.

This person wanted to take a deep nap. But whenever he was about to fall asleep, the flies would come and land on his face. It was so irritating and he could not bear it. Right then, the bear was in the yard, playing by himself. The man called the bear over and told it to chase away the flies whenever they would land on his face. Since the bear was chasing the flies away, the master thought, "Alright," and he laid down, and fell asleep, snoring loudly.

Whenever a fly would land on the master's face, the bear would chase it away. Now, if a fly is shooed away, then it shouldn't come back. But it would come back and sit on his face again and again and again. The bear became angry. The bear looked around and there was a block of stone which was used like an ironing board. The bear picked up that stone and waited for the fly to come back. If a fly landed on the master's face again, he wanted to slam down with the stone. The master was sleeping but felt something strange. When he opened his eyes, he saw that the bear was ready to slam down on his face with the stone. He was shocked and woke up. "Are you crazy? Are you trying to kill me?" he yelled at the bear.

The bear did not understand what was so wrong about trying to kill the fly with the stone. "I was just trying to do what the master told me, and shoo the flies away. But that fly kept on irritating my master while he was trying to sleep. So I wanted to kill it. What's so wrong about that?" In the eyes of the man, it was so clear that the bear was terribly wrong. But the bear is not smart enough to realize that. Even though he chased the flies away like the master had told him to, the flies kept coming back and sat on his face no matter how often he chased them away.

That's why he tried to take the block of stone and kill that fly.

Everyone, there is a difference of intelligence between the bear and the man. In the same way, there's also a great difference of intelligence between God and man.

That's why, even though you may be smart and you may be great, you can only remain at the level of man. But compared to the level of God, we are nothing. That's why when we live spiritual life, it cannot be done through our diligence or determination. Instead, we must know and we must learn the heart of God that is within the Bible.

Sin, Which Cannot Be Realized Through Man's Senses

What does Leviticus chapter 4, verse 27, say?

And if any one of the common people sin through ignorance, while he doeth somewhat against any of the commandments of the Lord concerning things which ought not to be done, and be guilty;" And verse 28 says, *"Or if his sin, which he hath sinned, come to his knowledge…*

Everyone, when you hear this, you don't understand what it means, right?

If you sin, you already know that it's wrong. So you may be thinking in your heart, "What does it mean, 'when the sin comes to his knowledge?'" When you steal something, is there anyone who does not know that's a sin? Does anyone not know that committing murder is a sin? You would be nothing more than a bear if you didn't know these things.

When people commit theft, murder, or adultery, they all know that, "Yes, that is a sin." But that's about as deep as man can realize about sin. So then, how do we come to the realization that stealing, committing adultery, and murdering is sin? It is because these things are relative.

For example, suppose I bought land and I farmed on it to prepare my children for marriage and saved up $100,000. If someone stole that from me, imagine how angry and upset I would be. That is why a thief feels guilt in his mind when he steals. "If I steal this, it will cause the owner of that house grief." When you hit somebody, you feel guilty in your conscience because you also know the feeling of pain when you are hit.

When a person commits adultery, what is the reason that he feels it was a sin?

If you were to rejoice and be happy when your wife commits adultery with another man, then you would not feel any guilt. But you do feel the pain. That's why when you commit adultery, you feel pain also because you know you are inflicting the same pain that you would feel if your wife were to cheat on you. In this relative manner, man realizes sin.

However, the Ten Commandments tell us, *Thou shalt have no other gods before me. Thou shalt not make unto thee any graven image, or any likeness of any thing that is in heaven above, or that is in the earth beneath, or that is in the water under the earth. Thou shalt not take the name of the Lord thy God in vain. Remember the sabbath day, to keep it holy.* These four laws are laws concerning God.

Honor thy parents. Thou shall not commit murder. Thou shall not commit adultery. Thou shall not steal. Thou shall not lie. Thou shall not covet. These six laws are laws concerning man.

Because we are human, these kinds of sin concerning our relationship with other people are easily recognized even if we don't spend much time talking about them. However, we don't feel the guilt of sin so easily when we sin against God. People who don't read the Bible will not feel guilty when they don't keep the Sabbath. They will not feel guilty for serving an idol. With your conscience, you cannot realize on your own that not keeping the Sabbath or serving idols is wrong. But, sins against God can be realized when you know the heart of God. People realize the sins we commit against other man. The lies, theft, and adultery: it is only concerning these kinds of sins, that we can relate to. But, the deeper world of sin cannot be realized simply through man's senses. That's why Leviticus chapter 4, verse 28 says, *Or if his sin, which he hath sinned, come to his knowledge....* It means that, to realize sin, it's not something you can do on your own, but someone else must bring knowledge of sin to you.

"I lied today, committed adultery, or committed murder. I've committed sins. God, please forgive these sins. Help me to not commit these sins again." Understanding sin in this manner is not truly realizing what sin is.

That's because, this much, anyone can realize without understanding what sin truly is.

Something Beyond the Wisdom of Man Is Necessary

There is an elder that I know who runs a small electronics company. When they build large factories in the Gumi industrial complex, and he is in charge of installing equipment in those factories. That's what he's paid for and that's how he runs his company.

Once, LG was building a factory there and this elder won the bid for the contract to do electronic installation in that factory. So he began his installation work. In the process of his work, he needed to install a transformer for this project. People could not lift up the transformer. But there are certain companies that specialize in moving this kind of heavy equipment. He requested one of these companies to move this transformer. But while that company was working on moving that transformer, one of the workers was struck by the transformer by accident. He was seriously wounded and moved to the hospital, but soon after he died. The peculiar thing about the situation was that the other company was responsible for moving the transformer. So, it should have been that company that would take responsibility for this accident. But because that company was such a small company, they were unable to give compensation for this accident. However, if the elder, who was in charge of this project, also claims no responsibility, since this happened while building an LG factory, this problem would be passed on to LG.

People at the Gumi industrial complex found out about this situation, and everyone was curious to see how the situation would unfold.

The elder's company is not very big. So they also did not have enough to handle such a situation. But the elder, who is Chairman Ahn, took out $100,000 loan to pay for all the hospital expenses of the man who had passed away, to pay for all the funeral expenses, and also to give his family some compensation. People would say, "Chairman Ahn, you didn't have to do all of that. It was not your mistake, Chairman Ahn. It was the mistake of that other company."

As the people in the Gumi Industrial district found out about this, they began to say, "If you give Chairman Ahn work, no matter what it takes, he'll get it done." At that time the IMF (International Monetary Fund) Crisis broke out and the amount of work available decreased more and more at the industrial complex. In particular, many small electronics companies had to close down due to the lack of work. But whenever new factories were being built or there were new electronics projects in the industrial complex, the directors in charge would always ask for Chairman Ahn. Other companies were closing down, but the elder's company kept growing with more work and projects. Their revenue increased more and more and their company got bigger and bigger.

Ultimately, the person who died during the transformer incident was not even an employee of that elder's company. He didn't have to take that responsibility.

But he, being a person who believed in God, could not just ignore that situation when this person who worked for the small company died. That's why he paid for the hospital and funeral expenses, and also gave compensation to the victim's family members. This became the driver by which his company would rise and flourish.

However, in today's world, people don't have this kind of wisdom. We only know how to take what's immediately in front of us. We don't know how to give out what we have. If you did have this wisdom, the way you live in this world would change dramatically. When that kind of wisdom comes upon you, that is when you can live true spiritual life.

It is such a foolish thing to be vaguely thinking, "Oh, if I just pray hard, everything will be fine."

In James chapter 1, it says, *If any of you lack wisdom, let him ask of God, that giveth to all men liberally, and upbraideth not; and it shall be given him.*

Even if you're great and intelligent right now, there is a limit to what the bear can understand, and there is a limit to the wisdom of man. For us to live spiritual life, a wisdom beyond our own wisdom is needed. That wisdom must come in order for us to precisely see our own spiritual lives and to clearly understand why our spiritual lives do not work out. However, people don't think about these things at all. They simply think that their spiritual lives are not working out because they did not try hard enough. They think, "Ok, then. One of these days, when I tithe, I'm going to fast with all my might and do overnight prayers. And if I do all that, my spiritual life will be well." Many people think of it in this manner. Even when it comes to sin, people simply think, "Oh yeah, I stole, I committed adultery. That's why I'm a sinner." Therefore they end up saying, "God, please forgive me for stealing. Please forgive me for the sin of committing adultery." But by saying these things, you can only remain at the level of man.

Through the Bible we must gain the wisdom of God. We must receive the Holy Spirit of God into our hearts. We must receive the heart of God into our hearts.

When this occurs, you will receive a wisdom that is beyond any wisdom you will ever know.

With that wisdom you will read the Bible and get to know God. That's why this is something that cannot come about through us trying to realize on our own. The realization has to come to us. It must come to our knowledge. We need to receive the grace of God.

The power and the wisdom of God must be upon us.

Ddobyul Which Was Discovered by the Wisdom of God

We conduct youth activities through an organization called IYF. One of our IYF teachers is Chairman Young Woo Jin. He is a plant biologist. Although he's very busy, whenever there is an IYF World Camp, he volunteers to take one month off from his work so that he can serve as a teacher and be with the students.

One day, he read a thesis about taxol, which is used as an anti-cancer substance. Taxol is extracted from yew trees and has proven to be a very effective form of treatment. But four 100 year-old yew trees must be cut down to extract 1 cc of taxol. That's why more and more yew trees are disappearing off the face of the earth. I heard that in China, they are planting yew trees on expansive lands. Many scientists all over the world have researched ways to artificially cultivate taxol. But no one has been successful. Chairman Young Woo Jin read a thesis stating that it was impossible to cultivate taxol. But when Chairman Jin read this thesis, he felt something in his heart.

"Pastor Ock Soo Park gave a sermon saying that God does that which is impossible with man." He had the heart that if this is impossible with man, then he should receive the help of God. Chairman Jin then started to research this together with the chief researcher at his lab. Amazingly, God gave him wisdom.

There are certain cells that live forever in plants called "immortal cells." Chairman Jin developed the technology to extract these cells. Right now, the only person on this earth who can extract immortal cells is Chairman Young Woo Jin. But, he is not a very famous plant biologist. He graduated from Woosuk University in Jeonju, and he runs a small laboratory. But he was able to develop this amazing technology. We named this immortal cell, Ddobyul. The amazing thing about Ddobyul is that when cancer patients were administered Ddobyul, many of them were healed of cancer. My son's father-in-law, about two and a half months ago, was on the verge of death with stage-4 lung cancer. He took Ddobyul and his condition improved tremendously. He was hospitalized at Hanyang University Hospital.

While other patients were getting worse and worse and dying, my son's father-in-law was getting healthier. The people around him were curious and would ask what medicine he was taking. Now, he is almost completely healed. Patients who took Ddobyul were also healed of leukemia. Right now, we are studying it as a treatment against AIDS. They have developed a partnership with Edinburgh University in England, to jointly research this together. There are about a hundred people right now waiting to take Ddobyul. Right now, Ddobyul can only be produced inside a laboratory, in small quantities. That is what we use for a few people, and so far it's been very effective. But, soon, they will be looking to buy a large building and produce large quantities of Ddobyul to supply to many people. In the future, we want to make a cultivating facility as large as a soccer field so we can supply this Ddobyul to people all over the world. Chairman Young Woo Jin, even today, says that it is God who gave him this wisdom.

The Spirit of the Man Will Sustain His Infirmity

At our church, we have an elder named Hyo Jung Hwang.

He is a doctor of Chinese medicine. He treats eczema very well. Eczema is a disease you cannot get to the root of. When you take medicine, it gets a little better, then the disease relapses. There are lots of eczema patients who suffer from this disease that you cannot bear to look at. So Elder Hwang would ask the people in Gangwon province to bring some sponge gourd to him. He would take the concentration from the sponge gourd to make the medication to treat eczema.

Once, I told the elder, "Elder Hwang, run an ad in the newspaper, saying 'Eczema, Worry No More.'"

Then the elder said, "Oh, Pastor," while showing disapproval.

"What's wrong?"

"I would need to be able to treat eczema to the root, before I can run such an ad. But that's very difficult to do."

Afterwards, the Unhwa Chinese Medical Center moved to a larger office. Because I was unable to prepare a gift for them when they opened their new office, I wrote a Bible verse for them.

The spirit of a man will sustain his infirmity; but a wounded spirit who can bear? (Proverbs 18:14)

I posted this verse on the door of the hospital and told them to look at that verse every time the patients would come in. One day, Elder Hwang sat down and read this verse.

The spirit of a man will sustain his infirmity.

The elder was shocked. The word spirit in the Chinese character means heart.

The spirit sustains infirmity. The heart sustains infirmity.

Up until that moment, when the elder treated eczema, he was unable to rid the toxins in the body. That's why it was difficult to completely rid the eczema. To get rid of the toxins in the body, he would prescribe medication that focused on the liver. That was how he treated his patients. But it could not completely heal the disease. But at that moment his thoughts changed. As he read the words from Proverbs chapter 18 verse 14, he felt in his heart, "I need to strengthen the heart." He eliminated the medication that focused on the liver and replaced it with the medication that helped the heart. When he began to treat his patients with this new medication, the patients began to show signs of amazing recovery.

When the eczema patients took the original medicine, they got better for a little while, but then the disease came right back. But when they took the medication that Elder Hwang prescribed, the eczema that was hidden throughout body began to reveal itself. At first, it seemed as though the disease was getting much worse. When the patients saw this, they felt that their disease was worsened upon taking the medication. But, Elder Hwang would tell them, "Wait just a little bit. Now, what's inside is all coming out. All of it must come out. Then the disease can be completely healed."

When I go to Elder Hwang's hospital from time to time, he opens his laptop computer, telling me, "Pastor, welcome. Please sit here. Pastor, you know, this patient, when he first came to our hospital, his body was like this. But after taking our medication for three months, he became this clean. Look how clean he's become." Elder Hwang is so joyful to be working as a Chinese medicine doctor.

These eczema patients have such bad symptoms on their faces that they are forced to wear a large hat, and walk around with their heads down. Unable to marry, they would scratch themselves so much, that their blankets would be all stained with blood. I guess, to see such patients being healed from their illness brings Elder Hwang so much joy. I went there another time, and he said to me, "Pastor, do you know what this is? This is a gift from the mother of a baby who's eczema was completely healed. She sent this as a gift."

You Need A Leader Who Will Make You Realize

When the wisdom of God enters into your life, your life is bound to change. If your IQ improves by 30 points, that alone will change your life significantly. Living life in the world would be much more comfortable.

In Korea long ago, we were unable to build engines so we had to purchase engines from Japan to build our cars. Nowadays, I hear that Japan purchases Hyundai engines to build cars. Also, there are many models from the German Mercedes Benz company that purchase and use Hyundai engines. The Korean people are one of the smartest and one of the most talented people in the world. That's why even though Korea cannot produce a drop of petroleum, the country is able to eat and live well.

We import the expensive petroleum we need, and with that drive around our cars, and do everything. No matter what country you go to, the Korean people are very noticeable. They're smart, they're impatient, and they are very skilled with their hands. Once you look at the way they live, you can tell that they're Korean. If you go to America, you can see most Americans have lawns at their homes. But Koreans, they go and remove all their lawns, and instead, plant peppers, cucumbers, and tomatoes. When you go to America, and look at the yard, you can tell, "Ah, a Korean person lives there." Koreans are also one of the most impatient people in the world. If you want to find a Korean person at the airport, they say you can tell when you're at the bathroom. Americans, when they go to the bathroom they use the toilet, they wash their hands, they comb their hair, and they come out. But when you see a person zip his pants as he walks out of the bathroom, he is probably Korean. In this way, it is easy to see that Koreans are very impatient, very smart, and quick.

But even with that kind of intellect, you cannot enter into the world of spiritual life. A greater wisdom is necessary. There needs to be the guidance of the Holy Spirit. You need to receive that understanding. There's a limit to what we can realize on our own. You may say, "Pastor, what are we suppose to realize? If I've sinned, I know that I've sinned. You think I don't know of my own sin? I know. Yes, I know. Of course I know. Why wouldn't I know." But you only know, up to a certain point. In order to reach the spiritual world of God, a wisdom beyond your limits must come and make you realize your sins. That wisdom must come and free you from your sin. That wisdom must come and have you receive the grace of God. That's why we need the guidance of the Holy Spirit. We need the guidance of the Word of God. We need a revelation. We need the shepherd to have us realize these things. We need a guide.

The brothers and sisters in our church experience their lives change after receiving the forgiveness of sin. Just as the life of a person who's IQ is 100 will differ from the life of a person with an IQ of 130, people who receive the wisdom of God are also different. People without the wisdom of God become servants to their ambitions. They become servants to pleasures and servants to desires.

Even if you studied very well in school and possess several PhDs, you can only remain a servant to your flesh and will not be freed from it without the wisdom of God. But this changes the moment the wisdom of God enters into you.

I Threw Away My Boat and My Net for Jesus

So, let's continue talking about this. Right now, we are talking about sin coming to your knowledge versus realizing sin yourself. Can you tell the difference between the two? When you realize sin yourself, it means you can only realize it within the boundaries of what you can realize. But to have it come to your knowledge means you are being led into a world you would not be able to realize on your own, but by the Word of God and the Holy Spirit.

Let's discuss an example, Peter. Peter met Jesus at the Sea of Galilee. He cast his net all night long and could not catch a single fish. Jesus came and said, "Cast the net in the deep end and you will catch fish."

Peter thought, "There can't be any fish in the deep end. But I labored all night, and caught none. So let me follow His words and cast the net once more, into the deep end." He did so, casting the net in the deep end, and he caught a tremendous amount of fish. Peter was shocked and said to Jesus, "Lord, depart from me. For I'm a sinner."

Then Jesus said to Peter, "Follow me. I will make you into a fisher of men." Upon hearing this, Peter threw away his boat, his net, all of the fish, and followed Jesus.

This story is not in the Bible, but let's talk about the situation facing Peter's wife . That morning, Peter's wife made breakfast, and was waiting for her husband, who had gone out to catch fish, to come home. Usually, he would come home at around sunrise, but that morning he had not come home yet.

"Where is Peter?"

She goes out to search by the sea. She then gets a bad feeling. "What if his boat capsized in the middle of the night? What if he's lost, or fallen into the ocean?" She is worried as she goes, and a kid from the neighborhood runs over from the other side. Peter's wife asks him, "Did you see my husband over there? "

"Oh, yeah, I did see him."

"What was he doing?"

"Oh, your husband? He threw away his boat, and all the fish that he caught. And you know that guy Jesus, who walks around with nothing? He went and followed Him."

Peter's wife was flabbergasted.

"Oh, my…"

At least Pastor Ock Soo Park has a nice suit on. But our Lord, he only had one set of clothes. Do you think Jesus slept at a hotel in Jerusalem? Do you think he slept at an inn? Jesus always wore the same clothes, and he would sleep at the Mount of Olives. Let's take a moment to imagine Jesus. Do you think Jesus washed his hair with shampoo? Do you think he brushed his teeth often? Do you think he showered often? Do you think he washed his clothes? Quite different from the Jesus we imagine, Jesus at that time, must have been very pitiful. You can afford to sleep at an inn in Jerusalem if you have a little bit of money. But Jesus didn't get along so well with the inns, since he was young. He could not even enter the inns. When she heard that Peter followed that Jesus, how do you think Peter's wife must have felt?

"Has this man completely lost his mind? How could he just leave all that fish that he caught, his boat, his net, and follow that Jesus, who has nothing?"

What kind of heart do you think Peter had inside?

"I threw my boat away for Jesus. I threw my net away. I threw my life away. I threw my family away for Jesus."

And surely, that's the heart that Peter must've had inside. That's why Peter could think, "I have faith. I'm a good believer of Jesus. Is there anyone else who believes in Him as well as I do?" That's the heart that he must've had. There must be people like that among you also.

"See, I tithed. See, I gave offering. See, I prayed all night long. See, I gave help to others in need. Do you think I helped others because I had money to burn? Do you think I gave offering because I had so much money? I did all of this for God."

There are a lot of people like that. When the wisdom of God does not come, people think living spiritual life in this way is good.

I Lived in Prison for 14 Years for Jesus, and You Are Saying I Can't Go to Heaven?

Once, when I went to Vietnam, I met a pastor from an underground church. He was famous. When I met him, sadly, he was not born again. He did not know about the forgiveness of sins. I told him, "Pastor, by doing that, you cannot be born again." This person was so famous, and he's known by all the Christians in Vietnam. There was no one who would dare to say or criticize anything about his spiritual life. But when I said that to him, he didn't know what to do.

"Pastor, I was in prison for 14 years. Do you know what that life was like? I went through all that pain, and I wasn't the only one who went through that pain. My son became a beggar. My wife starved every day, and she had to pick out of the garbage to eat. And I endured all of that for Jesus. Still, you're saying that I cannot go to heaven?"

I said to him, "Pastor, I'm sorry but, the Bible clearly says that we cannot go to heaven through our works. The Bible tells us that there's nobody who can enter into heaven through their own good works. In Ephesians, chapter 2 verse 8 it says, *For by grace are ye saved through faith; and that not of yourselves; it is the gift of God, and not of works.* It says that salvation is not of works. In Titus, chapter 3 verse 5, it says that we being born again is not of works.

He then said to me, "Pastor, if believing in Jesus is not of works, then is it ok to commit sin and commit adultery?"

"I'm not saying it's ok to do that. But, no matter what we do, with our works, we cannot enter heaven."

He had no idea what to do. He then said, "I cannot talk to you anymore," and he left.

Everyone, with our works, we cannot be saved. Let's talk about the story of Heungbu, a traditional Korean folk tale. When the good guy, Heungbu, planted the gourd seed and opened up the gourds that were born, they were filled with gold, silver, and treasures. But when the wicked Nolbu opened the gourd, all these terrible, nasty things came out from it.

Everyone, there's another story that goes like this. There was this poor man who used to gather wood in the mountains. While he was gathering wood in the mountains, he dropped his ax into a pond. A lumberjack cannot gather wood without an ax. And if he's unable to sell wood, he will go hungry. He was sitting there weeping and wailing. Right then, after he lost his ax in the pond, a wizard suddenly appeared.

"Why are you crying?" asked the mysterious wizard.

"Oh, I made a mistake and I dropped my ax into the pond."

Right then, the wizard went into the pond, and brought out a big, shiny golden ax and asked him, "Is this your ax?"

"No, my ax is just an iron ax."

Then the wizard went back into the pond, and brought forth a silver ax. He asked, "Is this ax yours?"

"No, my ax is just made out of iron."

Again, he went into the pond and pulled out an iron ax.

"Is this your ax?"

"Yes, that is my ax."

So the wizard said to him, "Oh, you are such a good person. You may keep the golden ax and the silver ax, as well."

This is a man-made story. The stories that people make up are about the good guys who do good things and are blessed. That pretty much completes the whole story line.

I read the 66 books of the Old and New Testament many times. Nowhere in the Bible is there a story of being blessed by doing some good deed. Look for it. Nowhere in the Bible is there a story of a person doing good deeds to be blessed.

But the very interesting is, the Pharisees or the priests who did good things could not receive blessings. Instead, the woman who committed adultery, the man with infirmities for 38 years, the thief at the cross, and Zaccheus the publican, such people who committed sins, were blessed. This cannot be understood with our own understanding. The words in the Bible and the thoughts of man are so different.

Me? Deny the Lord? I Will Not

Everyone, we think that if we just simply blend man together with God, go to church, do good things, and live honestly, then we'll be blessed. But that is not the case. This is the limit of man's understanding, through man's own wisdom. When the revelation and guidance of God comes to you, you can discover from the Bible how man, who commits evil sins, can become blessed.

Everyone, do not be deceived. You are all evil people. This is not Pastor Park saying this to you, but this is the Word of God. We are all the descendants of Adam. In the same way, we are all the descendants of sin. We cannot do good deeds. People who labor and strain, and try to do good their entire lives will go to hell when they die. That is why we need Jesus. We need Jesus because we cannot do good. Jesus wanted Peter to realize this. But what heart did Peter have?

"I threw my family away for Jesus. I threw my boat away. I threw everything away. I only looked to Jesus and followed Him. I'm not like the other disciples. I'm a good believer of Jesus. I'm loyal to Jesus," were the kinds of thoughts that Peter had.

In the eyes of Jesus, Peter who thought this way of himself was in big trouble. Jesus wanted to use Peter as a precious worker, to make him into a fisher of men. But with this heart of Peter, this will not happen. Why is that so? It is because Peter trusts himself. He thinks he can serve Jesus well, and serve God well. But, that's why he cannot receive the grace of God.

Jesus wanted to teach Peter what kind of person he truly was. He wanted Peter to realize, "Peter, you trust in yourself, but you need to see how foolish and stupid it is to trust yourself." But Peter did not know these kinds of things.

Finally at the last supper, Jesus opened his mouth. "Tonight, all of you will be offended because of me." Peter was shocked.

"What? We will all be offended becauase of you? Sure, Andrew or Philip may, but not me," thought Peter. "Though I die Lord, I will never be offended because of you," he said.

Jesus said to Peter, "Simon, before the cock crows tonight, you will deny me three times."

"Nonsense. Why would I deny you Lord? Though I die with you Lord, I will never deny you. I'm the kind of person who says, 'I'll do it,' and I really do it. I threw everything away to follow you Lord. Why would I deny you? I will never!"

Peter still had no idea who he was. He only knew what he did well. He only knows of himself as the person who threw the boat, the net, and his family away to follow the Lord. But, he does not know exactly who he is. Peter cannot realize this on his own.

Jesus wanted Peter to realize what kind of person he was. He said, "Before the cock crows tonight, you will deny me three times."

"Lord, is that all you think of me? I'm so disappointed. I'm not that kind of a person. Why would I deny you Lord? Even if I die, I'll never deny you,

Lord," answered Peter, who was full of determination.

When the soldiers came to Jesus at Gethsemane, all of the other disciples ran away, but Peter could not. He could not run away because he said he would not deny the Lord, even if he dies. Had he run away, he would not have denied Jesus. But he was caught because of himself. He followed Jesus from afar. Jesus entered the house of the priest. Because John knew the high priest, he spoke to the porter, and Peter was able to enter in as well. Right then a damsel saw Peter, and said, "Oh, this person. Isn't he part of the same group as Jesus? Isn't he also His disciple?"

Peter thought about it, and there was nothing that he could say. He said, "What are you talking about? I am not His disciple." He felt pricked in his heart. And somebody else also came to Peter and asked him if he was a disciple of Jesus. Peter said that he was not. When he was asked the third time, Peter cursed Jesus and said that he didn't know Him. We don't know what he said as he cursed Jesus, but while he was denying Him the third time, the cock crew, "Cock-a-doodle-do."

So, who was right? Of course, Jesus was right. Until that point, Peter did not know himself. Why didn't he know? Because of what he did well, he did not have the eyes to see himself.

Peter Who Realized Who He Was Through the Guidance of Jesus

This is also true with us. When you give offering, when you pray or fast, or stay up to pray all night, and when you go to the early morning service, or help others, Satan makes you remember each of those things.

"I went to the early morning service. I fasted and I prayed. I prayed all night. Oh, I'm not like Deacon Lee. I'm a good believer."

When you have that kind of a heart, you lose the eyes to see yourself. You say to yourself, "I'm a good believer." However, your spiritual life does not go as well as you planned. You say, "Oh, it's because, this time, I didn't try my best. But from the New Year, from the first day of the first month, I'm determined to live a spiritual life. Then I'll do well."

"From this moment, if I repent all of my sins, keep from sinning again, and just live according to the words in the Bible, then I'll be able to keep the law and believe well."

You say such things, because you don't know yourself.

Jesus wants to show the people who think of themselves to be great, their true image. Jesus wanted to show Peter his image. The Peter who thought that he was great, and that he believed well. That's why Jesus said what He did at the last supper. He created the opportunity for Peter to deny Jesus three times. Right then, Peter realized what kind of person he was. Then, the heart to believe in himself came crumbling down. Peter wept and wailed, "Oh, I was so foolish. Even though I had nothing, I alone thought that I believed well, I was so arrogant." Right then, Peter was so disappointed and embarrassed with himself. He thought, "I'm no apostle. A person like me? I can't be a disciple of Jesus. No, I can't. I'm just a fisherman. I'm just a fisherman. I'm not worthy to become a disciple of Jesus." Peter thought that he was the greatest among all of the disciples that followed Jesus, and he thought that he was the best. He thought that he was different from the others, that he was faithful and loyal to Jesus. But when Jesus led him to realize himself, Peter saw who he really was. Then Peter thought, "I'm not worthy to be a disciple of Jesus. I've been so uplifted all that time. I'm not an apostle." For three years, he followed Jesus. Now he realized how much he had been boasting and how he had been lost in his own greatness. He thought, "No, I'm not worthy. I'm just a fisherman. I should be fishing."

Peter told the other disciples, "I'm going fishing. I'm not worthy to be a disciple of Jesus." Peter returned again to the Sea of Galilee. Afterwards, when he met Jesus who had resurrected, Peter felt ashamed and he also realized what he had done, boasting that he would not betray Jesus. He felt as though he needed to say something to Jesus.

"Lord, what you said was right. I thought that if I tried, then I could do it. I thought if I tried to not deny you, then I would be able to not deny you. But now, I've discovered what a foolish man I was. Lord, forgive me."

I'm sure that's what Peter must have wanted to say. But when he met Jesus, he could not say anything. He just hesitated for a little bit. He was unable to bring himself to say anything. He became a Peter who was completely different from the previous Peter. Jesus wanted Peter to realize his own image. Peter did not realize this on his own, but he was able to realize this through Jesus.

Loving folks, just like the grace that Peter received, you also need to receive this revelation that comes, not from your thoughts, but that comes from the Lord. With your thoughts, you cannot realize what is wrong with you. Your thoughts only go so far as to say, "Oh, I sinned yesterday. But I shouldn't sin anymore. Oh, I should be good. I should pray hard and live a good spiritual life." That's as far as your thoughts go. But that realization must come to you. It means, you need to receive the grace of God. But because we are high-hearted, we simply think, "What, all I have to do is try harder." What does the Bible say? Does it tell us that to receive the forgiveness of sins, we need to have that knowledge?

"God, I committed adultery, God, forgive me. God, I lied. Please forgive me. God, I committed fraud. Please forgive me." Is that what the Bible is telling us?

You Must Precisely Realize

Leviticus chapter 4 tells us about the forgiveness of sin. Loving folks, just as Jesus allowed Peter to realize, if God has you realize, then you can precisely discover yourself. The image that you have seen until now, just like Peter, has only been one side of yourself. You have not seen yourself as a whole. When you get to realize this through the Holy Spirit of God, only then can you see your image precisely, and then become humble. Your heart can become lower. Then, you can accept the Word of God, accept the salvation of God, and you can also have the heart to accept the power of God.

The Bible does not tell us to realize. It says, *Or if his sin, which he hath sinned, come to his knowledge....* The fact that we have sinned means that sinfulness has already entered our hearts. But afterwards, not only do we need to have realization outwardly about the sin that we've committed, but we need to discover it in the core of our hearts. And we need to precisely realize what kind of person we are.

Peter, after discovering himself, discovered the power of Jesus, and became a powerful servant of God. Everyone, once again, objectively look at your heart. Isn't your heart dirty? Isn't your heart evil? Isn't your heart lustful? Isn't your heart deceitful? With that dirty, evil, lustful, and deceitful heart, how could you do any good? How do you think you can follow the will of God? You need to be freed from yourself. And shed off all the good things and bad things that you have done. You need to be freed from yourself and you need to gain the new heart of Jesus. You need to have realized these things through Jesus. And the wisdom of Jesus must be upon you. Then, you can become one with God.

CHAPTER 3
Bring a Kid of the Goats, a Female Without Blemish

Just as a doctor heals a disease, the one that heals our lives is Jesus. But people live spiritual life while having built a wall between Jesus and them. Then, they strain to become clean, honest, and holy on their own. But no matter how hard they try and labor, and although it seems like things are going to work out, ultimately, they don't. The female goat without blemish does the work of washing our sins away. Becoming holy is only possible through Jesus who is without blemish. No matter how hard we try, labor, pray, and make an effort, we must realize that it cannot be done.

Hello, everyone. It's good to see you. Today, as well, we will talk about Leviticus chapter four, about the sin offering.

And if any one of the common people sin through ignorance, while he doeth somewhat against any of the commandments of the Lord concerning things which ought not to be done, and be guilty; Or if his sin, which he hath sinned, come to his knowledge: then he shall bring his offering, a kid of the goats, a female without blemish, for his sin which he hath sinned. And he shall lay his hand upon the head of the sin offering, and slay the sin offering in the place of the burnt offering. And the priest shall take of the blood thereof with his finger, and put it upon the horns of the altar of burnt offering, and shall pour out all the blood thereof at the bottom of the altar. And he shall take away all the fat thereof, as the fat is taken away from off the sacrifice of peace offerings; and the priest shall burn it upon the altar for a sweet savour unto the Lord; and the priest shall make an atonement for him, and it shall be forgiven him. (Leviticus 4:27-31)

Sister, You Are One Step Behind

The sin offering for the common person recorded in Leviticus chapter 4 verse 27 says, *…and if any one of the common people sins through ignorance*, and it begins with how they commit sins. Then, in verse 31 it tells us, *and it shall be forgiven him*, which is the end result of this. When we read the Bible, it often starts with where man commits sin, and then many different things happen along the way, and then the sinner receives the forgiveness of sins and becomes holy. That whole process is the general storyline of all the passages in the Bible.

Ever since Adam and Eve committed sin in Genesis chapter 3, the history of mankind continues on as a history of man fighting with sin. Then man received the forgiveness of sins, and in Revelations chapter 21 and 22, man enters a state of being without sin. That is the whole process that the Bible is showing us about. All of the stories in the Bible tell us about these things. As we talked about before, this is also true with the story of the prodigal son in Luke chapter 15.

A certain man had two sons. The younger said, "Father, give me the portion of goods that falleth to me," and that's how the story begins. There must have been many words exchanged between the father and the son. The son then takes the wealth and goes to a faraway country. How can something like this come about? Whether a person commits theft, commits adultery, or has spiritual life, no matter what he does, all of those things start from the heart. Theft doesn't just happen out of nowhere. From the heart, man makes his plans, "Oh, I would like to have that thing. When would be a good time to steal it?" Such plans are first formed in the heart. A person who commits adultery, when he sees a certain woman, immediately says, "Let's commit adultery."

"Sure!"

That's not how it happens. First, the lustful heart arises. In the beginning, there is resistance in his heart telling him he should not commit adultery and he is conflicted by it. Then when he's defeated by the lustful heart, that heart begins to drag this person around. He thinks, "Ah, this is how I should go meet women. Ah, I can go commit adultery like this." With that he begins to plan. He follows through, and the sin of adultery becomes established. This is also the same with murder, and also the same with the world of faith.

Simply saying, "Let's believe in Jesus. Let's not sin. Let's keep the law. Let's tithe." Saying such things will not do. The foundation to be able to believe in the Lord must first be built in the heart, and then spiritual life can develop. When you read the Bible, it tells us in detail how spiritual life can develop and form inside of our hearts.

The younger son one day says to the father, "Father, give me the portion of goods that falleth to me." Even the older brother could not dare say such a thing, but how was the younger brother able to say this? Satan exalts our hearts and continually strikes up the heart in us to make us think that if we do something, we can do it well.

Today, many Christians in Korea are deceived by the heart Satan puts in them. They simply think, "If I pray all will be well. From now on I will pray in the mountains. I'll fast and pray, and I'll go live my spiritual life and I'll be fine. From the start of the New Year I'll be able to tithe well. And if I go to church every Sunday beginning with this Bible conference, things will be fine." They just vaguely think that if they are determined to do well, they can do well. They are deceived into thinking it will be well. So many churchgoers in Korea today are so endlessly deceived in this way. They continue to try and fail, try and fail. They repeat this over and over again.

Satan put into the heart of the younger son an arrogant heart of thinking, "You are great." That heart entered into him and after some time when that heart settled in the younger son, he became able to ask for the portion of the wealth from his father. He said, "Father give me the wealth. I'm different. Father, do you always only think of me as a little child?"

Because he is high-hearted, he cannot listen to anybody else. And finally, the father gave him the wealth.

When you become high-hearted, you end up indulging, and you end up becoming corrupt. As I served the Lord, He gave me so much grace. Among the grace that I've received, He has upheld my heart. I'm a pitiful person, but there are times when I would also exalt my heart. At times I would feel in my heart, "Wow, this college student camp was great. Oh, the theme this time was really good. Wow, a lot of people received grace from reading my book." But each time that would happen, the Lord would bring me great difficulty. I feel in my heart that God is saying to me, "So, you think you did that well? Then why don't you try this too?" When I exalt my heart, often times the Lord would give me hardships. I would become high-hearted, and then I would be shocked, saying, "Oh! This is not it! I was not the one who did this; God did this!" God would then change my heart. It was God leading me so that I would be able to remain within grace.

One day, D.L. Moody was coming down from the pulpit after preaching the Word. One lady came to Moody and said to him, "Mr. Moody, the sermon tonight was so graceful to me. I've never been so blessed in my whole life."

Right then, Moody smiled and replied to her, "Sister, you are one step behind."

"No, Mr. Moody. I listened to your sermon tonight and really, I received so much grace."

"That's right, Sister. You're one step behind."

"What? What do you mean?"

"Sister, before you came to me, the devil was one step ahead of you and came to me and said that to me already. He said to me, 'You gave a graceful sermon tonight.'"

Moody received the grace of God. In that kind of a heart he was able to work with humbleness. When you become high-hearted, you indulge and you begin to have confidence. That is why when the younger son lived riotously eating and drinking with the harlots, he was able to spend money wastefully. Once you become riotous and indulge, you are bound to fail. The younger son failed in everything and went down to the pigpen. Once you fail, pain comes about. Once pain comes, you begin to remorse even if you don't try to. There was no one telling the younger son, "Hey younger one! What you did was terrible, so repent!" As he ate the husks that the swine fed on, the younger son began to realize and fell into remorse on his own, saying, "You're so crazy. How could you give that pile of cash to those harlots? If you hadn't, you wouldn't be going through this kind of suffering. You were crazy!" Once he realized this, he was able to turn around, and the younger son returned home.

If you repent and turn around with a true heart, the grace of the father comes upon you. This is a rule of the Bible. This is the way it works in the Bible. Many people in their spiritual lives go through this process their whole lives. Some people's lives end while they remain in arrogance. Some people's lives end while they have failed in everything and remain in pain. Some people's lives will end while they're on their way back. The Bible tells us the world of our hearts.

The Change of a Certain Biology Doctor

The female goat without blemish that we are talking about represents Jesus who has become the sin offering for us. Jesus lived in this world for 33 years, and not once did he commit sin. He was without blemish. Everyone, just because you are a nice person doesn't mean that you do not commit sins. When sin enters your heart and tempts you, you will not sin if you have the power to overcome it. We look at the people around us and when we see good people we say, "That person can live his life without laws. He's so good and so kind." We say that from time to time. However, the standards of man and the standards of God are very different. There may be many people who are good and without blemish according to the standards of man. But there is no one who is without blemish in the eyes of God. There's no one among us who can stand boldly before God without blemish in His eyes. There is only one person who can come before God: Jesus Christ. Through Jesus Christ we become washed and we become holy. This cannot be done through our good efforts or our works. But people don't realize this.

There was a biologist in the United States. His wife was a very fervent churchgoer and a true believer of Jesus. Because his wife had faith and respected the pastor of her church and exalted him so much, this biologist became upset. He thought, "This woman is crazy about her church. You know what? I'm a doctor. How is that pastor any better than me?"

One day, this doctor had a plan to embarrass the pastor. He told his wife, "Honey, if the pastor of your church is such a great man as you say he is, then let's invite him to our home for dinner one night." His wife was shocked. She was so happy to hear that her husband, who had always been critical of her church, was inviting the pastor over for dinner. She was so happy and excited, and with a joyful heart she prepared dinner and invited the pastor.

At the dinner, the doctor spoke to the pastor, "Pastor?"

"Yes, Doctor?"

"Pastor, do you believe that Jesus was born from the body of a virgin?"

The pastor smiled and answered, "I do believe. Jesus is the almighty God. I'm absolutely sure that Jesus came to this earth through the body of the virgin, Mary."

The doctor thought, "I've got him," and opened his lips, saying, "I had never dreamt that the pastor of the church that my wife attends would be this ignorant. How could a virgin have a child? I majored in biology, and that biologically makes no sense. Pastor, please make some sense!" The doctor began to corner the pastor.

The pastor listened to all he had to say, and said, "But I do believe that the almighty God could bring a virgin to have a child." That was how the dinner ended and they said their goodbyes.

Afterwards, this doctor was conducting some research upon the request of a certain company, and he failed. He went through great hardship. As he went through hard and painful times, his heart crumbled down and he received salvation. He began to go to church every day and listened to the pastor's sermon. One day, this doctor said to his wife, "Honey, let's invite the pastor over for dinner."

"Sure, let's do that."

So, at the exact same place where they had dinner 10 years earlier, they all sat down and were eating. Then the doctor asked a question, "Pastor, do you still believe that Jesus was born from the body of a virgin?"

"Yes, I do. The almighty God had Jesus to be born from the body of a virgin so that He may save us."

"I believe that as well. It is more than proven biologically that a virgin can have a child. Hens can lay eggs even without the rooster. The almighty God who made that possible, why wouldn't He be able to have Jesus be born from the body of a virgin?"

"Before, you said biologically that it was impossible, and now you say it is possible. What's wrong with your biology?"

"Pastor, before, with the petty knowledge that I had, I thought to go against the Word of God. That's why I thought in a manner that made it seem impossible. But now, I have submitted to the Word of God and I accept the Word, and I think in a manner that makes it possible. And that's why it can be more than proven."

When people have certain thoughts, they are more than capable of thinking in the wrong direction. When your heart settled and organized, your thoughts will move in the same direction as the thoughts of God. But when your heart is wrong, your thoughts will move in a direction that's the same as the thoughts of Satan, even though you are still the same person. That's why the Bible humbles the arrogant and proud hearted. Through that, our hearts must flow together with the heart of God. Then we can live a happy, blessed, and graceful life. That's what the Bible is telling us. It also tells us the process by which faith becomes established in our lives.

Jesus Who Is the Offering Without Blemish to Make Us Holy

Nowhere in the Bible did God see man and call man perfect. What God said upon seeing man can be read in Jeremiah chapter 17: *The heart is deceitful above all things and desperately wicked.* In Genesis chapter 6, God writes: *And God saw that the wickedness of man was great in the earth and that the imagination of the thoughts of his heart was only evil continually.* Then in Psalms 14 it says, *The Lord looked down from Heaven upon the children of men to see if there were any that did understand and seek God; they were all gone aside, they were altogether become filthy, there is none that doeth good, no not one.* If so, everyone, then how does spiritual life come about? How can spiritual life be achieved in our hearts?

Yesterday evening a friend of mine came here. About ten days ago this friend had called me. He was a friend that I grew up with from elementary school.

Bring a Kid of the Goats, a Female Without Blemish

He said, "Let's go get some dinner together."

I said, "Sure. Let's do that."

He told me to come to the subway Surak-san Station by six in the evening, and I went. That friend bought meat for several of our friends. We ate and enjoyed it very well. Then we went to the house of another one of our friends. This friend's wife had passed away ten years ago, and he was living in difficulty with just his younger son. He said, "Hey Ock Soo, you're a pastor. Since you've come to my home, why don't you say a prayer of blessing, to bless my home." So, I opened the Bible and first preached the Gospel to them.

Right then, among my friends, one named Jinyoung told me of his pain. "Hey Ock Soo, I have a younger sister and things are very difficult. From a long time ago she has been suffering from suspicion of her husband's faithfulness and her life has been like hell. No matter how much I talk to her she doesn't listen to me. Her husband just wants to kill himself now. And she is a pastor herself." When friends get together they tend to only want to talk about good things. They don't want to talk about such things. But this friend of mine opened his heart to me so I preached the Gospel to him. Before heading home, there was a copy of the book, *The Secret of Forgiveness of Sins and Being Born Again* in my car, so I gave it to him.

Even though this friend of mine is old, he still drives. Whenever he would have a little bit of break time from driving, he would read that book, then put it away, and read it again. After reading the whole book, he said that his heart was unlike before. This friend had so many difficulties in the past and he would drink so much. I said to him, "Hey, at this age how can you drink so much? Do you still think that you're young? Stop drinking so much!" But after this friend read the book and after Jesus came into his heart, whenever he wanted to drink, he was reminded of how he drank in the past and of the dirty mistakes that he made. This kept him from drinking and he began to drink less and less. That's what happens when Jesus Christ enters into our hearts.

It's not that I'm trying to make myself clean. It's not that I'm trying to make myself whole. It's not about me, making myself more honest. If Jesus makes me clean, and He upholds my heart to make me whole, then it is Jesus who makes me holy. It is not the common person who can cure diseases, but the doctors at the hospital who treat and heal diseases. The one who heals our lives is Jesus. But people today have built walls between themselves and Jesus, and that is how they live their spiritual lives. They strain to make themselves clean, to make themselves more honest, and to make themselves more holy. But no matter how much they labor and strain, no matter how much it looks like it's going to work out, it doesn't work and they fail. Ultimately, you fail. That is why Jesus must do it.

So, what is the meaning of the female goat without blemish mentioned in Leviticus chapter 4? Is it not the offering to wash our sins away? It means that it is the female goat without blemish that washes our sins away. Becoming holy is only possible through Jesus, who is without blemish. We must realize the fact that no matter how much we labor, try, pray, and strain, we cannot do it ourselves. If we don't realize that truth, we will continue to try to go to heaven by laboring to do good. We will continue to try to keep the law and try to be faithful. However, this kind of spiritual life cannot work out. Ultimately it fails. Many people today don't realize this so they just believe in their own thoughts.

"These days I've been so busy with my business and I tell some lies. After I'm done raising my kids and getting my kids married, and once I'm done with my business and start to live a good life without lying, I'll do a better job of believing in Jesus." That is how people always think. But it's not about you doing something.

When Jesus enters inside of you, everything changes. That is why I carefully search the Bible about how Jesus, who is without blemish and holy, meets with us. Interestingly, when a person who is wearing clean clothes hugs a person who is covered with ashes from a charcoal factory, what will happen? Does the person who is covered in charcoal ashes become clean? Or does the person who is wearing clean clothes become dirty? In the world, when clean things get together with dirty things, the clean things become dirty. No matter how clean it is, if dung gets on it, it becomes dirty. It becomes dirty when dust gets on it, and it becomes dirty when dirt gets on it.

The Bible is so amazing; when the clean Jesus met the dirty woman taken in the act of adultery, what happened? Did Jesus end up committing adultery? Jesus not only defeated the evil and the dirtiness, but He also cast out the lustfulness inside of the woman of adultery. The woman who committed adultery became clean. In the world, if lepers lived mixed in with healthy people, there's a chance that the healthy people will catch leprosy. But when the lepers met Jesus, the lepers were made clean. These are the ways of God, which are completely different from the ways of the world. In the world, when dirty things and clean things come together, it is the clean things that become dirty. But in the world of God, when the dirty sinner gets together with the clean and holy Jesus, the sinners become holy. In the Bible, there are many stories of how the dirty man gets together with Jesus who is clean. The woman taken in the act of adultery was being dragged to be stoned to death when she met Jesus. The thief at the cross met Jesus while he was hanging on the cross. Simon Peter met Jesus at the Sea of Galilee. Apostle Paul met Jesus on his way up to Damascus. Through meeting Jesus, all of these people changed.

Where Is that Place Where You Can Meet Jesus?

If so, where is that place where we meet Jesus? Where must we go to meet Jesus? There are many people who have gone to church for decades and have yet to meet Jesus. Must you go to prayer houses to meet Jesus? If you look in the Bible, it records of the place where you can meet Jesus.

In Luke chapter 10 verses 30 through 33, it says:

And Jesus answering said, A certain man went down from Jerusalem to Jericho, and fell among thieves, which stripped him of his raiment, and wounded him, and departed, leaving him half dead. And by chance there came down a certain priest that way: and when he saw him, he passed by on the other side. And likewise a Levite, when he was at the place, came and looked on him, and passed by on the other side. But a certain Samaritan, as he journeyed, came where he was: and when he saw him, he had compassion on him. (Luke 10:30-33)

The good Samaritan represents Jesus in these words. Jerusalem is located 800 meters above sea level and Jericho is in a very low-lying area. Where along the way between high-elevation Jerusalem and the valleys of Jericho is this place where we can meet Jesus? Where was Jesus going? Then, where is that place? "Where" is the place where that certain man fell among thieves and was dying and could do nothing at all. When you, through the

Bible, realize this and your heart reaches that "where," then tonight you will meet Jesus, have your sins washed clean, become holy, and become born again. And when you get to that place, you can receive the blessing of walking with Jesus your whole life.

We're talking about the female goat without blemish in Leviticus chapter 4. Jesus is the one without blemish and we are people with many sins. An artist said to me this one time, "If only men sit along a long bench, because the men have broad shoulders, it becomes tight along the shoulders. But if only women sit along that same bench, because women have wide hips, it becomes very tight along the hips. That's why if they sit alternating one man, then one woman, one man, then one woman, then it will not be tight along the shoulders, nor along the hips, and it will be just the perfect fit." That is how God made man to be. I really felt like that is true. Jesus came to save sinners. That is why Jesus must be holy, and we must be filthy. Jesus must be good. We must be evil. Jesus must be perfect, and we must be full of blemishes. Then it's a perfect match. But, we keep on straining, trying to not become a sinner.

If the Leprosy Spreads Through the Whole Body, You're Clean

I'll read just one verse in the Bible. Leviticus chapter 13, verse 13:

Then the priest shall consider: and, behold, if the leprosy have covered all his flesh, he shall pronounce him clean that hath the plague: it is all turned white: he is clean.

These words have tremendous meaning. If a person begins to show signs of leprosy, in the Old Testament, the priest examines him. If there is leprosy that is growing on his head, on his back, or on his chest, or his leg, or his hand, the priest declares that person unclean and kicks him out of the camp.

When that little bit of leprosy on his back begins to spread and covers his whole back and spreads down to the legs, and spreads to the chest and reaches to his head and spreads all over from head to toe, then his whole body would be covered with leprosy and he would be filthy and nasty. So he should be terribly unclean, right? But what the Bible says is that if the leprosy spreads throughout the whole body, then that man is clean. At first, I thought, "Was this verse incorrectly translated?" I searched other Bibles.

I searched the King James Version, the Living Bible, the Revised Standard Version, the Amplified Bible, I searched them all but this was what they all said. I thought, "Why is this? If you have a little bit of leprosy, it says you're unclean. So if it spreads to the whole body, then that person should be more unclean." But the Bible says that if the leprosy spreads throughout the whole body, then you're clean. I could not understand. But when we read the story of the prodigal son, in the book of Luke, this all begins to make sense.

In Luke chapter 15, the prodigal son was eating and drinking with the harlots and ran out of money. He was hungry so he went to herd the swine. Right then, what did the younger son do? He regretted that he had wasted all that money on the harlots. He realized how wrong he was; how evil, how dirty, and how foolish he was. He made up his mind, saying, "Okay, I'm never going near the harlots again. And from now on I'm going to herd the swine and satisfy the master. And if he pays me, I'm going to buy some nice clothes and wear them. And I'm going to buy some gifts for my father and I'll return to my father." Not only does the younger son feel this way, but we also feel the same way.

As we commit sin, we think, "Oh I was terribly wrong. I should never do this again. And from now on, let me read the Bible and be good and live by faith." Is that a bad thing to do or a good thing to do? Everyone thinks of this to be good. But when the younger son, with the heart of remorse, tried to herd the pigs well, did the blessing come upon him? Not so. While the younger son was in the pigpen, he was thinking, "From now on I'm never going to the brothel again. From now on I'm going to be diligent. I'm going to take good care of these pigs and make some money." While he was doing that, he dropped down to the position of starving, until he was at the point of death. Do you know why that is? Suppose the sin of the younger son going to the harlot's house was leprosy. Living as a good person represents the parts of the body without leprosy. This means the younger son only had leprosy on half of his body. Right? Is that clean or unclean? That's right. Unclean. Do you understand what I'm saying?

Everyone, by nature we have hearts that are dirty, but we try to realize the sins that we committed and try to move forward by attempting to be good. That's the kind of heart that we have. People with that kind of heart think that if they begin to live truthfully, from this point forward, it's going to work out. But that's what it is to be deceived by Satan. In the eyes of God, even when you make up your mind to become truthful, you're still unclean and still dirty.

Who were the people who met God? They were the people who became full lepers. It was terribly wrong of the younger son to commit sins with the harlots, live riotously, and waste the father's wealth. But on the other hand, trying to be good from that point on is also evil. People don't realize that fact. That's why they think that if they live truthfully they can become truthful. They think that if they live honestly, they can become honest. Because they're unable to realize that they're filthy like a full-body leper, they try to stand in the position of trying to do good. That's why they're unable to meet Jesus.

Everyone, Jesus is the sin offering without blemish. We must come before God as the filthy, dirty man that is full of blemish. But we try to live honestly. This does not make us truthful. But, the more we try to realize in our hearts, the more pitiful it makes us. So, when the thought, "From now on, if I try, it will be well," falls apart, and when you have no hope, that's when Jesus comes to us. When did the man who fell among thieves meet Jesus? He had fallen among the thieves and he was dying. When the priest was passing by, he thought that the priest would save him. But the priest just passed him by. Then the Levite was passing by, and he hoped that the Levite would save him. But the Levite, as well, just passed him by. Now he was all out of hope. Jesus comes to such a person.

In John chapter 5, Jesus went to the man with the infirmity for 38 years. The other sick people nearby wanted to enter the pool first when the angel came down to trouble the water. They were staring at the water and thus were unable to meet Jesus. The man with the infirmity for 38 years could not even enter the water, even if he were to see the angel troubling the water. Because he had no way and had no hope, Jesus came to him.

The woman taken into adultery met Jesus. How did He meet her? This woman who was caught in adultery and was being dragged over to be stoned to death had no hope at all. She thought, "Now I'm dead." When she had no way and no method, Jesus came looking for her.

Where did the thief at the cross meet Jesus? He met Jesus while he was hanging, crucified on the cross. While on the cross, he had no hope at all. How could he have any hope when he was dying? Many people believe that if they realize their sins of committing adultery, theft, living riotously, and they turn from these sins, they will somehow become good. The younger son also felt this way in the beginning. What you must clearly know is that people are fooled into thinking this. Even if we do realize that and turn around, we can only continue to do evil. We must give up on the thought of trying to be good. Then Jesus can come. Jesus must come, for us to become good. But because people try to be good themselves, Jesus cannot come to them.

When a leper has only a small amount of leprosy, he says, "I'm going to take medication and be healed quickly," and tries to be healed. After one night, the condition seems to get better and he begins to have hope. After another night, the disease spreads more and he becomes more disappointed. When the leprosy spreads throughout the whole body, there is no place in the body without leprosy. Even the last bit of skin remaining is all covered with leprosy and he no longer has any hope. He can only say, "Now there is no way I can be healed of this leprosy." The Bible calls such a person clean. Why is that? People who think that they can do even the smallest bit of good, try to do it themselves, and with that, they block Jesus from being able to work and Jesus is unable to work.

You may think of spiritual life as, "Since I'm lacking, I'm going to read the Bible. I'm going to pray a little more." And if you keep the law more, you think that your spiritual life will be well. That is being deceived by Satan to think backwards. You have to be lacking for spiritual life to be well. The more you try to do spiritual life, the more you will fail. Spiritual life is saying, "Lord, I don't have any more ways. There's nothing I can do. I can only face destruction. Lord, now have compassion on me." That's what it is. For you to have that kind of spiritual life, you must try it and realize the fact that you cannot do it. I'm sure you must have been determined to quit smoking, quit drinking, and live a good life in the church from the New Year. Is there anyone who has not made those kinds of resolutions before? You made the resolutions but did they work? They did not. Why did they not work? They must not work in order for Jesus to fix you.

"Even though I try, I can't do it. Even though I tried to read the Bible, I can't do it. Even though I prayed, I can't do it. Even keeping the law, even tithing, even going to church on Sunday, I cannot do it. I cannot do it anymore. Jesus, you must do it." This is the confession that we must make.

Hey, Why Did You Mess with It and Put Us Through All This Misery?

As you well know, there is a great difference between a fisher who owns his own boat, and a fisher who doesn't. Fishers, who own their own boats, can keep all of their earnings when they sell the fish they catch. But people who don't own their own boats must give half of their catch to the owner of the boat. That is why it's a fisher's dream to own his own boat and go fishing with it. But does a boat cost ten or twenty dollars? Because the boats are so expensive, many fishers can't even think of buying their own boat and they must use other people's boats.

One day, a boat captain bought a new boat and put his old boat on sale. Three fishermen heard about this and said, "Oh this is our chance!" and the three of them bought that boat. Although it was an old, junky boat, because it was their own boat, they were so happy. They, so excitedly, took the boat to the ocean and began to let down the net to catch fish. That day, they caught so many fish. "Alright, now we made a lot of money," and saying that, they tried to turn on the boat's ignition to return to the port.

The engine, vroom, vroom, vroom, turned on. But soon after, it turned off. They tried to turn on the ignition again. Once again, the engine turned on for a little bit then turned off. All day it went, "Pang, pang, poof," and turned off. The weather was so hot, and the fish began to rot. They were thirsty and it was driving them crazy.

"I guess you get what you pay for. We were so happy that the boat was so cheap, but I guess this was why it was so cheap." They said that and complained but it didn't help them at all. The three of them continued to just wrestle with the boat and became exhausted. They spent the night and it became morning, but still, the boat would not turn on. Now the fish were all spoiled and they needed to return to the port, but they were unable to. They were out of water and were completely lost. But from the other side a big ship was passing by. They waved and screamed to call that ship over. That ship came close and asked what was wrong. They said, "Our boat has broken down. So please help us."

"Our ship is on its way to Incheon. Is it okay if we take you to Incheon?"

"Yeah. Whether it be Incheon… just take us to any port."

"Then throw us your rope." The fisherman threw the rope and the men tied it to the large ship.

Then the ship went, "vroom" and went on its way, and the other boat was simply pulled along. Everybody let out a sigh of relief saying, "Now we've made it." They began to talk amongst each other about whether they should sell this boat or get a new engine. After talking about that for a little bit, they had nothing else to do, so they became bored. Among them there was one fisherman who knew how to deal with engines, and he opened up a grease rag. With a wrench, he began to disassemble the engine and lay out the pieces of the engine, one by one, on top of the grease rag. Then he wiped down and cleaned the parts, one by one, and began to reassemble it. When he turned on the engine, it went, "vroom, vroom, vroom" and the ignition turned on.

When the ship in front that was pulling them looked behind and heard the engine turn on, they saw that the boat's engine was running and smoke was coming from it. So they untied the rope and just left. But not long after the big ship left, the boat went, poof and stopped working. No matter how hard they tried, the ignition would not turn on. Then a fight broke out inside of the boat. "Hey, what's wrong with you? If you're going to fix it, then do it right. Why did you even touch it and put us through this misery?"

"Hey, I didn't mean to do that. This is just what happened."

"Of course, I'm upset. We're about to die of thirst."

Everyone, the large ship pulls what kind of a boat? It pulls the boat with an engine that does not work. But if the boat makes a sound, then the ship releases it and just leaves. So if the boat is going to be fixed and makes the pang, pang, pang sound, then it should surely be able to go all the way to its' destination on its own. If it can't, then it shouldn't even make that sound to begin with. But if it makes that sound, though it can make it all the way, it's a path to failure.

Live Perfectly or Completely Keep Your Hands Off

Spiritual life is the same. If you're going to live spiritual life well, then don't commit a single sin and live perfectly. Or completely let go of it from your hands. One or the other. But because you live a spiritual life that's neither this nor that, spiritual life becomes difficult. If you're confident in living a spiritual life, then keep every single Word of God from Genesis chapter 1 to Revelation chapter 22, and do not break a single one of them. Jesus said that if a man looks at a woman and has lust in his heart, then he as already committed adultery. Then don't have lust in your heart. Don't covet, and don't get angry. Then you can go to heaven. Who would ever stop you from doing that?

But if you can't do it, you must say, "Lord, I am unable," and let go. The problem is that, even though people are unable, they act like they can. Even though they are unable, they think that if they try, they can do it, so they continue to try. Why is that? It is because they have not arrived at the end result yet. The younger son failed. When he wasted all of the wealth, had he turned around and returned to the father's house, he would not have suffered, he would not have gone to the pigpen, and he would not have had to eat the husks. But the younger son tried to do well on his own in order to return to the father's house. That's the problem. If the fisherman just remained idle, the ship would have just taken them to Incheon or Youngpyeongdo or anywhere. All they needed to do was just get pulled. But why did they put their hands on the engine? If they're going to fix the engine, they should have fixed it well enough so they can get home all the way, or if they had not touched it or did nothing to it to begin with, then it would not have been a problem. But they put their hands on it, even though they couldn't fix it completely, and that's what became the problem. This is also exactly the same with your spiritual life. When you feel, "Pastor, I can't do it. I can't keep the law. Even if I try to do it, I can't. Honestly, I'm so dirty inside. The dirty heart arises inside of me. And the lustful heart arises in me. What can I do? I cannot do it," Jesus comes and works. But though they can't even do it, they try to do it themselves. The very frustrating thing is, after failing three or four times they should be able to realize how vain their efforts are. But even though they've failed their whole lives, they feel that this time, if they try, they can do it. People are dragged by the heart that this time, if they try, they can do it well. People who gamble feel that if they gamble this time, they can win.

People live spiritual life the same way. They have the heart that at this revival, if they are determined to do well, then they can do well. That is not becoming the full leper. For example, if you have leprosy on your chest, you can cover it if you put something over your chest. People try to cover it up in that way and they try to be healed. But if the leprosy covers you from head to toe, it cannot be hidden. How can you hide it? No matter how hard you try, you cannot. Just like the full-bodied leper, in front of God, we are people who are completely crushed by sin. But Satan continually deceives us to make us think that we can become good if we try hard. He deceives us so that we are unable to become the full-bodied leper. That's why God cannot work inside of you.

Everyone, there is the female goat without blemish, which is the sin offering. There is no one on this earth that is without blemish in front of God, that can be acceptable to God. Not even Pastor Park, here. Not even Pastor Sung Hoon Kim, who is the emcee. In front of God we are all dirty human beings. The difference is the dirtiness inside of you, whether much of it was revealed outwardly or not. But at the core, we are all the same, we are all dirty human beings.

When you read the Bible, the interesting thing is, there is nothing prepared for the good person. There is nothing God has prepared for the good person. But God prepared everything for the person who committed sin, for the dirty, for the diseased, for the filthy people. Leviticus chapter 4 was prepared for whom? The person who committed sin? The person who has realized sin at the core of his heart:

"God I am just a bundle of sin. Not only did I commit theft, not only did I commit adultery, there are so many conditions in my heart to have me commit sin. Because I'm just covered with blemishes, it is impossible that I become good or truthful."

The Lord always came upon people like the woman taken in adultery, the man who fell among thieves, or the thief at the cross, and He poured grace upon them.

I Have Failed. Lord, Now…

Loving folks, if tonight you have the heart, "I'm going to go to Pastor Ock Soo Park's service and listen to the Word, receive grace, and live truthfully from now on. From now on, I'm not going to commit sins and live a good spiritual life," Jesus can never come anywhere near you.

A person who feels, "God, because deep inside I am dirty filthy and evil, I cannot do good. Everything I do is only evil and only dirty. I have tried to do good, but I can't. I've tried many times, but it does not work. I cannot do it. That's why Jesus you must do it," is like a person who has the full-bodied leprosy. God calls this person clean. This is a person who Jesus can quickly heal. But a person who thinks he can live to become good, can only remain in his filthiness and shortcomings. Jesus cannot live and work inside of this kind of person.

Until now, as I preached the Gospel to many, many people, the most difficult thing for people to do was crumble down the heart of thinking, "if I try hard, I can do it." But, no matter who that person is, after that heart crumbles down, from that moment on, Jesus begins to live and work inside of him. As we talked about yesterday, among the sixty-six books of the Old and New Testament, there's not one person who became good and honest by trying to become that way. There's nobody who was blessed through that method. In the Bible, it was the filthy, dirty, evil people who committed sin, but were blessed. Jesus did not come to call the righteous, but He came to call the sinners.

Everyone, spiritual life is not something that has to look good in your eyes. It's not something that you have to do better than Deacon Kim, or Deacon Lee. It has to fit the standard of God. There's not even one person who is perfect according to the standard of God. Whether that person is more good or more evil, they all fall short according to the standard of God. But people who think of themselves to be good, go on and exert their own goodness, and make it more difficult for them to receive the grace of God.

This is what the Bible says. While the younger son remained in the pigpen, he continued to labor. But once he realized that, ultimately, he could only starve to death, the blessing came upon him. When you know the fact that you cannot do good, and when you trust in God, that's when He works. But many people try to do good themselves; and it becomes difficult to receive blessings. Everyone, do not try to feel this with your emotions. Do not try to feel something burning in your heart. Examine it deeply in your heart and evaluate it in your heart.

"Indeed, am I good? Indeed, can I do good? Indeed, am I righteous? Indeed, can I truly do well?"

Everyone, if you deeply evaluate yourselves, you will realize the fact that you are evil. We are the descendants of sin. As descendants of Adam, we are all evil. Now, give up on yourself trying to be good. When you trust in Jesus with your heart, Jesus will work inside of you from that point on. Then you can really live a blessed and graceful life. You cannot compare the work that you do to the work that Jesus does. When I gave up on the good that I tried to do, Jesus came and led me to live the good life. Even in raising my children, when I did not try to raise them well, but entrusted it to Jesus, I could really see that He led and raised my children really gracefully. When I did not prepare for my elderly years, but entrusted it all to the Lord's hand, I could see the Lord blessing me and pouring grace upon me.

Everyone, tonight I sincerely ask of you, let down everything that man tries to do, and trust in Jesus to work inside of you. And with that, acknowledge that you have failed.

"Lord, I did not keep the ten commandments. I committed sin. And I tried to live to be good, but I could not. Therefore, I trust my life in your hands. Holy Lord, have compassion upon me and take charge of my life and lead me." If you have that heart tonight, from this evening God will work inside you and truly you will easily be freed from sin and live a holy life. And I believe you will live a blessed life.

CHAPTER 4
And He Shall Lay His Hands on the Head of the Sin Offering

The laying on of hands is placing sin onto the head of the goat. The Bible says, *And he shall lay his hand upon the head of the sin offering.* So, it is meant to place sin upon the goat through the laying on of hands. If the sin offering is given without the laying on of hands on the head of the goat or the lamb, could that be considered an offering? No, it could not be. Because the sin has not been transferred over, even if the offering is killed, the sin still remains on you. It is when you do the laying on of hands that the sin is moved over onto the goat. When that goat sheds its blood and dies, that sin is taken care of.

Today, we will again read Leviticus chapter 4 verses 27 through 31.
And if any one of the common people sin through ignorance, while he doeth somewhat against any of the commandments of the Lord concerning things which ought not to be done, and be guilty; Or if his sin, which he hath sinned, come to his knowledge: then he shall bring his offering, a kid of the goats, a

female without blemish, for his sin which he hath sinned. And he shall lay his hand upon the head of the sin offering, and slay the sin offering in the place of the burnt offering. And the priest shall take of the blood thereof with his finger, and put it upon the horns of the altar of burnt offering, and shall pour out all the blood thereof at the bottom of the altar. And he shall take away all the fat thereof, as the fat is taken away from off the sacrifice of peace offerings; and the priest shall burn it upon the altar for a sweet savour unto the Lord; and the priest shall make an atonement for him, and it shall be forgiven him. (Leviticus 4:27-31)

The message the Bible is sharing with us is intended to set us free from sin, to make us holy and righteous. Because people do not know what they must do to become holy and true, they simply labor to keep themselves from committing sin, in order to become holy and righteous. Many Christians live like that today. But, the more they live that way, the deeper they fall into sin. Truly becoming holy and righteous can never come about through your determination or willpower. Unless Jesus Christ enters inside your heart, it can only be engulfed in darkness, filth, and deceit. No matter how hard you try to chase the darkness out of a dark room, it will not work. However, if you turn the light on, the darkness automatically goes away.

In the same way, if Jesus, who is the light, enters into our hearts which are full of darkness, no matter who we may be, our hearts will become bright, joyful, and renewed to the point where we may think it is strange. It 's so ludicrous to say, "Ok, I'm going to be joyful from now on. I'm going to love." Love is something that must flow from your heart. Joy must spring forth from the depths of your heart. We can only be at peace when peace remains in our heart.

Douglas' Fingers that Were Molded Together

There is a brother named Douglas in the Gracias Choir who sings bass. He is from Ghana, Africa. If we get the chance, I wish we could listen to Brother Douglas singing. His voice is very soft and nice. It's a sound that is difficult for Korean people to make; it's a very envious sound. Brother Douglas and a few other brothers got together and formed a vocal group called Black Pearl in Ghana. Their voices and the songs of Africa go together very well. The director of the Gracias Choir wanted to recruit Brother

Douglas and so this brother came to Korea to attend the World Camp last summer. The director would not let him return, and had him stay. Now he is singing as a member in the Gracias Choir. The director was so happy to see the bass section of the choir improve so much with their newest addition.

Once, I saw this brother, and I noticed that the fingers on his right hand were all folded and fused together. I asked him what had happened. He said he had fallen on a fire when he was five years old and had burnt his hand. At that time, they did not take him to the hospital, but just left him as he was. So, his fingers just folded together and hardened.

Twenty years passed by with his hand in such a state. I asked him to stretch out his hand and I looked at it carefully. Within his hand, all of his fingers were there, with about one centimeter at the end sticking out. With the part that protruded out, he could use his hands to hold scissors and such. It was so saddening for me to see that. I wanted to call him into my room, give him some anesthesia and then just separate all of his fingers one by one. It may sound funny, but I had given a long and hard thought about that brother's hand: "How to reconnect the blood vessels? What to do with the bones? How to reconnect the nerves? What to do with his skin, if he were to get his fingers separated?" When I thought about those things I thought they would be too overwhelming for me. But then I thought even if it would cost us some money, we should take him to the hospital. So I took him to the plastic surgeon at Hanyang University Hospital. The chief doctor carefully looked at Brother Douglas' hand. He said that since all of his fingers are there, it could be unfolded. He also said he would need some more skin, but he said he could get skin off of Douglas' thigh or buttocks and graft it to his hand and fingers. He said it would take two or three surgeries. I also asked about the cost of the surgeries. Later on, I met the head plastic surgeon and he said that this brother would be able to use his fingers again. I was so happy to hear that.

However, just to get some more information, I went to the orthopedic surgeon. But the orthopedic surgeon said things that left us not so optimistic. He said that since the fingers had been stiffened that way for 20 years, even if you were to separate them through surgery, they would not unfold. He said, "Even if you do the surgery, the fingers will be useless." He said that it would be painful and costly, and that it didn't make sense to carry on with the surgery.

This brother is also very handsome. People from Africa are very handsome. The face tone of Koreans look faded in the sunlight, but people from Africa are very handsome and their features are very clear. They look especially good in photos. They have big eyes, and when I stand next to them, I feel so ugly.

But the real sad thing was that if his fingers were separated just a little bit when he was first burnt, then those fingers would be usable today. However, they didn't do that back then, and that's why his fingers are bundled up into a ball like this. As I touched his hand many times, it broke my heart. Occasionally, when I return home from Africa and I come to our church to have service and see many church members sitting there, it upsets me. I think, "Why must we be sitting here? We should all be in Africa. There's so much work to be done in Africa. We need to preach the Gospel. But when we see the people in that vast land, suffering without houses, it's very saddening." Does Africa have winters and is it cold there? You don't need heating or cooling systems. You just need to take a shipload of pre-assembled panels and take it to Africa. I want to take a few of our brothers there and assemble the panels into houses and give them to the people of Africa. They do not have enough water there, so they often drink unsanitary water. But if we could study how to install running water, if we could study their underground water, and if we could dig up the ground water and have the water spring forth abundantly, the people would be so happy.

But the more heartbreaking thing than this is that there are so many disabled people in Africa. You know, it really breaks my heart to see that there are so many people who do not have to become disabled, but they end up becoming disabled. And now they have to live like that. Also, malaria is a disease that can be healed if you just take the medication. One dollar is such a small amount of money that we often do not even consider to be money. But there are so many people in Africa who die because they do not have even that amount of money. I think about how we could gather some money at our church and buy a truckload of malaria medicine pills and put them in African villages, where anybody who catches malaria can come and take the medication.

In Korea or America, there are people who appear to be fine outwardly but are mentally ill. People who would be able to turn their hearts around with just a few words fall into their thoughts, suffer autism, and endure much difficulty and pain. When I see these things it really breaks my heart. Even if I were to live this life a hundred times over, I'd live as a pastor. Drug addicts, gambling addicts, game addicts. If these people hear just a few words from the Bible, they can be free from these addictions. Simply telling the game addicts, drug addicts, and gambling addicts to quit will not have any power to actually change them. But if the Word is preached to them and Jesus Christ enters into their hearts, they amazingly change. Jesus defeats drugs and He defeats gambling. Jesus gives freedom to the people who are game addicts.

We formed the organization, IYF, through which we are educating the youth. We hold our World Camps and Global Camps for two weeks at a time, and I tell our teachers, "Think hard about what the students would like to do for two weeks. Let's think about what we must do to make them joyful and happy. Let's give them a joyful time that they will remember forever." The teachers figure out what it is the students enjoy, and do it for them. At the camps, I preach the Word once in the morning and once in the evening, just twice a day. I don't tell them, "Stop stealing, stop drinking, stop getting addicted to games!"

There is no one who does not change when the Word enters into them. Becoming strong-willed and determining to not sin doesn't work. My friend who came to the first night of the conference used to live very well, but he went through many hardships. Even I could see that because he went through so much pain, he started to drink a lot. He had no choice but to drink. But he read the book that I gave him, *The Secret of Forgiveness of Sin and Being Born Again*, and the Word of God inside of the book came upon his heart. He then quit drinking. After he read the book and the Word settled in his heart, whenever he wanted to drink again, the memories of how he had drank, made mistakes and had done nasty things would come to his mind and it made him dislike drinking. Quitting drinking by allowing Jesus to come into us, and quitting drinking by your own efforts is completely different.

The First Step in Spiritual Life: Repentance

Today, I want to tell you how each Word in the Bible, one by one, can work inside of you. Our ancestors Adam and Eve went against God and united their hearts with Satan. From that point on, a channel of the heart was formed between Satan and man. Satan continually puts evil thoughts, desires, and ambitions inside of you. He places a heart completely different from the heart of Jesus inside of you. Without even knowing it, you are being led by Satan. Your heart has stiffened as you live in this manner. That's why, when you listen to the Word of God, the heart to refuse the Word begins to arise in you. Even though you try to live a spiritual life, it doesn't work because your heart and God's heart do not match up. Then what must you do? You need to break your heart. You must deny your heart.

There is a king named Saul in the Bible. God established him and made him the king of Israel. But while Saul was serving as the king of Israel, his heart did not get along with God's. One day, the Philistines attacked. Although God said that He would protect Israel, Saul was afraid, thinking, "What if God does not protect us?" Because he did not have the heart to believe in God, Saul gave an offering to God on his own accord and struck up wrath from the heart of God. Afterwards, God told him to destroy Amalek. God commanded him to destroy the Amalekites' sheep, cows, donkeys, children—to destroy them all. Then, all Saul has to do is destroy them. But while destroying the sheep and cows, Saul looked at the fatted and good things, and thought, "I shouldn't kill this cow. It would be good to give this as an offering to God." He felt that way in his heart. Among the sheep and the cows, those that were ugly and pitiful he killed, and those that were strong and fat he kept alive. In this way, God's thoughts and Saul's thoughts were different. God wanted to use Saul and God gave him many chances but Saul could not put his thoughts away and followed his own thoughts. Ultimately, God was unable to use him and threw him away.

Everyone, the thoughts that you have regularly don't just come out of nowhere. They are formed while you are being led by Satan. That is why although you may appear to be normal, your thoughts do not fit with God. That's why before you enter into spiritual life, repentance must first be achieved. Then how is repentance achieved? Repentance is completely emptying all of the thoughts that arise within you, and accepting the Word of God. This is the first step in spiritual life, as well as the most important step.

What kind of people received the grace of Jesus? One day, Jesus said to the man with the infirmity for thirty-eight years, "Rise, take up thy bed and walk."

The man with the infirmity for thirty-eight years would think, "He told me to take up my bed and walk. Am I able to take up my bed and walk? My legs are all withered like dried twigs. If I could get up and walk, why would I be lying here? That makes no sense." Truly what Jesus said didn't make sense. In his eyes, he wasn't just lying there for one or two years, but rather he had been lying there for thirty-eight years. His thoughts told him, "I've tried so hard to get up and walk but it didn't work. This is nonsense. I cannot walk. I'm not lying here just because I don't want to walk. My legs are all withered and they have no strength. This is not going to work."

But the Words of Jesus were telling him to take up his bed and walk. If the man with the infirmity for thirty-eight years believed in and followed his thoughts, then he would just remain lying there. But he denied his thoughts, and accepted the Word of Jesus by faith. "It is true that I cannot walk, but since Jesus is telling me to walk, I should walk." Because he threw his thoughts away and followed the Word of Jesus, he was able to walk through the power of Jesus. This is how the works of God in the Bible come about.

One day, Jesus went to a wedding at Cana of Galilee. At the feast, they had fallen short of wine. Jesus then told the servants to fill pots with water. When the servants filled them up with water, He said, "Draw now and serve unto the governor of the feast."

The servants couldn't understand it. They thought, "How is this wine? Surely it was water that we scooped up and poured in here. This should not be drawn up and served. We need to serve the governor of the feast wine! How can we give him water?" If the servants had spoken their own thoughts, they would have said, "Jesus, I don't think you really know what's going on here. But this is not wine; this is fresh water. This is water! At a feast, wine should be served. We cannot serve water." That's what they would say. But the servants did not believe in their own thoughts, and they served according to the Word of Jesus. And, the water became wine.

Give All of that Money to Pastor Ock Soo Park

Everyone, once you know what spiritual life is, it is actually very easy. If you only learn this, God will work inside of you. I moved to Daegu in 1973, the day after my daughter's first birthday. We were quite poor when we first moved to Daegu. We were very poor. Once, it was two days before New Year's Day, and we were out of charcoal and we were out of rice. That is a complicated way of saying it, but simply put, we were out of money. That is how we barely got through each day, and now it was the day before New Year. All we had at home was some kimchi that we had made for the winter. That night, I prayed so much to God. My mother-in-law had come from Seoul, and she had brought a lot of money with her. But in a poor home the money runs out quickly, doesn't it? My mother-in-law needed to return to Seoul, but she didn't have the travel fare to get back to Seoul, so I couldn't fall asleep that night.

When I was being trained, I was taught to think, "Since you're a servant of God, do not stretch your hand out to man, but pray only to God. Believe that God will give it to you. Do not seek man for your needs, and don't even signal to them of your needs." Hunger was bearable, but it wasn't easy to act as though I was not hungry. Because if I act out my hunger, it would be signaling to others and asking for money. That night, I prayed all night long, but we were unable to gain anything. I woke up in the morning and had some radish from the kimchi. Because it was salty, I rinsed it in water, had a piece of it, and picked up my Bible to go witnessing at the Daegu train station. It was the day before New Years and all the people had crowded the station, wearing colorful clothes and had bags of gifts in their hands. When the trains would come, all of those people would leave with the trains and the station would become completely empty. Then soon after, people would gather one by one and pack the station. Then, they would again all disappear when the trains would come. That's what I saw all day long, and I preached the Gospel to the people. But rather than putting my heart into preaching the Gospel, I was hoping that the people hearing the Gospel might be touched and give me some money. But all the people were so excited about going back to their hometowns, that they didn't listen well when I preached the Gospel to them. That was how I witnessed until the evening.

Actually, that was not witnessing. I was preaching the Gospel hoping that God would give me money through someone because I had prayed the night before. Because I didn't have any bus fare, I had to walk about 4 kilometers to get home. I saw my wife's face. You know, my wife smiles when good things happen, and her expressions are very clear and obvious. When I came home and saw how quiet she was, I could tell, "Ah, she must have had nothing to eat all day as well." I was tired and we laid out the blankets to go to sleep. We did not light any charcoal for heat and the room was cold. We laid out all of the blankets we had on the floor. When we first got married, my wife had brought along with her many thick blankets, which was nice to have at least those laid out on the floor. We laid down to go to sleep, and at about 10 o'clock that night, there was a "ding dong." Someone had rang our doorbell.

My wife turned the light on, got up, and went outside. It was a sister who attended our church. My wife spoke with that sister for a long while. After the talk, my wife came in with an envelope. This was a time when the 10,000 won ($10) bills were first issued. There was a 10,000 won bill inside of the envelope. At the time 10,000 won was a lot of money. That sister, while handing that envelope to my wife was giving her testimony, and that is why they were out there for such a long time. That sister was a professor at Gyeongbuk University. It was New Year's Eve, so all of her family had gone to her in-laws' place for New Year's Day. She was home alone because there was some work she had to do at the school. That night, the sister had the heart, "Today, I'm going to say a prayer to close out this year." Earlier, she had cleaned her whole house and after locking the doors she began to pray in front of God. After praying for a while, she was unable to pray. She kept hearing a voice in her heart, "You, go give that money to Pastor Ock Soo Park."

This sister started praying again, "God, tonight I don't want to do anything else. I just want to pray to you, God."

But still, inside she heard the voice telling her, "Go, give that money to Pastor Ock Soo Park."

This sister said, "I don't know where Pastor Park lives and it's late now.

When the day breaks, I'll ask where he lives and go give it to him then. But tonight I'm just going to pray."

She said that and wanted to pray, but still in her heart, she kept hearing the voice that said, "Go, give that money to Pastor Ock Soo Park." The sister could not bear it anymore, so she put the money in an envelope, put it in her wallet, and came out to the big road without even knowing where we live. But while she was out there on the big road, a brother from our church passed her by.

She asked, "Brother! Do you know where Pastor Park lives?"

"Yes, I do."

"Please show me where he lives."

That was how that sister found my house that night. She handed this envelope to my wife and said, "This money is not my money. It's money that God told me to give to you. And from now on I'll be in charge of pastor's living expenses." She said that and left. My wife brought in the envelope and gave us this testimony. My mother-in-law heard it and cried, saying that God is really alive.

Spiritual Life Is Easy and Fun

Even though I do not have the faith to believe in God, when in difficulty, I pray. I would think, "Will somebody give me some money? If I go somewhere, won't they give me some money? If I go somewhere, won't they give me some food?" My heart would be divided into those kinds of thoughts. That's why God could not work powerfully inside of me. As I experienced many situations like what I had just told you, in my life, the more I experienced them, the more I could see that it was foolish to believe in myself. It became more and more clear and established in my heart that God was living inside of me. Normally, I'm a person who believes in my own thoughts, who believes in my own ways, and who lives doing whatever I want. But while I served God, He led me in faith. No matter what thought arises within me, no matter what path I walk, so that I may throw those things away and live by faith following after the Word of God, I could see that is how God was leading me.

Everyone, spiritual life is extremely easy. Spiritual life is a lot of fun. When Brother Douglas hurt his hand, had they gone to the hospital and had the doctor treated the burn and separated all the fingers that were bundled together, all those fingers would still be usable. However, that did not happen. A few days ago, I received a phone call from the plastic surgeon. He said, "So, Pastor, have you decided on the surgery?"

"Yes, the orthopedic surgeon said this and this to us. So what do you think we should do?"

"Still, don't you think it's worth a try?"

"Okay, I'll make some time to visit again." That was the end of our phone call.

How great it would have been if he had received even just a small bit of treatment when he was younger? I see so many people like that when I go to Africa. When I go to Africa, I give them my watch, my shoes, my clothes. More than that, I have the heart to help the people whose lives can change so much from just a little bit of help.

When we look at the reason why people are living inside of pain and not living by faith, it's so foolish in the eyes of God. You working versus Jesus doing the work—who would do a better job? Please answer me. You raising your kids versus Jesus raising your kids—who would do a better job? You caring for your future, versus Jesus caring for you future—who would care more? It's Jesus. But when Jesus works inside of you, He doesn't work according to your thoughts. He works according to God. When you learn this fact, spiritual life becomes so easy and so fun.

You get answered every time you pray, and the Lord takes care of you every time you are in difficulty, and you get to see how people listen to what you say and become changed. How wonderful it is. How fun it is.

Pastor, Do Not Tell Me to Get Back Together with that Woman

One time, a sister in our church in Seoul went through a divorce. The husband said that his wife was going to a heretic church. He would often bully her around and it ultimately resulted in a divorce. Later on, we found out that the husband was actually having a relationship with another woman, but he just made her church-going into an excuse in order to get a divorce. As soon as they were divorced, the husband began to live with this other woman.

I did not know about any of this, but one year after their divorce, I got a phone call at two in the morning. It was the ex-husband of that sister. He started cursing, "Pastor Park, you punk!" While in the middle of cursing, he would sometimes call me "older brother."

Because he was younger than me, I told him, "Hey, when you're in a good mood, you call me 'older brother' and when you're in a bad mood, you call me a punk?" I thought about it and realized it must not be so easy for him to be awake at two in the morning and call me on the phone. I thought about how much pain he must be going through to be acting this way. So I listened to what he had to say.

He said to me, "Pastor, do not tell me to get back together with that woman. I will not live with that woman." I had never even mentioned it to him. As I analyzed those words, I could see that after he cheated on his wife and began living with the new woman, he began to miss his first wife so much. So he began to regret his actions. He didn't even last one year with the new woman and they broke up. Now he began to miss his wife. But he couldn't bring himself to say, "Pastor, I'm so sorry. I was terribly wrong." Instead, this was the way he was behaving.

That's what I came to realize, so I simply said to him, "Hey, let's get some sleep. I need to get some rest," and I hung up the phone.

Then a few days after, he called me again. He said, "Pastor, I clearly know your heart. Don't even think of getting me back together with that woman. Even if I die, I'm never going to live with her."

As I heard that several times, I thought, "Ah, this guy cannot forget his ex-wife." That's what I felt in my heart. At that time, I was living in Daejeon. I told him, "Stop just calling me whenever you want day and night, but why don't you come down here to Daejeon?"

Then he quickly changed his attitude and quickly asked, "Really? When should I come down? Pastor, when do you have time?"

"Come at 12 o'clock, this Saturday."

"Yes, Pastor, I'll be there this Saturday."

So he promised to come at 12 o'clock on Saturday. I then called that sister. I said, "Sister, come to our church on Saturday."

"Yes, Pastor."

This sister had no idea what was going on. That Saturday, I was out in some other area and there was traffic, so I came back around 1 o'clock.

When I got back, the two of them were sitting there, talking. I sat with them and spoke with them.

The husband then said, "Pastor, why did you tell her to come? You were going to tell her to get back together with me, right?" Even though he was happy about it on the inside, that was what he was saying on the outside. He said, "You know what? There's no way I can live with this woman. The whole world knows that the two of us got divorced. How can we get back together and live together again?"

I said, "How is that a problem? If that's how you really feel, come down to Daejeon and live here."

"Oh really? Would that be okay? Will you find a place for us to stay?"

"There are lots of realtors in Daejeon."

"When should we come down?"

When I saw the two of them getting in the car and leaving together, they looked so happy. That sister, after being persecuted by her husband, got divorced and remained quietly in the church. And the husband had experienced living with a woman in the world. From then on, he began to realize how precious the sister from our church was, and how she quietly served her in-laws.

The great thing about being a pastor is, in the middle of the night you answer a few phone calls, say a few things, and get to bring back together a couple that was torn apart. If you are not a pastor, it would be difficult to reunite people who are already broken up. When I see these things, I want to meet more people who are divorced. On their own side, they think, "I cannot live with that woman." It's a big problem in their own eyes. Often times, in the eyes of the third party, it's absolutely nothing. When the heart opens, you begin to understand, saying, "That's how all people are." It's so precious to see that's how people's hearts change.

Many college students go through change. It's great speaking with college students. Because they are bright and honest, you can clearly see what's inside of their hearts. I often say to them, "Hey, that thought is wrong. It's supposed to be like this."

"Oh really, Pastor? Is that so?" Then they start to change.

At our church, I often say, "What fun do you have in this world, if you're not a pastor?"

What fun do the unbelievers have? Buying a car, making money and traveling—that stuff is really no fun. What's so great about going to Hawaii? It's just so-so. But try being a pastor. You get to see people who are mentally disabled, changing to reconcile with the people around them.

I get to see a father and son who used to be enemies, and the son was planning to kill the father. But I get to see the son change and say, "Father, I was so wrong." When I see these things, it sometimes make me wish I had twenty bodies so I can work everywhere as a pastor.

If You Throw Your Thoughts Away and Accept the Word of God

Even if a little bit of the Word enters your heart, it works. What does the work?

It is the Word that works.

In the beginning God created the heaven and the earth. And the earth was without form, and void; and darkness was upon the face of the deep. And the Spirit of God moved upon the face of the waters. (Genesis 1:1-2)

In beginning, the earth was without form, void, and in deep darkness. If man were to try to change that, how difficult would it be? But the Word of God said, *Let there be light. Let there be a firmament in the midst of the waters, and let it divide the waters from the waters. Let the earth bring forth grass, the herb yielding seed, and the fruit tree yielding fruit after his kind.* Each time the Word was spoken, the earth changed.

In the story of the prodigal son in Luke chapter 15, when the son became a beggar and returned to the father's house, the father said, "Bring forth the best robe and put it on him. Put a ring on his hand. Put shoes on his feet. Bring forth a fatted calf and kill it. Let us eat and be merry." Each time the Word was spoken from the father's lips, the son's image changed. This is also true with our lives. When the Word of God is spoken to us, we change.

We are finishing our conference this Saturday. I hope that by Saturday, the Word will be received in all of your hearts so that by then, all of us would be born again and able to live a happy and blessed life. There's only one reason why this cannot happen to certain people. It's because they place the Word and their own thoughts in front of them. Then they look, calculate, judge, and conclude that their own thoughts are better. People who stubbornly exert their own thoughts and do not accept the Word, cannot be changed.

No matter who you are, whether you are a dirty sinner who committed more sins than anyone in Korea, or whether you are this terrible woman, deemed the most wicked woman in the world. Or even if you are a person who committed adultery or murder... even if you are such a person, there is not one person who will not change when the Word of God enters them.

There's only one reason why you are not changing inside and why the miracles do not happen in you. It's because you are rejecting the Word of God. With your own thoughts you say, "Oh, that makes no sense. How is that going to work? That's not possible." And with saying that you refuse the Word. That's why. Whether it fits your heart or not, if the Word enters you, all of you can change. If the Word of God enters in, but if you don't change, God has to be responsible for that.

I can say this with God's name on the line. You do change. You become joyful. You are freed from sin. You become happy. In the Bible, what happens when man meets God? Because the thoughts of man and the thoughts of God are different from each other, they clash with one another. One day, God said to Abraham, "Abraham, your wife Sarah shall bring you a son." Abraham just needed to say, "Amen, Hallelujah," and accept it. But with his own thoughts he looked at himself and said that he is too old and his wife Sarah was also too old. Abraham listened to the Word of God and then looked at Sarah. He saw this old, elderly lady walking with a cane saying, "Oh, old man, I don't know why my legs feel so cold these days. I guess it's almost time for me to go now."

Abraham thought in his heart, "How could an old woman like her have a baby? It's scary to think that she might actually have a baby." Since Abraham was looking at it with his own thoughts, he laughed. He thought, "Shall a child be born unto him that is an hundred years old? And shall Sarah, that is ninety years old, bear?" Then he said to God, "Oh, that Ishmael might live before thee!"

Soon after, God spoke again, saying, "Abraham, where's your wife Sarah?"

"Behold, in the tent."

"I will certainly return unto thee according to the time of life; and lo,

Sarah thy wife shall have a son."

Sarah laughed. She said, "After I am waxed old shall I have pleasure, my lord being old also?" In her own thoughts, it seemed that she could not have a child. She was unable to accept the Word of God that said that she would have a child.

If we had an x-ray machine of the heart, I wish we could take an x-ray of the heart. I would say, "Sister in the front, please come forward. Hold your breath. One, two, here we go." Snap! "Oh look, see? You have so many sins and you're so fleshly. If you act stubborn like that, it's not going to work. You're going to go to hell." If there was an x-ray machine that could really take a picture of the heart, I want to buy one, no matter how expensive it is, set it up in front of the chapel, and take pictures of all the people coming in.

I would say, "Have you gotten your sins washed away?"

"Yes."

"Come here. Hold your breath. One, two…"

Snap!

"Ah, all your sins are washed away. Okay, goodbye."

Because we do not have such a machine, we cannot see our hearts with our own eyes. Everyone, if you only throw away the thoughts of your heart and accept the Word of God, He will work inside of your life. Amen? But people are unable to do that, although it is so easy. Because I know very well that the Word of God does not fit my thoughts, I often throw my thoughts away. Because, if I trust in my thoughts, I will fail, so I don't believe in my thoughts. From that moment on, God begins to work inside of me.

Everyone, spiritual life is so easy. Before I got saved, I went to church and did terrible, bad things. I tried not to do them, but it didn't work. But I received salvation and Jesus entered into my heart. It's been 50 years since I have been saved. In the last 50 years, I've been so happy as I lived my life together with Jesus. Of course, at times I've been poor. At times, it was difficult. At times, it was very hard. But I wasn't alone. Jesus was with me. Even in difficult times, the grace of the Lord protected me. That's the life I want to lead you to. There is only one way that you can live that way. When your thoughts and the Word of God differ, it's about throwing your thoughts away and accepting the Word of God. If you only do that, God will work inside of you. If you don't do that and only try to do good things—trying to tithe or whatnot—it becomes meaningless. Of course, I'm not telling you not to do those things. But it should not be about you trying to do it alone, without Jesus.

Ock Soo Park, You're So Dirty! You're So Filthy!

Everyone, I was truly a person who couldn't do anything. Filthy and dirty thoughts were always within me. Because I would always tediously argue, I was not popular among my friends. One time, a friend of mine took one of my things and broke it. I was so upset and angry, so I fought with him. Another friend standing by said, "Hey, Ock Soo, you're his friend. Don't be like that. I'll just give you mine." I was so embarrassed. I was really such a bad guy. I know that I'm worse than any person. When I look back, there is not one good thing that I've done. I was shorter than my friends, I was ugly, I had a bad personality, and I did poorly in school. There was nothing I could boast of. But still, because I went to church, I thought I was great. But the year I turned 19, I looked at my own image. I saw that I was a bad son—a problematic child in the family, who would always cause problems. I was this wicked person who did many bad things. I really hated myself.

I sat in front of the mirror. I looked at my reflection in the mirror. As I saw myself in the mirror, I yelled out, "Ock Soo Park, you dirty, low-life!" I hated the people who even looked like me. Actually I became a person who didn't trust in myself. Then, the heart of Jesus entered into my heart. As I believed the Gospel and received the forgiveness of sins, my heart started to change. This heart that I have now is clearly not my heart. After Jesus entered, my life changed.

When people read the Bible, many people, with their own opinions, go against God. In 2 Kings chapter 7, God sends a prophet to Samaria where people were starving. It says, *Tomorrow about this time shall a measure of fine flour be sold for a shekel, and two measures of barley be sold for a shekel in the gate of Samaria.*

A high official in whose hand the King relied on said, *Even if the Lord were to make windows in heaven, might these things be?* To him, the thoughts of man were even greater than the Word of God. Everyone, this life that we have lived with Satan for such a long time, has become something of a habit to us. Inside of us, ambitions arise, a deceitful heart arises, a lustful hearts arises, and evil hearts arises. Even so, we think of ourselves to be good and we continue living life that way. But if you truly, precisely see yourself, you come to realize that you are a person that cannot be trusted and you are able to deny yourself. When your thoughts collide with the Word of God, you get to throw your thoughts away and follow the Word of God. That's what repentance is.

Suppose I am living with a friend, and that friend always commits fraud, does bad things, and lies. When I don't know these things, I remain close with him. But one day, when I find out and I realize, "Oh this guy, all he does is cheat. I shouldn't believe what he says." From then on, no matter what that friend says, I wouldn't listen anymore. Turning around from believing in that friend—that's what repentance is.

Repentance isn't confessing, "I stole. I committed adultery." But knowing who you truly are, "I'm an evil and dirty human being. Not only are my actions filthy and dirty, but the core of my heart is dirty. If I live following that heart, then I can only become dirty and evil and cursed." Understanding this and turning around from the heart of believing in yourself, and believing in the Word of God, is what true repentance is. Many people beg and realize, asking for forgiveness. But because they do not turn from the heart of believing in themselves, they continue to live a dirty and filthy life.

The Lamb of God that Takes Away the Sin of the World

Today, we want to search out Leviticus chapter 4, about the laying on of hands onto the head of the sin offering. If a common person, sins through ignorance, and that sin that he had committed comes to his knowledge, then he has to bring over a female goat without blemish and do the laying on of hands upon the head of that goat. Why does he do the laying on of hands? Let's look at Leviticus chapter 16, verse 21.

And Aaron shall lay both his hands upon the head of the live goat, and confess over him all the iniquities of the children of Israel, and all their transgressions in all their sins, putting them upon the head of the goat, and shall send him away by the hand of a fit man into the wilderness: (Leviticus 16:21)

Here it says that Aaron does the laying on of hands upon the head of a live goat. This laying on of hands moves the sin over onto the live goat. Here it says, "Aaron shall lay both his hands upon the head of the live goat" and "putting them upon the head of the goat." Through laying on of hands, the sin is put upon the head of the goat.

In Leviticus chapter 4, they also do the laying of hands upon the sacrificial offering. When the sin offering is given without laying your hands upon the goat or lamb, can that be an offering? It cannot, because sin had not been moved over. It means that even if the offering is put to death, the sin still remains in you. When you do the laying on of hands, that is when the sin is moved over onto the goat. Amen? Now, when you do the laying on of hands upon the head of the goat, is the sin upon the goat or upon you? It's upon the goat. When that goat sheds its blood and dies, is that sin taken care of or not? It's taken care of. This is a foreshadowing of Jesus Christ.

When Jesus wanted to be baptized at the River Jordan, John the Baptist tried to stop him. He said, "Master, I have need to be baptized by you."

"No, suffer it to be so now. For thus it becometh us to fulfill all righteousness." Jesus had no sin. He had no sin to repent of. Then why was he baptized? The baptism that Jesus received is different from the baptism that we receive. As John the Baptist baptized Jesus and did the laying of hands upon the head of Jesus, John the Baptist, as the representative of mankind, placed the sin of mankind upon Jesus.

Everyone, when John the Baptist did the laying on of hands, was the sin placed on Jesus, or not? What did John the Baptist say when Jesus came to the river Jordan the next day?

Behold the Lamb of God who takes away the sin of the world. (John 1:29)

That's what it clearly says, right? Through Jesus bearing the sin of the world and dying on the cross, He took care of our sins. Now, let's just empty our thoughts and look according to the words of the Bible. Are your sins upon Jesus or not? If it's only according to the words of the Bible, did Jesus shed His blood and die for our sins and wash our sins away; or did He not wash our sins away? If it's only according to the words of the Bible, then do you have sins or not? But the devil deceives us to make us feel as if our sins still remain and makes us feel as though our sins are not forgiven.

Everyone, it's not that Jesus needs to be crucified every time we commit a sin. Billions of people commit sins everyday. Even if He were to go up and down the cross a thousand times in one second, it still wouldn't be enough. If Jesus was crucified every time we committed a sin, even if He were to die hundreds of millions of times, it would still not be enough. But Jesus isn't crucified and put to death every time we commit a sin. Rather, he gathered all of our sins from beginning to the end, all at once, and was crucified at the cross and forgave our sins forever. From the beginning to all eternity, He forgave us for all of those sins. If you are a person who believes in God, and if God says that your sins have been placed upon Jesus, then you should all empty your thoughts and simply say, "Amen. They have been placed on Him." Through the crucifixion of Jesus, the punishment for all of my sins have ended. That's what it means to believe Jesus. You should not add your own thoughts on top of this because within your thoughts is the plan of the devil.

John the Baptist clearly said that when he laid his hands upon the head of Jesus, all of ours sins were placed upon Him.

Behold the Lamb of God who takes away the sin of the world. (John 1:29)

He clearly says that He took away the sins of the world, right? Within the sin of the world are your sins, my sins, sins of your children, all of those sins. So what does it mean to be a sinner? It means that you do not believe in the Word of God. In the Word of God, our sins are all washed clean. Hence, God said we are righteous. If God called us righteous, then all we need to say is "Amen" and accept it. Loving folks, a person who believes in his own thoughts, believes in himself. The person who believes in the Word of Jesus, believes in Jesus.

Everyone, throw your thoughts away and just purely believe that your sins have been moved over unto Jesus. Amen? Simply believe that Jesus washed your sins away at the cross. Your sins no longer remain and at the cross they were all taken care of. Two thousand years ago, the punishment for your sins had come to an end. Jesus received the punishment for all of your sins until the day you die. Two thousand years ago the punishment ended. I hope you will believe that your judgment, your curse, your destruction, and your punishment have all ended.

Spiritual life is so easy. That's what spiritual life is. It's not amazing. It's so easy. But because you don' believe it and try to keep the Ten Commandments, it's so difficult. Because you don't believe, you go to early morning services and do forty-day fasting prayers. That's why it's tiring and difficult. I apologize, but, I'm not so good at fasting prayers or the overnight prayers. But I do believe Jesus. I believe that Jesus has forgiven my sins. I believe that He has washed my sins whiter than snow. There's a hymn that we used to sing quite often during revivals a long time ago.

I can sing now the song
Of the blood-ransomed throng
In my soul there is peace, rest and calm;
I am free from all doubt,
And I join in the shout,
I'm redeemed by the blood of the Lamb.

After singing that hymn and making the confessional prayers, people would cry out, "God, I'm a sinner. Forgive me." Just a little while ago, they sang a hymn saying that they were redeemed. Now they are asking for forgiveness. Good thing it's God they are talking to. If it were us, we would be confused. Without any thought, they are just living spiritual life with their mouths.

If you're redeemed, doesn't that mean you should have no sin? If you're not redeemed, then you should sing in the hymns, "I'm not redeemed by the blood of the Lamb." Now, let's stop living that kind of spiritual life. Let's throw our thoughts away and believe in the Word of God. I believe that God will work.

CHAPTER 5
Shall Take the Blood Thereof With His Finger, Put It Upon the Horns of the Altar

The priest takes the blood with his finger and puts it upon the horns of the altar. It is to erase the records of our sin on the horns of the altar. Why must the records of our sin be erased? They must be erased because our sins have been taken care of. Just as the lamb is put to death and its blood is put upon the horns of the altar to erase the sin, Jesus came not to the tabernacle that is on earth, but to the temple that is in heaven. He took His blood that He shed at the cross, placing it upon the horns of the altar, and sprinkling it upon the mercy seat. With that He has forever cleansed our sins and erased them. That is why God says that He remembers our sins no more.

Now, this is our fifth session. This evening I will preach to you about, *Shall take the blood thereof with his finger, put it upon the horns of the altar.*

When we read the Bible, at times, each word in the Bible gives us strength, life, and grace in our hearts. I'm so thankful to see that, and I hope that you will fall deep into the words of the Bible.

Once again, today we will read from Leviticus chapter four verses 27 through 31.

And if any one of the common people sin through ignorance, while he doeth somewhat against any of the commandments of the Lord concerning things which ought not to be done, and be guilty; Or if his sin, which he hath sinned, come to his knowledge: then he shall bring his offering, a kid of the goats, a female without blemish, for his sin which he hath sinned. And he shall lay his hand upon the head of the sin offering, and slay the sin offering in the place of the burnt offering. And the priest shall take of the blood thereof with his finger, and put it upon the horns of the altar of burnt offering, and shall pour out all the blood thereof at the bottom of the altar. And he shall take away all the fat thereof, as the fat is taken away from off the sacrifice of peace offerings; and the priest shall burn it upon the altar for a sweet savour unto the Lord; and the priest shall make an atonement for him, and it shall be forgiven him. (Leviticus 4:27-31)

Is It the Word of God, or the Voice of Satan?

This morning we talked about laying hands upon the head of the sin offering. When I read the Bible, from Genesis to Revelation, I can see God has spoken so many words to us. But man listened to another voice that is not the voice of God. It is the voice of Satan. God said to the first man Adam, "Man, if you eat from the fruit of the knowledge of good and evil, you shall surely die."

But Satan said to Adam, "That's not so. The day you eat of it, your eyes will be opened and you shall become like God. God knew that would happen, and that's why, to keep you from eating it, He told you that you would die." Man always has that fate of listening to both the Word of God and the voice of Satan. Right then, will you listen to the Word of God? Or will you accept the words of Satan? Your fate is decided, depending on who you listen to.

During the time of Noah's flood, God clearly said, "The sinfulness of man is great on the earth and I will punish this world with water." Right then what kind of heart did Satan strike up inside the heart of man?

"No, God's not going to do that. Why would God give us a flood?" Satan struck up that kind of a heart inside of man. As thoughts that were completely different from the Word of God rose up in their hearts, people from that point until the day of the flood, did not obey anything that God said.

When we read the Bible, there are many stories about how man goes against the Word of God. As a result, they met destruction. Satan guides people's hearts to go against God. In John chapter 13 verse 2, it says, that the devil put into the heart of Judas Iscariot, the son of Simon, the thought to betray Jesus. The devil does not speak to you directly saying, "Hey, go steal something. Go commit adultery. Or, go commit murder." But rather, he puts those kinds of hearts inside of you. Now, will you live according to your own heart? Or will you live according to the will of God? Or will you believe in your own thoughts that arise within you? Or will you believe in the Word of God? These are the most fundamental problems for spiritual life.

But sadly, although many people today listen to the Word given in the 66 books of the Old and New Testaments of the Bible, they believe in their own thoughts more than the Word of God. They believe in their own opinions more. That is why people struggle inside of darkness and inside of pain.

If the Sin Is Stripped Away, the Image of God Appears

The Gracias Choir sings at all of our conferences. The Christmas Cantata is Gracias Choir's hallmark performance and it is very popular. Not only do they hold performances in the large cities of Korea, but they also performed in Sydney, Australia; in Bangkok, Thailand; and many other cities all over the world. The Gracias Choir was not a choir that sang well from the beginning. But we invited the world's best vocalists from Russia, and we asked them to guide the singing of the Gracias Choir. When the choir did not have performances, the members went to St. Petersburg, Russia to study voice.

There is a choir member, a tenor, named Taejik Woo. This person could not sing very well. But the voice teacher, a vocalist from Russia saw Taejik Woo and was shocked. He said that Taejik would be a star in the world of music, but he's just here rotting away. In our eyes, we thought, "Taejik Woo is no star. He's not even a small twinkle of light." But the vocal professor said to Taejik Woo, "You really have a very good voice. But you don't know how to draw out that voice, so the voice doesn't come out as it should. Instead, it comes out scratched. That's why it sounds bad."

Taejik Woo laughed, "No, my voice is not that special."

"Yes, it is!"

Professor Anatoli and professor Galina who sang the solo tonight, they're with us at this conference. Professor Anatoli from time to time says to us, "A newborn baby's cry is the most basic vocal expression. When the sound comes forth from the stomach without any form of alteration, it creates the most beautiful sound."

As Taejik Woo learned from the professors day by day, he changed. Right now he's in the United States working for the music college, so he's not here today. But Taejik Woo, Ilyong Song, Wonhee Jeon, these and many members of the Gracias Choir have changed so much.

Among the old Korean poems, there is one that talks about a jade.

There was dirt on a jade, and it was cast away to the street side. All the people who went back and forth on the street only knew the jade to be dirt. Let them call it dirt. But just because it's called dirt, is it really dirt?

There is a poem that goes like that. I think it expresses the heart of the author. It was jade, but it was treated as dirt. As the Gracias Choir received instruction, they completely changed. Just as people have a good sound within, because you were built in the image of God, within you is the image of God. But, your hearts are covered with sinfulness. When that is stripped away and the inner heart is revealed, you will become like a shining star and become like God. We were all made by God so that we would lack nothing in being the sons of God. But we fell into sin.

Now, I hope you will throw away the thoughts that arise from you to lead yourselves. If you accept the Word of God, then change will arise within you from your heart. Judas Iscariot followed the thoughts that arose inside of his heart and he became cursed. During the time of Noah's flood, many people followed the thoughts that arose within them rather than the Word of God, and all of them met destruction. Like we talked about this morning, spiritual life is very easy. All you need to know is how to do this one thing. What is it? It is to not believe in the thoughts that arise within you, not believe in your heart, and not follow it, and then accepting the

Word. If you do that, then all of you will change. God has made you so that you can only be changed. That is how God made us to be.

The Sin of Stealing a Tool from the Temple!
Tonight I want to speak to you about taking the blood thereof and putting it upon the horns of the altar.

And if any one of the common people sin through ignorance, while he doeth somewhat against any of the commandments of the Lord concerning things which ought not to be done, and be guilty; Or if his sin, which he hath sinned, come to his knowledge: then he shall bring his offering, a kid of the goats, a female without blemish, for his sin which he hath sinned. And he shall lay his hand upon the head of the sin offering, and slay the sin offering in the place of the burnt offering. And the priest shall take of the blood thereof with his finger, and put it upon the horns of the altar of burnt offering, and shall pour out all the blood thereof at the bottom of the altar. (Leviticus 4:27-30)

It means that the priest should take the blood from the sacrificial sin offering that was put to death for our sins, take that blood with his finger, and put it on the horns of the altar. This is what we will be talking about today.

In 1980, I went to the Yeosu Aeyangwon Church and held a conference there for a week. Almost everybody knows about the Yeosu Aeyangwon Church. A long time ago, it was called the "nuclear bomb of love." It was the church where Pastor Yang Won Son used to serve in. It was a church of a leper colony. From the first evening, I talked about the process of how our sins become washed away.

At the time, the members of the Aeyangwon Church were all living their spiritual lives backwards. The one who washes our sins away is not us, but Jesus. The one who takes responsibility for our sins is also not us, but Jesus. But they were laboring to have their sins washed away, and they were laboring to try to be good. Because they were all living spiritual life backwards, they were very tired in their lives. Then they heard the Word of God. After receiving the forgiveness of sins and becoming born again through the Word of God, their lives changed. They would gather here and there and talk about the painful spiritual lives that they used to live.

There was one elder who used to live there. The image of how he used

Sin Offering: Freedom from Sin

to give his testimony is still very vivid in my mind. This elder used to be a deacon at a church before becoming a leper. He lived right next door to the church in a house that shared a wall with the church. So whenever he had time, he would clean the chapel, organize the flowerpots, plant flowers, and he cared for the chapel.

One day, he was looking for a hoe to take care of the small farm at his home. So he borrowed the hoe from the church and used it. After using it, he wanted to put it back in the church. It was too late that day so he just left it at home. But at the church a rumor begin to spread that someone had stolen the church hoe. He heard this, and then became afraid in his heart thinking, "If this continues, I may be labeled as the thief who stole the church hoe." All he needed to say was, "Oh, no, deacon, that's not it. I just took the church hoe to work on the farm at my house for a little bit and just hadn't put it back yet. It's at my house right now so don't worry about it, I'll put it back soon." Had he said that, it would not have been a problem. But he didn't want to hear that he had stolen the church hoe. He was afraid and hid the hoe in a bundle of hay.

Also, he was afraid that the church members would come visit him at his house and discover the hoe hidden in the bundles of hay, and he became very, very nervous. Then one night, he waited until it was late and no one was around. He dug up a hole on one side of the farm and buried the hoe. Now nobody knew about this; the deacon didn't know, the elder didn't know, the pastor didn't know. Only he and God knew. But from then on, whenever he would go to church to have service, in his heart, the sin of stealing a tool from the temple of God would not be erased.

This happened in his early thirties, and when I was having the conference at the Aeyangwon Church he was already past the age of 70. For 40 years, the elder's sin of stealing the tool from the temple of God had remained in his heart. He couldn't have peace, not even for a day, or even for an hour. He could not even tell anyone about this and he was always very uneasy in his heart as he lived in pain. But, as he listened to the words about the sin offering and received the forgiveness of sins, he was so joyful that he danced. He said, "If so, Pastor, that sin of stealing the church hoe, that must be forgiven too, right?" Everyone, do you think that sin is forgiven or not forgiven? Please answer. Do you think it's forgiven or not forgiven? Yes, it is forgiven. There's no sin the blood of Jesus cannot wash away. He was so happy.

You Lose Freedom When Sin Enters In

In Jeremiah chapter 17 verse 1 it says, *The sin of Judah is written with a pen of iron and with a point of a diamond, it is engraven upon the table of their heart, and upon the horns of your altars.* Once the sin is recorded in our hearts, we lose freedom. We cannot have peace.

Once, I was on my way up to Seoul from Daejeon. I was in the car together with my son.

"Yeong Kook," I said.

"Yes, Father?"

"I'm going to sleep a little bit in the car so why don't you drive?"

"Yes, Father, go ahead and sleep."

I was in the backseat trying to fall asleep. After a little while my son pulled the car over to the side. "Why are you stopping the car?" I asked.

"Father, the police is telling me to pull over."

"What? Did you do anything wrong?"

"No, I don't think I did anything wrong."

"Did you keep the speed limit?"

"Yes. I did not go above the speed limit."

The police officer came, saluted us, and asked to see my son's driver's license.

I opened the window and asked, "What did we do wrong?"

"You did many things wrong."

"What did we do wrong?"

"Why are you driving in the bus-only lane?"

"What day is today? Is it a Sunday?"

"Today is Memorial Day."

I thought the bus-only lane law was in effect only on Sundays and on national holidays like the Independence Day and the New Year's Day. But I had no idea that it was in effect on Memorial Day, too. In addition, there was no traffic that day so I could have just driven in any lane. But we didn't know about it, so we had driven in the first lane.

You know, even when we're committing sin, when we don't know that it is sin, we feel very free. Even before the police had pulled us over, we thought we had done nothing wrong. We only realized it when the police officer approached us and told us.

"You did many things wrong. Why are you driving in the bus-only lane?"

"What day is today? It's not a Sunday."

"Today is Memorial Day."

"The bus-only lane law is in effect even on Memorial Day?"

"Of course!"

When we learned that the law was in effect, we became sinners immediately. From that point on we had no choice but to be humble. We said, "Oh, we're really sorry. We had no idea." Even the police officer knew, because the roads were empty that day, that we had done this because we didn't know. Because he gave us a ticket, we had to make a payment at the bank. After going to the bank and paying the fine, we became free from that sin, because we had paid the price of that sin.

Everyone, while sin is alive in our hearts, it becomes a wall between us and God, keeping our hearts from having freedom before God. When the first man Adam was in the Garden of Eden, he was very free in front of God. When he met God, he would say, "God!" and be joyful before Him. But after Adam and Eve ate the fruit of the Knowledge of Good and Evil, and after committing sin, sin came alive in their hearts and Adam lost freedom in front of God.

God came to Eden, but He didn't see Adam there. God said, "Adam! Adam, where are you?"

"Yes, God, I was afraid because I was naked so I hid in the shades of the trees," Adam said.

"Who told you that you were naked? Did you eat of the fruit of the tree that I told you not to eat of?"

Everyone, before sin entered, Adam was so free before God. But Adam lost his freedom once sin entered in.

Once, when my son was in elementary school, somebody broke the lock on his wooden piggy bank and stole the money from it. When I looked closely at the piggy bank, it had been torn open with something like a spoon. You could tell that it wasn't done on one try, but on many tries; it had many streaks to show for it. It was clear that somebody who was not very strong had done it. Kids, who did not have much strength, had done it. I could tell that it was our kids who had done this.

I said, "Yeong Kook, did you take the money from this?"

"Oh, Dad, I have no idea. I don't know."

"Eunsook, did you do this?"

"No, I don't know!"

Now I became a detective. So I lied a little bit. I said, "You guys get over here and put your fingers on the clock. Then it will show your finger prints. If I check the fingerprints on this wooden piece right here, then I can immediately tell who touched this. I'm sure I can clearly find out who did this. You guys have to be honest with me."

"Uh, we didn't do it," my children said. But their answers began to lose more and more confidence. At first they said, "No! It wasn't me!" but their answers became weaker and weaker.

"Do you guys want to answer me after you get spanked? Or, if you tell me honestly I'll forgive you. So tell me honestly."

Having lost even more confidence they said, "It wasn't me…"

"You little rascals! I know!"

Then I separated my daughter and my son, and then I had them talk about each other. I asked, "Who said to do it first? Was it your older sister; or was it your younger brother? Who was it?"

Then my daughter said that it was Yeong Kook. You know my kids are all grown now, but there was a time when they used to be like that, a long time ago.

What is this sin? If they did not steal the money from the piggy bank, how free would they have been? They could say, "Dad, it wasn't me! What's wrong, Dad?" But because they have sin recorded in their hearts, even though they say, "Dad, it wasn't me," they have no confidence. When I pushed them further the second and third time, they began to lose more and more confidence. So I was easily able to catch the criminal. Of course the criminal was from my family.

Death Is a Really Good Thing

Sin influences our hearts. That is why, no matter who you are, sin should not be treated lightly, but every little tiniest bit of sin must be taken care of. If not, and if just a little bit remains, the boldness in your heart dies. Right now, things may feel okay. But when does it become difficult? When God is giving His judgment, everybody would be sitting there. The next one to judgement is called to stand in front of God.

"God, you know what, I had some sins, and…."

"Your name is not in the book of life."

"God, I was a pastor and I cast out demons!"

"Angels, throw him into hell!"

One angel takes his right foot, another the left foot, another the right arm, and another the left arm. They say, "One, two, three," and then they toss him into hell. Of course, I'm not sure if that's how they toss him in.

He screams, "Ahhh!" and falls into hell.

When you hear that sound you will become afraid. Even people that are pretty confident will begin to feel nervous and begin to break a cold sweat. At that moment, if you have even the tiniest bit of sin remaining, while standing before the judgment, you would probably faint.

But, suppose that your sins are clearly washed away. How bold would you be?

You would praise, "I'm redeemed by the blood of the Lamb," and be dancing. You would sing, "Happy day, happy day! When Jesus washed my sins away!" You would stand boldly.

About 20 years ago, my grandmother passed away and we held a funeral. I went down to the countryside and there were so many relatives, and I had to greet them. I couldn't get any sleep for several days. I spent the nights with only coffee. After the funeral, I came up to Seoul for a conference; and on the day it ended, my stomach hurt badly. At midnight I was hospitalized at the Hanyang University Hospital.

The doctor took x-rays and said that my intestines were all twisted, and he tried to stick in a tube. My stomach had been bulging forward, and all of a sudden, blue water gushed out of me and it was all over the doctor's white coat. They scheduled me for surgery on Monday morning. For the first time, I skipped Sunday service. I laid on the bed, and I could see my wife looking down on me with a worried look on her face. Then my wife's face started to become cloudy and fade away. I began to think, "Ah, I'm beginning to lose consciousness. I'd better snap out of it! No, I can't go out like this, I need to be strong!" But things became even cloudier and I began to fade away. It felt as though I was completely losing my consciousness. As that continued on I began to think, "Oh, I'm dying right now."

I thought that I should settle some things before I die. I thought, "Our church. Even without me our church has good pastors so I don't need to worry about it. My family. How will my wife and kids live when I die? God has cared for my family until now. Wouldn't He continue to care for them even after I die?" and even that wasn't a problem. I thought, "Thirdly, what about me? What will happen to me when I pass away?" I thought about death for the first time. At that time I felt inside of my heart, "I received the forgiveness of sins through the blood of Jesus. My sins have been washed even whiter than the snow. None of my sins remain and they are all taken care of at the cross. That's why if I die now I will cross the river of death and by the Tree of Life I will remain together with Jesus. As I leave this world I will meet Jesus in front of God, and I will also meet the saints who have passed on before me."

Before, it seemed as though it would be scary and painful when I die. Although I didn't die that day, my heart stood before death, and I felt so peaceful. I thought, "Wow. Death is a really good thing. I will be rid of this painful body. I will be walking at the glorious riverside by the Tree of Life!" I felt so peaceful and so happy.

Hey, What Are You Talking About? Let's Go!
Two years ago, I went to Orissa, India. Missionary Su Hyun Kim, in Orissa, prepared a Bible conference there and invited me. Orissa is the Hindu capital of the world. When Missionary Kim Su Hyun preached the Gospel there, hundreds of Hindus converted and came to our church. Many of the Hindus there also tried to kill Missionary Su Hyun Kim. These people, called the RSS, are Hindu extremists. They are people who are trained to use axes and swords to kill people who go against Hinduism. Because thousands of people were expected to come to the conference, Missionary Su Hyun Kim borrowed a large plot of land and built a stage there. The Hindus came and destroyed the stage, and planted a Hindu flag there. What that means is, "This is Hindu land, whoever comes in is staging an act of war." When Missionary Su Hyun Kim tried to go in there,

the police chief appeared and said, "No one can go in here. Neither the Hindus, nor the Good News Mission can go in here."

I was told about these things, but I still had to go there. I was the main speaker, how could I not go? Now, even death was something I had to be prepared for. I thought about it for a long while, "I'm not going to live a thousand or ten thousand years. One day I will die. What kind of a death would be good to face?" I didn't want to die just struggling with old age. I thought that it would be too pitiful to die in a car accident with a broken head, bleeding. It also seemed too ruthless to become all withered and in pain, dying of cancer. There is no path to death that I would prefer. So what I chose was, if it were up to me, I had the heart, "I want to be martyred while preaching the Gospel."

Because I had already made up my mind to be martyred, I went to India with the heart that it may happen while I'm in Orissa. After getting in the airplane and going to Delhi, I got on another airplane from Delhi and went to Bhubaneswar. When I arrived at the Bhubaneswar airport, Missionary Su Hyun Kim was there to meet me. From there, I needed to go 600 km into the mountains, so Missionary Su Hyun Kim had reserved a helicopter. But the police prohibited the landing of the helicopter because it seemed that if I went there, the situation would become a lot more intense, and they wanted to prevent that.

The missionary said, "Pastor, we're sorry but the helicopter has been cancelled."

"It's okay, let's go there by car."

"We didn't bring our church car, but we borrowed another car. Because the Hindus know our church car, it may be a target for terrorist attacks." Everything he said was so scary. "Pastor, before you came here, I could not decide whether to bring you to the conference area or whether to just send you back home."

"Hey, what are you talking about? Let's go."

We got in the car and drove through the rugged mountains, and at around 10 o'clock at night we arrived in Orissa. There were about a thousand people waiting there for me. They gave me a wreath of flowers to welcome me. I thought, "Wow." The weather must have been quite cold but they made this wreath of flowers in the morning, and they had been waiting for me. Because they thought the flowers would wither, they had dipped it in water. When they put it on me, I was drenched; yet, these people were still so excited.

We held the conference there beginning the next day. The police were afraid that we would have a conflict with the Hindus there, so they sent us armed police officers, and they guarded the area where we were having the conference. There was one squad of nine officers carrying guns to protect our conference. We were able to have the conference safely through their protection.

Many Churches in Korea Just Skip Over This Topic of Redemption

Everyone, my hometown is not this earth. It is that land. Because I have assurance that I can get to that land, it is not a problem when I pass away from this earth. When I was hospitalized at the Hanyang University Hospital, although I did not die, from my heart, I met death that time. I really thought that I was going to die that day. Usually, I could not feel it. But when I stood before death, I was so thankful that Jesus had washed my sins whiter than the snow. I was also so happy that I was facing death inside of Jesus.

The one thing terribly wrong about churches today is that they just generally skim over the issue of salvation and the issue of redemption. They say that Jesus on the cross forgave all of our sins; you will go to heaven if you believe that. That's it. The church members don't know the Bible precisely, it seems that their sins are washed away, but it also seems that they are not washed away. They are unable to have assurance.

Sometimes, when we listen to the sermons, we can hear the pastor say that we're all saved, and it feels as though our sins are washed away. Then at other times, when we listen to the sermon it seems like we have sins and it's not going to work. It's confusing. There's a secret of redemption that's hidden in the Bible, but because the pastors are unable to precisely talk about the Gospel, many people have no idea about how their sins are washed away. Because they don't know, they think, "Yeah I'll probably go to heaven. Look how much I've believed. I've poured my heart into it for such a long time, so I'm pretty sure God will remember me. They say that if you believe then you can go to heaven." With those kinds of vague thoughts, they just pass it by. But when they actually stand before death, they are afraid. There are so many people like that.

Everyone, even though you may not be sure about anything else, you must at least have assurance that your sins are clearly washed away. Even though you may not know other things, you must know with assurance about being born again.

This is the reason why Christianity today is corrupted. People do everything else well, but when it comes to getting their sins washed away, they just carelessly skim over it. Pastors do not think and study about the aspects of redemption recorded in the Bible and they don't even try to understand what the Bible tells us. That is why, when I try to preach the Gospel to the people, most of them say that this is their first time hearing such things.

The book called, *The Secret of Forgiveness of Sins and Being Born Again*, was a book that was written based on the 1986 Busan Mugunghwa Auditorium conference. The words that I preached there were made into a book. People read that book and they become completely stunned. They say, "We never knew these words had this kind of meaning!" because the realization comes to their hearts and they receive the forgiveness of sins and have assurance. From then on, their spiritual lives become so joyful.

Everyone, people who live without Jesus gain joy from eating, drinking, and traveling the world. But we, inside of Jesus, have joy and happiness that comes from Jesus, because that peace, joy, and happiness cannot compare to the corruptible things of the world. Therefore, even though you do not go on nice trips, do not live in a nice home, you can still be happy.

This Fraudulent Theology that Says You Are Merely Called Righteous Even Though You Are a Sinner

Sin builds a wall in the heart. It becomes the wall that separates God and us. You have a door to your heart and there is a door to God's heart as well. Brother Young Woo Jin, who developed this pharmaceutical called Ddobyul, said this to me: "Pastor, the amazing thing about cells is that all human cells have doors, but plants cells don't have doors. Because people's cells have doors, even though it's the same disease and you use the same medication, some people get healed and some people do not get healed. This is what's most confusing to the doctors. While someone with tuberculosis takes certain medication and gets healed, another person does not get healed. Because human cells have doors, if the doors are closed, no matter what good medication he takes, it's not going to be effective because the cells will not accept it."

I said to Brother Young Woo Jin, "That's why you need to serve the herbal medicine with a key so that it can open the door and get in."

That's right. Just as the doors of the cells must be opened, the doors of the heart must also be opened. To open the doors of the heart, the sins of the heart must be taken care of; sins must be taken care of. Everyone, when we sin, the doors of our hearts close. Moreover, on God's end, His heart closes too. He is closing the door towards sin because He cannot accept sin. A theologian once said to me, "We are sinners. God has just called us righteous." Called righteous. I heard him saying that. I said to him, "You may perhaps be a theologian, but you are not one who believes in God." Theology today leads us in a direction to not believe in God. Theologians just study the knowledge of the Bible, but they do not move forward with the faith to believe in God. The way they interpret the Bible is dragging them to the path that Satan guides them to. But sadly, even among theologians today there are so many of them who do not believe in God. There are so many theologians who say that the Bible is not the Word of God. Because they have not met the God that's inside of the Bible, they have no choice but to say that.

I asked that theologian, "If God could just call a sinner righteous, why would He have sent Jesus to die on the cross? All He would have to do is just call that person righteous. If God could call a sinner righteous, then God could never be a righteous judge. A righteous judge must call a sinner a sinner, and a righteous person a righteous person. Just because He knows a sinner and is close with him, if he calls a sinner sinless, how could that be a righteous judge? And if there is such a judge, then who would go to hell?" What we clearly need to know is that God never calls the sinner righteous. God calls a sinner a sinner, and God calls the righteous, righteous. If God could call a sinner righteous, then all He needs to say to the sinner is, "You are righteous. You can all go to heaven." But because God cannot just call a sinner righteous, He sent Jesus. Because God needs to punish sinners, He sent His son Jesus to this earth. Without punishment, sin cannot be taken care of.

For God to Be Just, and for Us to Be Just

Let's find Romans chapter 3 verse 25. It says, *Whom God hath set forth to be a propitiation through faith in his blood, to declare his righteousness for the remission of sins that are past, through the forbearance of God…* God wanted to declare His own righteousness. If God is righteous then He must punish the sinners. Then, He would be the righteous God. God could not just leave us as we are, so He made up His mind to punish us.

I'll read verse 26, *To declare, I say, at this time his righteousness: that he might be just, and the justifier of him which believeth in Jesus.*

Everyone, please listen to this. If there is a person who committed a sin, and if God called that person righteous, God could not be righteous. What is God thinking right now? God wants to be just, and also He wants to make us who have committed sins, just. If God sees us, who have committed sins, and tells us, "You're a sinner. You must go to hell," then that would make God righteous, but we as sinners would be destroyed. What must God do so that He would be righteous and make us righteous as well? He must punish our sins. To do that, He placed our sins upon Jesus, and had Jesus receive the punishment instead of us. Jesus was crucified on the cross and received the punishment for our sins. Now it is justified for God to call us righteous because our sins have been punished. Because our sins have been taken care of, we are righteous.

God wanted to look at us and say that we are righteous. He did not want to leave us in the state of being sinners and merely call us righteous. Therefore, while we were sinners, Jesus was put to death for our sins. Now, He can freely call us righteous because all of our sins were forgiven and we were made righteous through the death of Jesus on the cross. Because He has called us righteous upon seeing that our sins were taken care of on the cross, we can be called righteous. These words are kind of confusing, but do you understand? If you understand, please raise your hand. Everyone, thank you very much for understanding.

To reinforce what I'm telling you, if we are sinners and we say that we are sinners, we go to hell. But, God wanted to make us righteous;

He wanted to let us into heaven. However, if God allows sinners into heaven, He cannot be a righteous judge. God thought, "What can I do to make sure that, since I am righteous, I can make man righteous as well?" God decided to punish our sins. If God punishes our sins and gives the punishment according to that sin, God would be righteous. But if we were to receive the punishment for our sins, we would be destroyed, and it would not have worked. That's why the punishment that we should have received was placed upon Jesus, and God had Jesus die on the cross. Now, through the punishment of Jesus, our sins have been clearly washed away. Therefore, God is just and we are just, also. Amen?

Then let me ask you this: When God calls us righteous, does He call us righteous even though we have sin? Or does He call us righteous because we are righteous, with all of our sins washed away? Raise your hand, if you think that God calls you righteous even though you have sin. Not even one person? Then, Jesus was nailed to the cross and received all of the punishment for our sins, and that's why all of our sins are washed away. That is why we are without sin and are made righteous. Upon seeing that, God calls us righteous. If you believe that, then please raise your hand. Yes. Thank you. Amen. I think you are listening to me very well. Thank you. This was a little complicated, so it was difficult for me to explain, but thank you for understanding so well.

Who Can Reverse What God Has Made Righteous?

Our sins didn't just get washed out of nowhere in the Bible. Many theologians today, with their own thoughts, interpret the Bible in a very improper way. They say that God just called the sinners righteous, and that God is not the righteous judge. God cannot call a sinner righteous. Everyone, believe in God. God cannot lie. If God says that you are righteous, then you are righteous. God can never call someone righteous who is not righteous. That's why, for God to call us righteous, He had to make us righteous. And what did He do to accomplish that? He sent His son Jesus to this earth. Through Jesus' death on the cross, He washed our sins as white as snow. That's why when God sees us now, we are righteous. Amen? In the eyes of God we are righteous. That's why, in many places in the Bible, God has called us righteous.

Romans chapter 3 verse 23:
For all have sinned and come short of the glory of God; being justified freely by His grace through the redemption that is in Christ Jesus.

It says we were justified freely by His grace. Because God made us righteous, because God justified us, we are righteous. If God says that you are righteous, then, are you righteous or are you not righteous? You are righteous. We talk about this very often.

Once, the first president of Korea, President Seung Man Lee, visited a military base. The President asked the commander of that base, "Are your soldiers eating well?"

"Yes, they are."

"Do they sleep well?"

"Yes. They sleep very warm and comfortably."

The President wanted to see the rice storage. He said, "Show me the rice storage."

While the commander was taking the President to the rice storage, the commander's office called the rice storage facility.

"His Excellency the President is on his way, so get ready quickly!"

But, at the rice storage, a captain the night before had drunk all night long. That day, he was so sleepy, so he looked for a place to take a nap. He was taking a nap on top of the rice sacks in the storage facility. The rice storage was so hot inside that he had taken off all of his clothes down to his underwear and he was sleeping there. But a private, who had answered the phone, came running in.

"Captain Kim! We're in big trouble! His Excellency the President is on his way here!"

He was so shocked. He wanted to run away, but he wasn't wearing anything. If he runs out in his underwear then everyone will notice him, so he couldn't do that. He thought, "Oh, no. I'm dead." Right then he came up with an amazing idea. He quickly started carrying a sack of rice, placing it on the other side of the storage. He picked up another one and carried it over, and picked up another one and carried it over. He was soaked in sweat as he did this and then the doors opened. His Excellency the President, along with the commander and several officers, walked in. The President could see that there was someone in the rice storage carrying the rice sacks.

The President said, "You, come over here."

"Yes! Captain Kim reporting to His Excellency the President!"

"What were you doing over there?"

"Yes! I was moving the sacks of rice!"

"Is that what your job is?"

"No, sir! I have subordinates, but because this is tiring work I was trying it out to see how difficult it is."

It seemed that what he was saying made sense. The President heard this and he was touched. He said, "Wow, we have soldiers in our country who really love their subordinates! Do you usually do this?"

"Yes! I do this from time to time!"

"You're doing a great job."

"Yes, if it's for my country, no matter what it is, I'll do it with all my might."

This guy who had drunk all night long was such a good talker. The President was so impressed. "You, what is your rank?" he asked.

"Yes! It's captain, sir!"

"What's above that?"

"It's major, sir!"

"And above that?"

"Lieutenant colonel, sir!"

"And above that?"

"It's colonel, sir!"

"You be that."

The secretary quickly took down that captain's military number, his rank, his affiliation, and called the Army Headquarters immediately. He said, "This is the President's secretary's office. By the special order of His Excellency the President, promote Captain Kim to colonel." That day, that man became an army colonel. Afterwards, the rumor of this spread all over, and people would say, "Had we known that, we would have drunk all night, too!"

If the President says, "You, be a colonel," then you are a colonel. Even for a death row inmate sentenced to death, if the President says to not execute him, then that execution will not happen. This is what you call power. The President has that much power. How much more then, if God who is in heaven says that you are righteous, would you be righteous or not? You are righteous!

For all have sinned and come short of the glory of God; Being justified freely by His grace through the redemption that is in Christ Jesus. (Romans 3:23, 24)

God said that you are freely justified. Why? It is because Jesus died for our sins. If God says that you are righteous then you are righteous. Amen? Amen. It's not Pastor Ock Soo Park saying this. But believe the Word of God exactly as it is. No matter what other thoughts arise, other than the Word of God that said this to you, cast all those thoughts aside. "God you have called me righteous, so I am righteous." The person who is able to say this, is a person who believes in God.

In your thoughts, you think, "I committed adultery, I got an abortion, I committed murder." Even so, God knows all of those things, yet called you righteous. Then, you are righteous. Everyone, have you ever received the judgment? Have you received it, even one time?

This happened when I lived in Daegu. I had gone out for a house visit on a Wednesday evening and I was on my way home on my bicycle. I was quite young at the time and I was riding so fast, and the headlight on my bicycle had blown out. It was the kind of headlight powered by your pedaling. I was riding without the lamp on my bicycle. When I was about 100 meters from reaching the church, a traffic cop blew his whistle and called me over. I begged him to just let me go, but it didn't work. He took my bicycle to the police station, and the next day, he picked me up in a police car to take me to court.

The judge gave out his sentences: "So and so, two dollar fine. So and so, three dollars. So and so, five dollars." If the judge calls out your name and declares the fine, that's the law. The judge was doing exactly that, and after a long while he called on a person.

"So and so, stand up!"

"Yes?"

"Why did you get drunk and not pay for your liquor?"

"It's not that I didn't mean to pay."

"Are you still drunk? Five nights in jail!"

Then he would keep going, "So and so, three dollars. So and so, two dollars. So and so, four dollars." He would keep on going and then call out another person, "So and so, stand up! If you got drunk why didn't you just go home and sleep? Why did you walk around the whole neighborhood throwing fits and screaming out loud?"

"Oh, I didn't mean to be so noisy...."

"You still haven't snapped out of it yet? Five nights in jail!"

Then I could see what was happening. If the judge says something to you, you're supposed to say, "I'm really sorry." If you come up with excuses and say this and that, then you're going to get five nights in jail. If that happens, even paying the fine is not going to help you.

"Ock Soo Park! Two dollars!" I was sentenced to a two-dollar fine, so I paid the two dollars. There was no other explanation. If the judge says five nights in jail, it's five nights; if the judge says you're innocent, then you're innocent. There's no one who can reverse what the judge has decided in court. God is the righteous judge. If God says that you are righteous, then there's nobody who can reverse that. But by not listening to the voice of God, but rather, listening to the voice of Satan, people say, "No, God, I'm a sinner! Forgive me!" Saying that is not believing in God.

Erasing the Sin Recorded on the Horns of the Altar with Blood

In Jeremiah chapter 17 verse 1, it says,

The sin of Judah is written with a pen of iron, and with the point of a diamond: it is graven upon the table of their heart, and upon the horns of your altars.

Our sins are recorded on those four horns of the altar, and are also recorded on the table of our hearts. When the sin offering is given, you bring over the female goat without blemish to do the laying on of hands upon its head, and place the sin on it. Then you kill that goat and receive its blood. When the goat sheds its blood and dies, your sin is forgiven, but the record of that sin still remains. Where? On the horns of the altar. That's why the priest takes the blood with his finger and puts it on the horns of the altar. That is talking about erasing the record of our sins that is on the horns of the altar. Why did they erase the record of our sin? Because the sin is taken care of. By putting the blood on the horns of the altar, through the death of the sheep or the goat, our sins are forgiven, and the blood is the proof of it. With that blood, the record of sin is erased.

That is why no record of our sin remains anywhere in heaven. Everyone, just as the lamb is put to death, and by putting the blood on the horns of the altar the sin is erased, our Lord Jesus Christ went not into the tabernacle on earth, but went into the temple that is in heaven. He put His blood onto the horns of the altar in the temple that is in heaven. And, through sprinkling His blood on the mercy seat, He has forever purified us from our sins and erased our sins away. That's why it says that God remembers our sins no more.

It says that in a hymn as well:
He'll forgive your transgressions,
And remember them no more,
He'll forgive your transgressions,
And remember them no more,
"Look unto me, ye people,"
Saith the Lord your God;
He'll forgive your transgressions,
He'll forgive your transgressions,
And remember them no more,
And remember them no more.

Now, in the memory of God, your sins have disappeared. There is no record of your sin anywhere in heaven, but I'm sure you have the memory of sin on the table of your hearts. Now, what do we do with that? We erase it, by faith.

I remember the sin that I've committed now, but through the blood that Jesus shed on the cross, the sin is all washed away. It is to believe in that. It is not difficult at all. It is difficult to believe something that is not true, but what's so hard about believing what's true? God does not remember our sins, but we remember our sins. Even though you remember them, Jesus already paid for the wages of that sin on the cross. Just earlier, the Gracias Choir sang this hymn, right?

But he was wounded for our transgressions,
He was bruised for our iniquities:
The chastisement of our peace was upon him;
And with his stripes we are healed.

Everyone, Jesus bore all of our sins. He took the responsibility. Believe in that. The heart of God concerning our sins is all erased. On that day, when you stand before God and stand before death, just as I had rejoiced back then, I hope you will be able to stand on that day with joy. I hope that you will be able to stand with thankfulness. I hope that you will praise our Lord Jesus.

CHAPTER 6
It Shall Be Forgiven Him

In Leviticus chapter 4 verse 31, it says, *And the priest shall make an atonement for him and it shall be forgiven him.* It means that because the priest makes an atonement for him, that his sins shall be forgiven. In the same way, Jesus fulfilled the sin offering. That's how He accomplished the forgiveness of your sins. It is not that you should ask for the forgiveness of your sins. All you have to do is believe that your sins are forgiven. If they are not forgiven, you should not believe they are forgiven.

But, because it is clear that the blood of the cross forgave our sins, we must believe those words.

I cannot say how thankful I am that we are able to talk about the sin offering this time. I, too, for a very long time, was conflicted and tormented and suffered inside of sin. But these words of the sin offering freed me from all of my sins. Everyone, now you can practically memorize the words about the sin offering in Leviticus chapter 4, right? Even though you may not be able to memorize them, I hope you will be able to remember the process that they speak of.

Sin Offering: Freedom from Sin

And if any one of the common people sin through ignorance, while he doeth somewhat against any of the commandments of the Lord concerning things which ought not to be done, and be guilty; Or if his sin, which he hath sinned, come to his knowledge: then he shall bring his offering, a kid of the goats, a female without blemish, for his sin which he hath sinned. And he shall lay his hand upon the head of the sin offering, and slay the sin offering in the place of the burnt offering. And the priest shall take of the blood thereof with his finger, and put it upon the horns of the altar of burnt offering, and shall pour out all the blood thereof at the bottom of the altar. And he shall take away all the fat thereof, as the fat is taken away from off the sacrifice of peace offerings; and the priest shall burn it upon the altar for a sweet savour unto the Lord; and the priest shall make an atonement for him, and it shall be forgiven him. (Leviticus 4:27-31)

God Who Blotted Out the Records of Our Sin

Yesterday evening, we talked about how the laying of hands is done upon the head of the sin offering and, after, the sin is placed upon the goat or the lamb. Then we talked about how they kill that sin offering on the altar. They take the blood and spread it upon the horns of the altar. When the priest kills the lamb or the goat, he stabs the artery in the neck of the animal. He has a bowl in his hand and he receives the blood into the bowl. The priest then takes that blood with his finger and spreads it upon the horns of the altar.

I went to Mongolia one time, and they asked me if I would like to eat some sheep meat. I don't know if you've ever had sheep before, but it has a kind of foul stench. At first, the foul smell is unpleasant. But after you eat it once or twice, it becomes delicious. Missionary Jong Jin Park, who's in Alaska right now, and a few others bought a sheep, and ate it. Four people fed on one hind leg of the sheep, and missionary alone ate all of the front legs by himself. Of course, the hind legs are bigger than the front legs, but Missionary Jong Jin Park said that it was still a bit small.

In Mongolia, there are many people who walk around with their sheep. If you see one and you say, "I want to buy that sheep," they kill that sheep for you and give it to you right away.

When a sheep dies, it's very different from how other animals die. When you want to kill a chicken, it runs away. Some people break the chicken's neck, put it into boiling, hot water, then remove its feathers, and then lose control of it. Then, sometimes in that state, the chicken runs around naked. When a pig is about to be killed, the pig screams so loud that the screaming can be heard all over the village. When I was young, from time to time, we'd kill a pig. Several homes get together to kill one pig.

You tie up the pig's front legs and cut its neck with a knife. Kids shouldn't see these kinds of things, but when I was young, I saw a lot of that. When they cut the neck with a knife, the blood comes gushing out. The pig screams and screams and throws a fit. Most people cannot handle this very well. No matter how upright or polite the pig had been, its life is now on the line, and being polite and all that stuff goes out the window. It throws a fit. It's really not easy to kill a pig. Most cattle are gentle, for the most part. But when they feel the threat of danger, they strain and throw tantrums.

But sheep are not like that. A person who kills a sheep does not need to even tie it down, nor hold it up. When you hold a sheep by its ear and stab it in the neck with a knife, it stands there for a bit and then falls over and dies. In the Bible, we can see Jesus being expressed in the same way. It says that He did not open His mouth, like a sheep before its shearing. It means that Jesus quietly accepted death. At the place of the sin offering, the priest dips his finger in the blood and puts it upon the horns of the altar. Why is it put on the horns of the altar? As we talked about yesterday evening, our sins are recorded on two places: one on God's end and one on our end.

For example, if I buy something from a certain store using credit, then in my record book I write, "Oh, on this date, I bought this much on credit." The person I bought from will also keep the same record of it. Likewise, where are the records of our sin on God's end recorded? It's recorded on the altar. The Bible tells us that on our end, it's recorded on the table of our hearts.

Everyone, when you commit sin, it's recorded on the table of your heart.

Usually, you forget about your sins, but when it's time to gather your heart to pray to God, you remember your sins. Let's think once again about giving the sin offering.

A common person has done something against the commandment of the Lord. The sin that he sinned came to his knowledge and he realized that he was a sinner. Then he brought over a female goat without blemish and does the laying on of hands onto the head of that sin offering. Laying on of hands means that the sin is placed over onto the lamb or the goat. Then they kill that sin offering on the altar.

Once the lamb or the goat receives the sin and sheds its blood and dies, the sin is washed. The priest then takes that blood with his finger and puts it upon the horns of the altar. Our sins are recorded on the horns of the altar. It means that because that sin is forgiven, it is being erased. That is what we call, blotting out. To blot out is like painting over it to erase it. God has blotted out the records of our sin.

In heaven, there is a record of the sins we committed. How do you erase that? It is all erased through the blood of Jesus, who is the lamb that died for our sins. Why must this be done? Because when Jesus, who is the lamb, shed His blood, all of our sins were forgiven. This is what we spoke about yesterday evening.

Ock Soo Park, He's Full of It. He Says that He Has No Sin?

This morning I want to tell you about the part, *it shall be forgiven him*. At the end part of Leviticus chapter 4 verse 31, it says, *And the priest shall make an atonement for him and it shall be forgiven him*. So, once that sin offering is complete, the sin is forgiven.

Everyone, when you first go to church, it appears fresh and good. Although people who come to church may not be so clean and reserved on the inside, for the most part, they are on the outside. People are drawn by that freshness and they begin spiritual life. They go to church and begin to learn the Bible, but what do the churches teach? In elementary school you learn the most simple sentences like, "Tom, Jane, come here. Let's go to the playground." That's where it all begins. As you continue your studies, you learn step by step, and begin to learn more difficult things. This is how you learn math. This is how all subjects are. Likewise, there is also a process in spiritual life.

You don't go to church every day like school, but to have service you go a couple times a week. Although you may not learn it very often, there are principles in spiritual life. If you learn the process one by one from the very

It Shall Be Forgiven Him

beginning, even though you may not know other things, once you clearly understand this process, faith begins to arise in you. So, after you learn a little bit, you can live a clear spiritual life. You can also receive the grace of God. But the churches today are not doing so. Because churches are not divided into grade levels, people who've been going to church for 30 years sit there and listen to the sermon, and people who are there for the first time also listen to the sermon. Even elders and deacons and those who are there for the first time listen to the sermon together. People who are there for the first time just look around to see what everyone else is doing and simply follow that. As they do that, they just become used to the ways of the church.

A long time ago, there was a child whose parents passed away. He grew up under his uncle. He could not find rest anywhere, so he went to church. It was so nice going to church. So, he came home one day and asked his uncle, "Uncle, why don't you go to church with me one time?"

The uncle did not want to go to church, but when he quietly thought about it, he thought, "My nephew so badly wants me to go. If I don't, he'll think that I'm not going because I'm not his father. So I think I'd better go."

The uncle sat next to the nephew.

The nephew prayed, "Father God, Father God…"

He could not hear what he was praying about, but all he could hear was the "Father God."

"Ah, he's calling God, 'father.' If he's the father to my nephew, that means he's my older brother." So, the uncle said, "God, my brother. God, my brother." The nephew felt so embarrassed, he gave his uncle a poke.

After the service was over, the nephew said to his uncle, "Uncle, how can you call God your brother? You're supposed to say, 'Father God.'"

When he said that, the uncle said to him, "Hey, don't you know the family tree? If he's a father to you, it means he's a brother to me."

If a person could have that much logic, that person can live spiritual life well.

But people who go to church, for the most part, don't clearly understand and realize why they go to church. They just go, copying what the person next to them does.

Sin Offering: Freedom from Sin

Koreans are quite smart. They say Koreans are one of the smartest people in the world. That is why they are not sincere. Because they are very quick, they can adapt to anything very quickly. Even in spiritual life, they observe the situation and adapt to it very quickly. When others give offering, they also give offering. When they see other people singing praises, they sing praises, too. When others pray, they also pray. If others say, "God, I'm a sinner," then they also follow and say they're sinners.

When the pastor says, "God, today this sinner comes before you," they say, "Oh that's right. If the pastor says that he's a sinner, then I too should say I'm a sinner." Then they say, "God, I'm a sinner. Please forgive me." Even the elder says that he's a sinner and asks for forgiveness. Then who wouldn't follow and do likewise? If they don't know any better and just let time pass by like that, after about one year, they are awarded deaconship in the church.

In 1962, without anyone teaching me about this, I was conflicted because of sin. But, by the grace of God, I realized the forgiveness of sin. At that time, I was part of the church choir. I said this to all the choir youths while they were gathered there: "I was in so much pain and conflict because of sin. But I received the forgiveness of sin. Now all my sins are gone. I am righteous."

Right then, all of the choir members said, "Mr. Park. Me too! I too, like you, was suffering because of sin." They were suffering because of sin, but none of them knew what to do about it. One time, afterwards, I was about to open the door to enter into the room where all the youths were gathered, but I could hear the people talking inside. It seemed that they were talking about me. I listened and one young man said, "Ock Soo Park, he's full of it. He says that he has no sin? I know exactly how he lived. We went together to other people's houses to steal fruit. We committed sins together." That's what he said. They could not understand what it meant when I said that I had no sin. That is how the churches today in Korea are flowing. We can understand if we open the Bible, talk about how we became a sinner, and search step by step how that sin can be taken care of. But people now have a spiritual life of not doing that, but just following along with what everyone else does.

If You Just Have the Foundation of Spiritual Life

After I became born again and I read the Bible, what the Bible said and what the church said were completely different. I realized, "Ah, this is what the Bible says… and, this is what the Bible says," and began to empty all that I learned before. I began to read the Bible step by step starting with Genesis. Genesis, then Exodus through Revelation, and once again Genesis, then Exodus all the way through Revelation. Once, twice, three times, four times, five times, six times…. After I read it about the sixth time, the Word became very sweet, and it burned in my heart and deeply touched me. I got to know the heart of God.

From then on, no matter what anyone said, I lived spiritual life following the Word of God. That became so much fun. From then on, it was so much fun to see students changing, and the drug addicts changing from the words of the Bible I would speak to them.

Everyone, the foundation of spiritual life begins with the assurance of the forgiveness of sin. At this conference, we're talking, step by step, about the words of the forgiveness of sin. There are so many things to say about the sin offering. If you learn this, spiritual life becomes so easy. People say Leviticus is too difficult.

Everyone, what's so difficult about Leviticus? It's not difficult at all. It's difficult because people just skim over it. But if we read it, one word at a time, what's so difficult about it? It says, "A common person's sin." Is that difficult? "And that sin to come to his knowledge." Is that difficult? "The female goat without blemish." That's not difficult. "Laying on of hands on the head." That's also not difficult. "Killing that female goat and taking that blood and putting it upon the horns of the altar." Was that difficult?

The Bible is easy and fun. But if people say, "Leviticus is hard," then it does become difficult. When people read Exodus and it says, "Three cubits and six cubits," people say, "Oh this is difficult."

When people read the book of Matthew and read the, "Begat, begat, begat." People only look at it like that and it feels difficult.

However, even a person who has never driven his whole life, if his life is on the line, wouldn't he learn to drive? If you make up your mind to learn how to drive, then you can learn in one week. Sure, it differs from person to person.

Getting a driver's license in one month, even as you live your normal life, is completely doable. But if you focus only on driving, it wouldn't take you even one week. Likewise, all you need to have is the foundation of spiritual life set. When your sins become washed away, God enters you, and spiritual life becomes automatic.

If God is there inside of you, He does not just sit there taking naps. God does not have nap time built into His schedule. When students arrange their daily schedules, they reserve time for sleep. But God does not sleep. Because He is always with us, no matter what we face, God is with us. So, when you receive the forgiveness of sins this time, you will become free from sin. Then joy and peace will come to your heart. Everything of you will become God's. The very funny thing is that when everything of yours becomes God's, then it seems like your loss, right? Because it feels as though you're losing all of your things to God. But if God gets to have all that is yours, then everything of God's also becomes yours. Then it's really good.

Everyone, this morning I want to share with you how we can live spiritual life, how we can have the assurance in the forgiveness of sins, and how we can be born again.

I Received the Forgiveness of Sins Because I Suddenly Remembered All of the Sins I've Committed and I Repented of Them!

I have personal spiritual counseling with many people because I'm a pastor.

I want to talk to the people about being born again and the forgiveness of sins, so I ask them, "Have you received the forgiveness of sins?"

"Yes, I have."

"How did you receive it?"

"One night, I was sleeping and my whole body began to burn…" That's how their stories usually begin.

I would ask somebody else, "Did you receive the forgiveness of sins?"

"Yes, I did."

"How did you receive it?"

"I was praying in the mountains and all of a sudden, I began to speak in tongues and that's how I received the forgiveness of sins."

Sometimes I wonder if the Bible is there just for show. It's clear that they never once read the Bible. The Bible tells us clearly how to receive the forgiveness of sins. But they just cover up the Bible and only speak from their assumptions. With their thoughts, they think, "Well, since I've received the gift of speaking in tongues today, I must have received the forgiveness of sins." When you listen to the words of the people who claim to have received the forgiveness of sins and were born again, that's how most of their stories go.

In 1974, in a town called Hodang-li, Chongtong-myun, Yeongchungoon in Gyeongbuk Province, we had a retreat at a silkworm farm. A pastor named Hae Kyu Jung attended the retreat. He was 79 years old at the time. His youngest son was the same age as me. Because he was a pastor, he shared a room with me. So I asked that pastor, "Pastor, are you born again?"

He said, "I am."

"How did you become born again?"

"My daughter in Gyungsan is turning 60 this year. And one day that daughter asked me, 'Father, are you born again?'

'Why do you ask?' I said.

'I'm born again.'

'How did you get born again?'

'I was praying and all of a sudden the sins that I committed long ago flashed before me like a movie and it caused me so much pain, so I began to tearfully pray and repent. And that's how I got born again.'

"After she told me that, I was saddened because I'd never had such an experience. But about a month later, I too was praying when all of a sudden, all my sins came to mind and I repented of them. That's how I received the forgiveness of sins."

When you don't know the Bible, you think you are born again when you experience something strange. But that is not being born again. When you receive the forgiveness of sins and become born again, why do you need the sin to flash before you like a movie? Where in the Bible does it say that? Tearing in your eyes and crying cannot make you become born again. People want to be born again when they go out to the mountains and pray. When they feel their bodies burning up, or when they experience speaking in tongues, they try to gain the assurance of being born again through these kinds of things. That is believing in their feelings. That is not believing in Jesus. Spiritual life does not come about through feelings or emotions. Of course, if you receive the grace of God, your heart may burn. And you may get teary, you may be moved, you may rejoice. But that emotion cannot become the basis of your spiritual life. You must absolutely avoid living spiritual life relying on your emotions, because your emotions will change endlessly. You may feel good in the morning, and bad in the evening. You may feel down when the weather is gloomy, and then get excited when the weather clears up. You may be happy when things go well, and sad when things don't go well. When you rely on your emotions, your spiritual life will always go back and forth. That's why your spiritual life will not work when you live like that. When your heart begins to burn or feel touched as you pray, you have to just leave it at that. You cannot say, "Because I felt my heart burning, I'm born again or saved." It is a big mistake to call that salvation, because emotions change endlessly. Never rely on emotions.

Spatial Disorientation and Spiritual Disorientation

We have several pilots in our church. We have a brother who flies for Korean Air. Once, I was going to Mongolia for a conference and I got to ride in the plane that he was piloting. I was scheduled to come back to Korea four days later. That brother also stayed in the same hotel as we did. Four days later, we came back on the same flight. It felt as though I had my own personal pilot. Also at our church, we have pilots who flew fighter jets in the air force. Most of them now work for either Korean Air or Asiana Airlines. They once told me about their experiences while piloting the fighter jets. There's this thing that the fighter jet pilots experience at least once. It's called spatial disorientation. Passenger airplanes take off and land, and that's all there is to it. But. when the fighter jets go in circles in the air, what the pilots see and feel can be very different from the actual situation.

There are many different kinds of spatial disorientation. When you fly between mountains or near the hills, the airplane moves at a slant. But you feel as though you are moving upright. Then after flying the plane for a while, you become unable to distinguish between the ocean and the sky. That is most dangerous.

It Shall Be Forgiven Him

Recently, an airplane crashed into the East Sea. Upon investigating, it was discovered that the pilot had fallen into spatial disorientation and entered into the ocean thinking it was the sky. Even apart from that, there are many kinds of spatial disorientation. There's something called "The Giant Hand." The pilot's stick is normally very easy to move. But I heard that once you fall into this disorientation, you are unable to move the stick. You begin to break a cold sweat and it feels as though a giant hand is holding onto your hand.

Some airplanes fly in circles in the sky, and are unable to get out of it. Then it becomes very difficult once the pilot falls into that kind of disorientation. Once, a trainer was flying together with a pilot-in-training. A fighter jet has two control sticks. Whoever falls into spatial disorientation must let go of the stick. The trainer was a major and the pilot-in-training was a lieutenant. The pilot-in-training could see that the trainer had fallen into spatial disorientation. If the person who is caught in spatial disorientation flies the plane, both of them will die. The pilot-in-training yelled out, "Trainer, let go of the stick! Let go!" But the trainer was afraid of having the pilot-in-training fly the plane, so he could not let go. Later on, the pilot-in-training said, "You punk! Let it go! You'd better let it go!" and yelled and cursed at him.

The most important fact in spatial disorientation is that what you are sensing and feeling right now is wrong. When the airplane is flying at high altitude and velocity, and all of a sudden you reduce the speed by half, it feels like you are falling down even though the airplane is still moving forward. That is what disorientation is. If people who are caught under such disorientation fly the plane, they'll be in big trouble. The most import thing when you're caught in disorientation is to not trust in your feelings, but to look at the gauge. It feels as though, to me, the airplane is falling down, but what does the gauge say? You must trust in the gauge.

Let me tell you an example that is important about flying with a gauge. There was an American cargo plane that departed from Sicily, Italy and was heading towards Cairo, Egypt. There were six people on the plane. The pilot was tired and they were all exhausted. Usually, from Sicily to Cairo, it takes about one hour. But as soon as the airplane took off, they all fell asleep. The pilot fell asleep, and the airplane continued on its way to

Cairo. After a long while, the pilot woke up and looked at his watch. It was 45 minutes after take-off. He thought he would soon arrive at the Cairo airport, but the gauges indicated that he had passed the Cairo airport. But no matter how much further they went, there were lights to be seen.

The pilot thought, "It's only been 45 minutes. How could we have passed Cairo?" and assumed that the gauges were broken. Because it was nighttime, he lowered the elevation and looked for the lights of the airport.

Ultimately, in the dark night above the desert, the airplane ran out of fuel. The soldiers jumped off the airplane on parachutes and the airplane also fell. The six people in the middle of the desert were thirsty, hot, and died of exhaustion.

Later on, the rescue team arrived and saw what one of the people had written in his notepad: "On this month, this day, the airplane crashed. On this month, this day, it's too hot. I'm so thirsty." When the rescue team discovered the airplane and opened up the gauges, they were perfectly fine. But why did it take 45 minutes, when it normally takes an hour at that distance? The airplane was very much influenced by the wind.

Because the Prevailing Westerlies were so strong, a distance that should've taken one hour passed in less than 45 minutes. That's why at flight schools, they talk about these kinds of examples and teach the students that they must absolutely not believe in their feelings but believe the gauges. They say that 90% of the flight accidents in America come about from not trusting the gauges. Once the pilot falls into spatial disorientation, he should not try to snap out of it or do something about it. If he just throws his feelings away and follows the gauges accordingly, he will be safe.

Once you are caught under spatial disorientation, you should not believe in your feelings or emotions.

Spiritual life is also the same as that. What you see, what you feel, you must ignore all of that, because our judgment can be wrong and our emotions can be wrong. Satan, one by one, endlessly shows people the wrongful paths. Everyone, just because you're saved, does that mean that Satan doesn't work upon you?

As you live spiritual life, of all the thoughts that arise in you, 99% are the voice of Satan. Just as the devil put inside of Judas Iscariot the heart to betray Jesus, the devil puts thoughts inside of you as well. In order to live spiritual life and trust in God, this is what you must absolutely learn today: How you feel, how you think, and no matter what your heart is like, you must throw all of that away, and you must believe only in the Word of God.

There are many theology schools today in Korea that teach something so scary; that the Bible is not the Word of God. If the Bible is not the Word of God, then what do we believe? How could we believe God? Can we believe God, following our thoughts? Everyone, today I am clearly telling you, all 66 books of the Bible are the Word of God. Amen? Raise your hand if you say Amen. Yes thank you. God will be pleased.

In Isaiah chapter 34 verse 16, it says, *Seek ye out of the book of the Lord, and read: no one of these shall fail, none shall want her mate: for my mouth it hath commanded, and his spirit it hath gathered them.*

The whole Bible comes from the inspiration of God. The Bible records that it was written through the people of God who had received His revelation. The people who add more to this will be punished. And those who remove from it shall be removed from participating in the glory of God. This is the Word of God. The scary thing about theologians today is that, there are so many theoretical theologians who don't live spiritual life at all. That's the reason behind our establishing the Mahanaim college in America. We want to teach that the Bible is the Word of God. The difference between a person who believes in the Word of God as the Word of God and follows it, versus a person who just knows it in theory is like heaven and earth. If you do not believe the Word of God, you have no hope. I realized how to receive the forgiveness of sins through these words. I gained strength in these words, and I continually learn the heart of God, and I receive the heart of God in these words. Is that also the case with you? I hope that you will believe in the Word of God. God does not speak directly to us as He had spoken directly to Abraham and Moses. So if the Bible is not the Word of God, then how are we to hear the voice of God?

Satan, the Swindler, Who Deceives You After Making You Trust in Yourself

The topics we are talking about this morning must be established in your heart. Your emotions can be wrong. Your judgments can also be wrong. It's the same with me. A long time ago, I began many works thinking I was right. But after it was all over, I realized so many things I had done were wrong. I was so sure that I was right, but they turned out to be wrong. When you go to Haeundae Beach, there are many swindlers by the beach. Everyone, do you know what swindlers are?

They say, "Okay, who wants to make some money? Come and take a look."

They show you a poker card. They line them up here and there and shuffle them here and there, and if you find the one they first showed you, you can win money.

There was a man whose friend was having a wedding in Busan, so he together with his wife went down to Busan from Jeonju. I was driving one day, and I heard the wife tell this story over the radio. The friend's wedding was at Haeundae Beach in Busan. When they got in the car early in the morning from Jeonju and went to Busan, it was only 10 o'clock in the morning. Since the wedding was at 2 in the afternoon, they had time left over so the two of them went to Haeundae Beach. They had a lot of fun. She said, "Catch me if you can!" and on the beach they were having a great time running around. Then, they met one of the swindlers on the beach.

The wife was able to find the card that the swindlers showed them, and she won $20. She did not want to receive the money, but they said, "No, you won. So you deserve it. Take it." She received the $20. Then, the swindlers showed them once again another poker card, and after shuffling it with the other cards, they told her to find it again. But they told her that she has to bet money first. She bet $50. But when they actually flipped over the card she picked, it was the wrong one. Now she's $30 in the red, so she feels like she has to at least break even.

But this time, the husband said, "Move over. I'll do it." He picked the poker card. They said you have to bet money, so he bet $100. They flipped it over, and once again, it was wrong. After doing it a few more times, they lost all their money. The two of them got all the change they had together and they couldn't even go to their friend's wedding, but instead just got on the transit train to come back to Jeonju. They were thirsty, but they did not even have enough money for a beverage, and they just returned like that all the way back to Jeonju.

Everyone, these kinds of swindlers deceive your eyes. That's why it's difficult to win money from them. If people could get it right, would these swindlers go through the trouble of setting up all that stuff to do that work? These people are confident that once they draw in some customers, they will win their money.

Because they use trickery, they deceive your eyes.

People tend to pick one thing when they are sure that it's right, but it's not. Everyone, the devil is so much more sophisticated than these swindlers. When the devil deceives people into thinking what is false to be true, everybody becomes deceived. Smart people are deceived in a smart way. The foolish people are deceived in a foolish way. Clumsy people are deceived in a clumsy way. The devil can deceive anyone. That's why the devil likes people who believe themselves the most. When people think, "I'm confident. I can do this," they can be deceived.

Jesus, in order to free Peter from being dragged around by the devil, and to have him realize how foolish it was for him to believe in himself, told him, "You shall deny me three times." Right then, Peter said, "Though I die with you, Lord, I'll never deny you." When he did deny Jesus, the heart to believe in himself came crumbling down.

As that heart came crumbling down, Peter became a worker of God held by the hand of God. Everyone, you must empty the heart to believe yourself in order for you to receive the grace of God and for you to become a worker of God. No matter how right you are, you must ask, "Is this my thought or the Word of God?" You must have the heart that, if it's your own thoughts, it's wrong. It's so good to accept the Word with that kind of heart. But Satan, with your thoughts, strikes up tactics to confuse you and to keep you from living a spiritual life.

The Basics of Spiritual Life: Denying Yourself

Everyone, if you are someone who just goes back and forth from church and if you don't care whether you die and go to heaven or hell, you may simply say, "Jesus, you do it your way, I'll do it my way. I'll just go to church to get some rest." You may continue doing so. But if you want to have true faith and become one with God, and if you want to receive the forgiveness of sin, become born again, and go to heaven and live the glorious blessed life, you must learn this process.

What did Jesus say? "Whosoever will follow me…" Then what does He say?

Did He say, "…shall exalt himself, shall believe in himself?" According to Jesus, "Whosoever will follow me…" must do what to himself? Please answer loudly.

Yes, he must deny himself, carry the cross, and follow Jesus. But as you live spiritual life, you forgot all about that.

A long time ago, as I was going to America, I went with one of the eldery men in our Daejeon church. But this elderly man, upon arriving in LA and getting off the plane, he ripped up his airplane ticket to return back to Korea and put it in the trash. It was the day for me to return to Korea so I asked that elderly man, "We're going to get on the airplane today. So, is everything all ready?"

"Pastor, don't worry. My bags are all packed and I'm ready."

"Then, let me see your passport and ticket."

He brought it over to me, but the ticket was not there. "Oh, your ticket has been torn out."

"Do I need that?"

"That was the ticket to return on the airplane."

"Oh, I tore it out and threw it away."

I asked him where he threw it away and we tried to find it in the garbage. He had thrown it away a long time ago and the trash had already been taken out. We tried to quickly contact the travel agency to get the airplane ticket reissued. It was so difficult to get it reissued, and it really put us through a tough time. When you go abroad with elderly people, they occasionally give you these kinds of surprises. Even young people, when they don't know what's going on, they also really have a hard time.

When I go on witnessing trips, I gather the people together and explain to them, "This is the passport. This is something you give when you go through the entrance and exit. This is something you turn in when you get on the airplane. This is the airplane ticket, and you must remove one page at a time. To travel abroad, you must clearly check whether you have the passport, airplane ticket, and visa. And you must check whether the passport or visa has passed its expiration date or not. Then after that you can get on the airplane." Even after that, if you lose even one of those things, it creates a big problem when you get on the airplane.

Likewise, there are things you must absolutely do in spiritual life. But when you close the Bible, go to church, and follow everybody else's spiritual life, you will be unable to learn exactly what spiritual life is. If you learn it, step by step, with the Bible open, you can learn spiritual life the right way. For example, you will see that the most important step is receiving the forgiveness of sins; number two, how to pray; number three, how to obey the Word of God… If you learn it in that manner, it can be done. However, although you have heard many sermons, you have not learned any one of those things. People just look around and if other people pray, they pray. And if other people give offering, even though they don't want to, they also give offering. They live that kind of spiritual life.

Some people call our church heretical. Pastors, whose hearts are quite dark, become jealous when they see their church members moving to our church. To keep them from going, they slander and lie and call us heretics. I think, later on, those people will be punished in front of God. Then, people listen to those things and call our church heretical. They say, "What? That church? I heard they're heretical."

"What's a heretic?"

"I don't know. Our pastor says they're heretics."

To be a heretic, you have to at least deny the Bible, or to have killed people and bury them, or committed some other kinds of sins worthy to be all over the newspapers. We're neither this, nor that, but because they don't know the Bible, they just hear what other people have to say and call us heretics.

If you go to Africa, often it is the government that keeps the people uneducated. If the people become smart, the politicians cannot do whatever they want. So the few people who are in power live extremely lavish lives.

The remainder of the people live in desperate poverty. The countries do not want to give their people an opportunity at education, so they keep the cost of education very, very high.

So, most people remain uneducated. This is a part of the reason why we want to establish schools in Africa. Even though you may not know anything else precisely, what we need to learn this morning is that your emotions, your feelings, your judgments, that these things may be wrong. That is why, when you have a certain thought, you must open the Bible and check what it says. When your thoughts differ from the Bible, which should you believe? You should believe the Word of God.

Everyone, you want to receive the forgiveness of sin, right? It's very important to receive the forgiveness of sins and become born again. If you live spiritual life without receiving the forgiveness of sins, your whole life and your heart just remains dark and gloomy. If you receive the forgiveness of sins, your heart rejoices and your whole life brightens.

Then, how do you receive the forgiveness of sins? Just like a random luck of the draw, some people think, "Yeah, one of these days I'll somehow receive the forgiveness of sins." They think if they do overnight prayers, speak in tongues, and prophecy then that's what spiritual life is. Nowadays there are prayer houses that teach speaking in tongues. They tell you to bend your tongue inwards, and tell you if you keep repeating "Alleluia, alleluia, alleluia," you'll be speaking in tongues.

Everyone, receiving the forgiveness of sins is the basis of spiritual life. But, to receive the forgiveness of sins, you must first deny yourself. When you listen to the Word like you are this morning, at least you learn that you should deny yourself although you may not actually be able to. However, this will lead your spiritual life down a path of progression.

I'm a pastor. I've been ministering for 50 years. There has not once been a division in our church. There has not once been a fight inside of our church.

Do you know why that is? In other churches I've seen many divisions and many fights. It is because they all have their thoughts saying, "This is right. That is right."

They are just exerting their own thoughts. That's why those divisions came about.

At our church, I say every day, "Break your thoughts. Crumble yourself. Bend yourself. Deny yourself." That's why our church members, whether they have denied themselves or not, know that it is right to deny themselves. That's the basics. Even though their own thoughts proceed forward, because they know they need to deny their thoughts, they do not move forward with their thoughts. That's why our church is so very peaceful. We have many elders in our church. I think that they are so precious and I'm so thankful to them. I'm so thankful that I'm a pastor to those kinds of people. All of the elders in our church are amazing people. They're all humble and they deny themselves. Even when a husband and a wife get into a fight, it's not because of a misunderstanding that they fight. They fight because they're busy exerting their own selves. But, if you deny yourself, the fight between you and your spouse will disappear. The couples at our church are very happy. At our church, we have a negative divorce rate. Do you know why that is?

Rarely are there people who do get divorced. But more often, there are people who were divorced before they meet Jesus, and become reunited after coming to our church. They say that the divorce rate in Korea is 30%. That's the overall rate, and the rate is even higher among younger couples. Everyone, getting married and getting divorced, how painful is that? The parents and children become all scattered. By just looking at that, it's clear to see that it's good to deny yourself.

Before the sermon last night, Professor Galina sang. She told me that musicians from Russia often say that, to reach the highest level of music, they must deny themselves. When you are freed from yourself and become like a small child, who is crying for the first time, the voice can come out most beautifully. But she said that people don't really know about that. To make a good voice, it's not that they should put strength into their voice or scream. They must remove strength.

Even in that, it is important for singers to deny themselves. The reason they really like our Gracias Choir is that most of the members have denied themselves. Of course, it doesn't mean every member of our church has denied themselves. There are people who still need to fully deny themselves. There are also people who are fighting to deny themselves right now. Whether you deny yourself or not, that's up to you, but you understand that you need to deny yourself, right? Please answer. Yes, if you have understood that much, that means you have learned well for today. The Bible tells us that we must throw our thoughts and our opinions away.

That Sin that Remains With You For a Long Time to Torment You

Now, let's get to the point. Everyone, you don't know whether your sins have been forgiven or not. Even though you cannot remember all your sins,

Sin Offering: Freedom from Sin

on certain days you remember that terrible sin you committed. In my heart as well, there was one sin that tormented my heart terribly. If I tell you about all the sins I committed, you would not even look at me. Because I'm a very bad person, I'm going to confess to you, one sin I committed. It was when I went to elementary school.

It was 60 years ago. Back then, we did not have nail clippers and we used to clip our fingernails with scissors. But somehow, we had a nail clipper at our home. In my hometown of Sueonsan-eup, Gyeongbuk, the only home with a nail clipper was our house. That was the most precious asset of our home. My father put a nail on the wall and tied it to a rope and we would hang the nail clipper on the wall.

"Ock Soo," said my father.

"Yes, Father."

"After you're done using the nail clipper, be sure to hang it up there."

"Okay."

"Jung Soo, you too, be sure to hang the nail clipper."

"Yes."

But I wanted to take it to school and show off. So one day, when my father was not around, I secretly put the nail clipper in my pocket and brought it to school.

After the first period, I showed it off to the kids and all the kids began to crowd around me. I clipped their fingernails and they were so amazed. Nowadays nobody would even look at that, but it wasn't like that back then. It should have ended there, but one of my friends asked, "Hey, Ock Soo, can it clip even wood?"

"Yes, it can!" I said.

So they brought a piece of wood. We put it into the nail clipper and pressed down on it and broke the wood. It should have ended there, but one kid asked another question.

"Hey, can it clip even an iron nail?"

"Hey, how could it clip an iron nail?"

That's what I should have said. But I said, "Yes, it can!"

I felt very tormented inside.

"Hey, someone bring a nail in here," said one of the kids. One friend pulled out a nail from the wall.

I was thinking, "Please, don't pull it out. Please don't pull it out." But he pulled it out and brought it over. Can a nail clipper clip an iron nail? I knew that it couldn't.

But because I had already boasted that it could, I put the iron nail inside the nail clipper. Now I needed to press down on it, but it broke my heart. But the atmosphere was so that I had no choice but to press down on it. So I pushed down, but it wouldn't clip the nail. So I pushed even harder.

SNAP!

It broke the nail clipper. I could see my father's face and I was so afraid. It was so painful to think how I was going to be spanked. Right then, an amazing idea as a descendant of Adam came to mind. When I come home from school, I would always go out with my younger brother to go catch fish. I came home, opened my younger brother's book bag and put the broken nail clippers into his pencil case. I then closed up his book bag and came out. In the evening, my father came and the nail clipper was missing.

He asked, "Oh, where's the nail clipper? Ock Soo, you took it, right?"

"No."

"Jung Soo, you took it, right?"

"No," my younger brother said.

"You little punks! Bring me your backpacks." Father searched through my backpack, but it wasn't there. So he began to open my younger brother's book bag.

When the broken nail clippers came out from his pencil case, that shocked face on my younger brother's face... I can never forget that my whole life.

"You little punk! You broke this!"

"No, it wasn't me!"

"But look! It's broken inside of your pencil case."

Right then I should have said, "Father, it was me. Forgive me. My brother did nothing wrong." I was supposed to say that, but I didn't have the courage. So my brother was spanked very hard that day. For me, it was ten times more painful than my younger brother getting spanked. I said to myself, "You're so low. You're the one who did this and you cause your brother to get spanked?" 60 years have passed, but even now I still cannot forget it. My younger brother is 65 this year. After we became adults, I told my brother about it.

He said, "Older brother, when did that ever happen? I don't even remember."

My younger brother doesn't even remember it, but I remember that sin in my memory. Everyone, even though it's the same sin, the size of that sin in your heart differs. Some sins, you feel as though you are washed now. Some sins continually remain in your heart, they don't wash away and they torment you. There are sins like that, right? But the people in Seoul are so slick, they don't answer things if it seems it's going to be disadvantageous to them. They only answer things that will be advantageous to them. I was so tormented about what I had done so I asked God ten times, a hundred times, confessing to forgive me. But it still seemed as though my sins did not wash away and remained in my heart. 60 years have passed, but even now, what happened is so clear and vivid in my mind - when the nail clipper broke, when the friend who asked if it will clip even an iron nail, how I hated him and wanted to kick him, the thoughts that I had in my heart are still very clear in my mind. That sin had been recorded on the table of my heart.

The Priest Shall Make an Atonement for Him and It Shall Be Forgiven Him

In Leviticus chapter 4 verse 31, it says, *and the priest shall make an atonement for him, and it shall be forgiven him.*

The sin offering in Leviticus chapter 4 has shown the image of how Jesus would die for us on the cross. Jesus, just like the priest in Leviticus chapter 4, takes the blood that He shed on the cross to the temple in heaven. He puts it upon the horns of the altar and sprinkles it on the mercy seat. Through that atonement, we have gained atonement. *It shall be forgiven him.* Who is him? It is Ock Soo Park. It is you. Your sins are all forgiven. Are they not forgiven? Answer me loudly. Are they forgiven, or not forgiven? Yes, they are all forgiven. Yes, the Bible says they are all forgiven. But from our conscience the sin of breaking the nail clipper and having my younger brother get spanked has not been washed away. If so, is my heart agreeing with the words of the Bible or is it different from the words of the Bible?

It Shall Be Forgiven Him

Different. Right then, what should we deny and what should we believe? We should deny our thoughts and believe the Word of God. Amen? Satan continually makes us remember the sins that we committed in our hearts.

One time, a lady came to see me. She was crying as she told me about the sin she committed. She said, "Pastor, Pastor, I committed murder. Not just one or two. I'm a midwife. From a child that's one month old to nine months, I've taken many, many lives. Can this sin be forgiven?"

According to my thoughts, I want to say, "No, not that sin."

But in the words of the Bible, even for that sin, it says, *the priest shall make an atonement for him, and it shall be forgiven him.* If the priest makes an atonement, the sin is forgiven. Jesus became our priest and He went to the temple in heaven and sprinkled the blood He shed on the cross so that He can achieve the atonement. Are our sins forgiven or not forgiven? They are forgiven.

Everyone, the biggest problem in our spiritual life is not that you have stolen or committed adultery or not gone to church on Sundays, or whether you smoked or drank. It's not those things. You think those things are the problems, right? You think, "The problem is that I committed many sins. The problem is I drank so much." But those are not the problem. The problem is that you are not able to distinguish the Word of God from the sounds that arise from your your heart. That's why your heart goes back and forth from here and there. Today, from this moment on, no matter what thought arises within you, I hope that you will become true people of faith who will deny whatever thought you have in front of God and believe the Word of God.

The Word of God says, *the priest shall make an atonement for him, and it shall be forgiven him.* Jesus became our eternal priest, and with His blood that He shed on the cross, He did not go to the altar on earth, but rather He went to the altar in heaven. He put His blood on the horns of the altar in heaven and sprinkled His blood on the mercy seat and completed our sin offering.

That's why it says, *it shall be forgiven him.* Like those words, our sins are forgiven.

Are they not forgiven? They are forgiven. This is the Word of God. You must believe these words. Do not believe your thoughts. You will remember your sins in your thoughts. Who does not remember the sins that they commit? There may be sins that you have forgotten about among the ones you committed. But there may be many sins you remember in your hearts as well. Also, in your conscience you may think, "This sin may not be forgiven." But now, we do not believe in our thoughts but the Word of God. Amen? That is what it means to be people who believe in God.

Because many people today do not know the Bible well, they believe that their sins are forgiven if they cry and if they're in a good mood. But if their hearts are gloomy and dark, they believe that they have sin. Now let us completely throw away those emotions, but let us believe in the Word of God. Everyone, in Leviticus chapter 4 verse 31, it says, *And he shall take away all the fat thereof, as the fat is taken away from off the sacrifice of peace offerings; and the priest shall burn it upon the altar for a sweet savour unto the Lord; and the priest shall make an atonement for him, and it shall be forgiven him.* Surely it says that the priest shall make an atonement for him and it shall be forgiven him. According to these words, Jesus fulfilled the sin offering. That is how the forgiveness of your sins was achieved. It is not that you should ask for your sins to be forgiven. You must believe that your sins are forgiven. If they are not forgiven, you should not believe that they are forgiven. But we must believe these words because it is clear that the blood of the cross has forgiven our sins. Now, do not be deceived in your thoughts between this and that kind of word. But decide in your hearts upon this serious problem of getting your sins forgiven according to the Word of God.

God says, *And their sins and their iniquities will I remember no more.* (Hebrews 10:17)

Why did He say that? Because our sins have all been washed away. In the memory of God, through the blood of Jesus who is the lamb, all of your sins have been erased.

I hope that you will believe.

CHAPTER 7
People Who Were Destroyed Because They Did Not Have the Sin Offering

The people committed a sin. They made the golden calf. In the Ten Commandments, the first commandment is to "have no other gods before Me." They also broke the second commandment, which is, "thou shalt not make idols." They wanted to have those sins washed away. Sadly, they did not have the altar nor the mercy seat, yet. If a sheep or a cow were put to death, the sins that the people of Israel had committed, the sin of making the golden calf, could be washed away. But, because they did not have an altar, they could not give the sin offering. That was why the Israelites were put to death instead of a lamb. 3,000 people were put to death.

Hello everyone. I'm so thankful for this one week where we could share the words in Leviticus about the sin offering. God has also allowed us this opportunity to be able to share the Word from the pulpit. It has brought me much joy and blessing. Today, I will read from Exodus chapter 32 verse 25.

And Moses stood in the gate of the camp, and said, Who is on the Lord's side? let him come unto me. And all the sons of Levi gathered themselves together unto him. And he said unto them, Thus saith the Lord God of Israel, Put every man his sword by his side, and go in and out from gate to gate throughout the camp, and slay every man his brother, and every man his companion, and every man his neighbour. And the children of Levi did according to the word of Moses: and there fell of the people that day about three thousand men. For Moses had said, Consecrate yourselves to day to the Lord, even every man upon his son, and upon his brother; that he may bestow upon you a blessing this day. And it came to pass on the morrow, that Moses said unto the people, Ye have sinned a great sin: and now I will go up unto the Lord; peradventure I shall make an atonement for your sin. And Moses returned unto the Lord, and said, Oh, this people have sinned a great sin, and have made them gods of gold. Yet now, if thou wilt forgive their sin-; and if not, blot me, I pray thee, out of thy book which thou hast written. And the Lord said unto Moses, Whosoever hath sinned against me, him will I blot out of my book. Therefore now go, lead the people unto the place of which I have spoken unto thee: behold, mine Angel shall go before thee: nevertheless in the day when I visit I will visit their sin upon them. And the Lord plagued the people, because they made the calf, which Aaron made. (Exodus 32:25-35)

Elder Kwang Yul Kim From the Leper Colony

Throughout my ministry, I've met so many different people. There are many who I cannot erase from my memory. There was a time, in 1980, when I went to a leper colony, in Gyeongbuk Youngchun, and held a conference there. After the first evening service, I asked the people, who wanted to receive the forgiveness of sins, to raise their hands. About 40 of them raised their hands. It was cold that night so I invited them into the room that I was staying in. The 40 people completely packed my room. That night, I talked about the sin offering, which I was planning to talk about throughout the whole week, in just one night. I didn't have enough time, and so I talked with them until 1 o'clock in the morning. That day, most of the people received the forgiveness of sins. They truly rejoiced.

He has passed away now, but Elder Kwang Yul Kim used to attend that church. Although he had leprosy, he was very tall and handsome. He was

People Who Were Destroyed Because They Did Not Have the Sin Offering

in terrible pain because of sin. That night, he received the forgiveness of sins, and he was so happy. His son also received salvation the next day. The day after, his wife received salvation. The elder was so happy. He looked at me and he asked, "Pastor, why don't you go around leper colonies to hold conferences?"

He would call elders at leper colonies and ask them to hold conferences.

"Elder Lee, why don't you hold a conference? Elder Lee, hold a conference." Most of the churches in the leper colonies would say that they don't have enough money to hold a conference.

Elder Hwang Yul Kind would speak, saying, "I knew you would say that. I'm sure you don't have money. I'll pay for all of the expenses for this conference. Invite Pastor Ock Soo Park, whom I recommend, and hold a conference with him." That year, I went to six leper colonies and held conferences there. Elder Kwang Yul Kim was not a wealthy man. He ran a chicken coop, and he sold chickens. Through that, he prepared the funds for each of the conferences.

As that elder went to the conferences with me, he would fund the conferences by selling his chickens. Even though he had fewer and fewer chickens, he was so happy. But sadly, he developed rectal cancer. Soon after, he passed away. I remember the elder at his funeral, the relationship we had with our hearts. Although the time I was with him was very short, the relationship was so deep. Even when I think about it now, I can feel it deep in my heart.

I saw how that elder was saved, was freed from sin, was at peace and lived a blessed life. He caught leprosy and was abandoned by his family and relatives. He was an elder who lived at the leper colony, fed chickens, and lived without any hope. But one day, after he met Jesus and received the forgiveness of sins and became born again, unspeakable peace came to his heart. Until the day that he passed away, he lived in this world, inside of joy and thankfulness and peace. Then he passed away. What could bring this kind of peace to this elder?

Many sins had weighed down this elder's heart. Just like the words, *the priest shall make an atonement for him and it shall be forgiven him,* the sins which had weighed down the elder were all taken care of. Jesus Christ redeemed us when He was crucified. He brought redemption to the elder, becoming the priest for us. When He was crucified, he redeemed us, and also made the redemption for the elder. The words of forgiveness freed this elder from all sins. He was filled with freedom, joy, and peace.

I have spoken endlessly about the sin offering. I have given many sermons about it at conferences. I've talked so much about it personally also. Because the price of our sins have already been paid, there's nothing we need to do for sin. On and on, I talk about how the blood that Jesus Christ shed on the cross has already fulfilled the whole sin offering. As these words enter into people's hearts, I see them becoming freed from sin and enjoying freedom. I was so thankful in front of God to see that. Throughout my life till now, there are so many people to whom I have preached this Gospel individually and many have been saved. At times, I have hardships, and at times, I become tired. But when I quietly think about them, truly I am so thankful and joyful.

Will I Remember No More

Once, I went to Mt. Jiri because I had a conference there. We had the conference in the morning and then, after lunch, we had personal fellowship time. I would sit in my tent, and elders and deacons would come over and ask for counseling about forgiveness of sins. Since I would be sitting there for long hours, I wanted to get up and get some fresh air. There was this young lady, in about her 20s, who came to see me. I spoke about the Bible to this lady. I spoke to her about how Jesus gave the sin offering and how all of our sins were forgiven. I read to her the words of Hebrews Chapter 10, from verse 17 through 18. *And their sins and iniquities will I remember no more. Now where the remission of these is, there is no more offering for sin.* To this point, her eyes just opened wide, and she was just staring at me and listening while I preached the Word to her. But as soon as I read her these words, all of a sudden, she just fell to the floor and started crying. I had no idea why she was crying. Her whole body shook as she was crying. I really didn't know what to do. I just told her, "Please stop crying. Please calm down." I guess she couldn't hear me. She just kept on crying. I just let her cry for a long while and went outside the tent. I got some fresh air and came back after about 10 minutes. She was still crying. I told her, "Please calm down now." Then she got up and gave me her testimony.

People Who Were Destroyed Because They Did Not Have the Sin Offering

She told me that her mother passed away while she was in middle school. Not long after, a stepmother joined her family. But the stepmother had brought along a daughter who was the same age as her. Because the family was so poor, the family could not afford to send the both of them to middle school. She was the only one attending middle school. But the stepmother kept on signaling that she wanted to send her daughter to middle school. Then, one day, this young lady took her tuition money and left home. She packed her bags and went to Masan.

What a wicked place the world is. The people who approached this middle school student were from a brothel. They took her, and made her into a prostitute. She suffered terrible pain, was treated sub-human, and lived a despairing life. She tried to commit suicide several times. She was living day by day this way, without any hope and only in pain. But one day, hope came to her. She met a man, who loved her, although he knew that she was a prostitute. She was so thankful. She thought, "Wow, how could he love a woman like me?" It felt as though this man was an angel. Because her only hope was this man, she gave all of her heart to him.

One day, this man said, "Don't say a thing and just follow me."

She didn't know what was happening. She just followed him and asked, "Where are we going?"

"I said, don't say anything and just follow me"

"But still, you should tell me. Where are we going?"

"Just follow me. Don't you trust me?"

She couldn't ask anymore. She just followed him. They got in a car, switched to a different car, and finally arrived at a leper colony. This man's parents were lepers. This person was not a leper. He was not infected. But he was living in the leper colony. From then on, this woman also lived in the leper colony. For two years, it was such a happy, dreamlike time. The father-in-law was so good to her. The mother-in-law treated her like a princess. She would tell her, "Hey, that's hard work. Get some rest." There's a lot of farm work to do at the leper colony, but they did not have her do any work. They simply cared for her so much.

But that happiness did not last long. Two years into the marriage, the parents in law were hoping for grandchildren. We don't know who it was that said it at that time, but people begin to say that, because the woman was once a prostitute, she cannot have babies. From then on, nobody would even look at her. When she would bring in the food for her father in law, he would turn his head away. He would then eat it after she had left the room. When she would return to clean up the meal, he would again turn his head away. Whenever the mother in law needed to say something to her, she would close the door, and have her stand outside the door, while she spoke to her. She was in so much pain. When she would go to the neighborhood pump to draw some water, the women there would be talking already. They would turn quiet when she showed up. Then, when she took her water and walked away, they would shout out and laugh loudly. Several times, she contemplated dying. Because she was so tormented, she made up her mind on going to church.

But she was so afraid of the people's eyes that she couldn't go to church. She said there was nothing as scary as the look in the people's eyes. But still she wanted to go to church. After the service had begun, in the middle of the sermon, she would arrive late and sit in the back. As soon as the sermon was over, before the end of the service, she would return home.

She then came to the Mt. Jiri conference, and the words of Hebrews Chapter 10 that she heard while she was counseling with me, deeply touched her heart.

And their sins and iniquities, will I remember no more. Where the remission of these is, there is no more offering for sin.

This lady wanted to erase her past. The fact that it was recorded in people's hearts, that she was a prostitute in the past, she wanted to erase all of that. But how could she erase that? The love of Jesus not only forgave all of this woman's sins, but also told her that God remembers her sins and iniquities no more.

Why does God remember our sins no more? Because the sin offering for our sins was fulfilled at the cross, all of our sins have already been forgiven. That's why God does not remember anymore the many sins that this lady committed.

If we are in heaven and God remembers our sins, we would not have any freedom. We would say, "God, how are you?"

God would laugh and say, "That punk, he used to steal, he committed adultery." We would have no freedom at all. We would feel very burdened before God. The difference between God and man is, even though man says he doesn't remember, he does remember. If somebody came to your house and stole something, and gets caught, even though you may say, "Alright, let's just forget about this," it still remains in your memory. But God is not a man. He does not do that. If God says He doesn't remember them, He doesn't remember them. That is the difference between God and man. That's why when you go to heaven you might worry, saying, "What if God remembers my sins. I'll be put to shame. What am I going to do? God's going to know my sins." There's no need for you to be afraid, worried, or concerned about that. God does not remember your sin.

The Mercy Seat, Where Sin is Redeemed

When the Israelites came out of Egypt and went to Mt. Sinai, God called Moses to the top of Mt. Sinai. While Moses was on Mt. Sinai for 40 days, God gave Moses the two tablets of stone that had the Ten Commandments recorded on them. God told Moses to go down with them. But before Moses came down with the two tables of stone with the Ten Commandments, what did he do for 40 days on Mt. Sinai? Through the revelation of God, he saw every detail of the temple that is in heaven.

God showed Moses, "This is the altar. This is the water pot. This is the candlestick. This is the bread table. This is the place of incense. This is the ark." Afterwards, Moses, according to the Word of God, made the tabernacle on earth in the exact image of the temple of heaven. That is where the Israelites have their sins forgiven. Within the tabernacle that Moses built, there's this place called the mercy seat. Underneath the mercy seat is the ark. The ark, as it is called, is a chest. On top of that chest, in pure gold, is a lid that is two and a half cubits in length, and one and a half cubits in width. They made a lid of that size to cover the top of the ark. On top of that lid, there are the angels on both sides spreading their wings to cover the ark. That lid is called the mercy seat. Repeat after me. Mercy seat. Mercy seat means the place where sins are forgiven.

The Bible tells us precisely why it is called the mercy seat and why blood must be sprinkled there. The two tablets of stone that have the Ten Commandments recorded on them are inside of the ark. Sin was not recognized as sin when the Israelites did not have the Ten Commandments, because they did not have the law. Whether they served gods other than God, or whether they kept the Sabbath or not, no matter what sin they committed, it was not considered sin. It is the law that formed sin. Although sin was there before the law, sin cannot be considered as sin until the law is put in place.

Now Moses had come down with the two tablets of stone, the Ten Commandments. Meanwhile, the Israelites had built the golden calf. Among the Ten Commandments, number one is, "thou shalt not have other gods before me." Number two is, "thou shalt not make unto yourself other idols." Now, these two laws had been broken. That was the sin that the Israelites committed. Until then, they did not know how to give the sin offering. Because they did not know, 3,000 Israelites were put to death. Had they known how to give a sin offering, they would've given it and they would not have had to die.

God Who Wanted to Cover the Ten Commandments with the Mercy Seat

The people were able to give the sin offering as the tabernacle was built. They killed lambs or cows, and sprinkled the blood on the mercy seat. Why does sin get forgiven when the blood is sprinkled there? Because within the ark are the tablets of stone, the Ten Commandments. The people break those commandments and commit sins. It says thou shalt not murder, but people murder. It says thou shalt not commit adultery, but they commit adultery. That's why these tablets with the Ten Commandments, which formed sin, were placed inside of the ark.

There are two cases that can make the Ten Commandments unnecessary. First, even if you have the Ten Commandments, if the people don't sin, then you don't need the Ten Commandments. The commandments say do not steal, do not commit adultery, do not commit murder. It is the people who commit these sins that are influenced by the law. People who do not commit those sins are not influenced by the law at all. Sometimes, as I drive, I'm pulled over by the traffic officer. When the police pulls me over, I begin to think in my heart. "What did I do wrong?" If I'm driving freely, and the police officer turns on his lights and pulls me over, I would think to myself, "Why is he pulling me over? What did I do wrong?"

People Who Were Destroyed Because They Did Not Have the Sin Offering

Then the police officer salutes me and says, "We are cracking down on drunk drivers. Please blow into this machine." In other instances, I may not be so confident. But when they ask me to do that, I feel very confident. Hoooooo~ I breathe hard with all my might. But the people who drank will get nervous. When they are told to blow, they will just blow very lightly.

Even though they are told, "No, you must blow out harder," they still blow very lightly. I'm comfortable when they are cracking down on drunk drivers. I blow out very hard. The law that requires people to get arrested for drunk driving applies to people who drank. But for me, because I'm not drunk, it doesn't matter to me whether that law exists or not. Recently, I read the newspaper, and saw that there was a pack of cigarettes that cost $10. Excuse me, but I don't know how much a pack of cigarettes cost. Once, one of our missionaries was doing mission work in China. While he was on his way back home, he was arrested by the police.

They said, "You're not a Korean. You're Chinese, aren't you?"

"No, I'm Korean."

"Prove that you're a Korean."

"Here's my passport."

"This passport looks like a counterfeit."

"No, I am Korean."

The police had arrested this missionary, thinking that he was Chinese.

They asked, "How much is a pack of cigarettes in Korea?"

"I don't smoke cigarettes."

"If you don't know how much a cigarette costs, how can you say you're Korean? Then what kind of cigarettes do they sell in Korea?"

He had no idea. So they arrested him and gave him a very tough time for a long while, before they finally released him.

If you ask me about cigarette prices, I know nothing. I know that long time ago, when I was in the army, they had these cigarettes called Pagoda cigarettes, which cost about 4 cents a pack. If a pack of cigarettes cost $10, smokers would get worried. But for me, even if cigarette prices become $1,000 a pack, I'm not worried at all. If smokers are told that a pack of cigarettes costs $1,000, they would probably faint. But if I'm told a pack of cigarettes costs $100,000, all I would say is, "Wow, cigarettes are expensive." That would pretty much be it. It has absolutely nothing to do with me because I do not smoke cigarettes.

No matter how much they crack down on drunk drivers, because I don't drink, it has absolutely nothing to do with me. No matter how many laws there are, if you do not commit those sins, those laws have nothing to do with you. In the same way, if the people of Israel do not commit a single sin, the two tablets of the Ten Commandments become meaningless. The first of the Ten Commandments is, "thou shalt have no other gods before me." Second is, thou shalt not make idols unto yourself. Third, "thou shalt not take the Lord's name in vain." Fourth, "thou shalt remember the Sabbath, to keep it holy." Fifth, "you must honor your parents." Sixth, "thou shalt not murder." Seventh, "thou shalt not commit adultery." Eighth, "thou shalt not steal." Ninth, "thou shalt not give false testimony." Tenth, "thou shalt not covet."

If the Israelites kept all ten of these laws, if there's not a person who broke any one of these, these laws would not be necessary. The law is necessary for the people who break the laws. But it's not necessary for the people who don't break the laws.

Here is the second instance where we don't need the law. Even though sin is committed, if the punishment for that sin is received, then that law becomes unnecessary. For example, if I break a traffic law and pay the one hundred dollar fine, then that law no longer applies to me. It's as if I had not committed the sin to begin with. Everyone, what the Bible says is, the tablets of stone with the Ten Commandments were not laid out in front of the Israelites. But rather, they were placed in a box with the lid on top of it. That is the ark. Nowadays, people read the Bible backwards. They even record the Ten Commandments in the front part of their hymnals. But God did not want the Ten Commandments to be opened and laid out. God wanted to cover the Ten Commandments because God did not want to fight with us using the law. To cover the Ten Commandments, God made the law and put it in the ark and covered it with the lid. That lid is the mercy seat.

Why is that lid called the mercy seat? Sins are all forgiven. Now, because you don't have sins anymore, you don't need to pull out the Ten Commandments anymore. The sins are all taken care of, so the law becomes useless. That's why it was covered with the lid. Do you know the reason why they sprinkle the blood on the mercy seat? To pull out the law, you must remove the mercy seat. When they would reach to remove the lid, there would be blood all over it.

"Oh, why is there blood here? Ah, the price of sins that the Israelites committed, which is the blood of death, is shed all over this place. That's why we don't need to pull out the law."

Remember, we're not people who live under the law. But we are people who live under the law of the Holy Spirit. Amen? Now, it is no longer the law telling us not to murder, do not commit adultery, do not steal. But it is the Holy Spirit that enters into us and leads us to hate such sins.

All Misunderstanding Ends Through the Forgiveness of Sins

There's a person named Elder Hyung Mo Lee in our church. This elder, a long time ago, persecuted his wife for attending our church for 8 years. He didn't just persecute us, but he systematically studied our church. He studied very closely, and realized that there was nothing wrong. Then after 8 years, he saw that his wife's spiritual life was much better than his.

One day, God worked. Because Elder Lee's wife was sick, Elder Lee's mother came to help out with the housekeeping. The mother-in-law was very upset as she made her way to her son's house because her daughter-in-law was not healthy, even before getting married. She came, thinking, "My daughter-in- law has gone crazy, falling into heretics. The house must be a mess. She's crazy and she's gone mad running around." With that upset heart, she arrived in Daejeon. But when she came, she saw that things were actually completely different. She thought the house would be a mess, and that the daughter-in-law would be crazy about church. But the house was nice and orderly. The children were upright. Elder Lee's mother's heart completely changed.

Elder Lee's wife used to be a teacher. When she got married, her in-laws had some debt and she paid off that debt for them. The husband's mother was so touched by this. She thought, "Oh, with this kind of frail body, you used to go to work?" She was so thankful.

The daughter-in-law came and said to her, "Mother, our church is having a conference. Won't you come with me?"

Sin Offering: Freedom from Sin

"Sure, I'll go."

She came to our church and listened to the Word. She was so happy and rejoiced, but did not receive salvation. Afterwards, she stayed at her daughter's house in Gwangju. She started becoming sick, and was about to pass away. It was so heartbreaking for Elder Lee to see his mother passing away. Before, he had no idea. But while he was persecuting the Good News Mission, he could tell whether a person is saved or not, and when he saw his mother, he could tell that she was not saved. He wanted his mother to enter into heaven, and he needed someone to lead her to salvation before she passed away. But the pastors of the Presbyterian churches could not speak about salvation. He was getting desperate inside, but because of his pride, he was unable to bring himself to say to his wife, "Please, bring a pastor of the Good News Mission church to preach the Gospel to my mother."

One day, he was at work and his wife called him. She said, "Honey, I'm going to go down to Gwangju."

"Why are you going to Gwangju?"

"I'm going to go there, to preach the Gospel to Mother, and make her some food that she likes."

He was so happy and joyful to hear that. But he didn't want to show that, so he replied to her very ruggedly. He said, "Okay, fine. Make some food for her, and come back home." Inside, he was so happy to think that his mother was going to get saved.

Not long after, he got a phone call from Gwangju.

"Honey, Mother received salvation."

He was so thankful, he wanted to cry, but because of his pride, he said, "Okay, hang up the phone. Goodbye."

It seemed that his mother would soon pass away, but she did not. I guess, maybe because she said that she was not done with what she needed to do. He brought her to Daejeon, to his house. His wife called me.

"Pastor, my mother-in-law is in Daejeon right now."

I went to go see her. I went there and Mr. Hyung Mo Lee was there, looking very upset. I didn't care. I went to the room, where his mother was. There we had service and sang hymns. Mr. Hyung Mo Lee didn't like me. But this was the last service, before his mother passed away, so how could he not come? He came in as well and sang hymns also. We sang hymns, I prayed, and I preached the Word. The mother was already unconscious, and was unable to listen. I preached, so that Mr. Hyung Mo Lee could listen. A few days later, the mother passed away. The sisters of our church went and helped out with the arrangements. The sisters of our church are very good at making food and those kinds of things. Even in my eyes, they are very talented.

In the middle of the funeral, the pastor of the church Mr. Hyung Mo Lee attended came. The atmosphere turned quite strange. He was lost for a moment, and he asked, "Mr. Lee, shall we have a service here or not?" Right then, Mr. Hyung Mo Lee felt in his heart, "What kind of pastor would ask, if he should have a service? Pastor Ock Soo Park, from the Hanbat Central Church, gives service without asking. Pastors are supposed to have service. What else are they supposed to do?" After the funeral, Mr. Hyung Mo Lee began to come to our church. Then, soon after, he received salvation. Now, he is an elder. It's like a dream to me.

These days, because of the conference, I have been sleeping at Elder Lee's house. I'm sorry, but I have pushed Elder Lee out of the master bedroom, and I am sleeping there now. As I think to myself in that room, I think, "Is this a dream or reality?" All of the misunderstanding in his heart had ended through the forgiveness of sins and the blood of the cross.

That Thy Sins May Be Forgiven Thee

Now, I don't need the Ten Commandments. All my sins are taken care of and I'm fine without the Ten Commandments. From now, I live receiving the guidance of God. That's why they put the Ten Commandments inside of the box, and covered it with the lid. That lid is the mercy seat. Sins are all washed away. What did they cover the Ten Commandments with? They covered it with the mercy seat. Now that sins are all forgiven, no sin can be committed even if there is the law. The law is no longer necessary. If somebody tries to remove the lid, because there is blood on the lid, the mercy seat, that person's hand will be all covered with blood. Then he would say, "Oh, there's blood on my hands. What blood is this? Oh, Jesus shed His blood to forgive all of our sins. Oh, then we don't need to pull out the law." The relationship between God and us is not formed through the law. The Bible tells us that it is a relationship that is formed through the law of the grace of the Holy Spirit.

Now everyone, we no longer live a life of being tied down to the law. There are many people today who are suffering, tied down to the law. Because all sins of breaking that law have been taken care of, we live the life of true freedom and receiving grace. We have been freed from the law.

But what we read in Exodus chapter 32 today is different from us. Sadly, although the two tablets of stone and the Ten Commandments have come down, the tabernacle had not been made yet. Although the law had come, the altar and the mercy seat were not yet made. In addition, the sacrificial lamb had not yet come. That period is called the period of the law. The people at that time died every day because they did not have the mercy seat. Now, they committed sin. They made the golden calf. The first commandment of the Ten Commandments is, thou shalt have no other gods before me. They broke the second commandment, which was, thou shalt not make idols unto thy selves. They wanted to get those sins washed away, but sadly, at the altar, they did not have the mercy seat yet. If they killed a lamb, if they killed a cow, the people of Israel could have the sins that they committed, the sins of making the gold calf, washed away. But because they did not have the altar, they were unable to give the sin offering. That is why, instead of the lamb being put to death, the Israelites were put to death. 3,000 Israelites were put to death.

Now, let's look at Exodus chapter 32 verse 30.

And it came to pass on the morrow, that Moses said unto the people, Ye have sinned a great sin: and now I will go up unto the Lord; peradventure I shall make an atonement for your sin.

Moses did not say, "Now I will go up to the Lord and now your sins will become forgiven." He said, "Peradventure I shall make an atonement for your sin." In Leviticus chapter 4 verse 31, did it say, "the priest shall make an atonement for him and peradventure, his sins will be forgiven?" Is that what it says? No! It says the priest shall make an atonement for him, and it shall be forgiven him. Here, it doesn't say peradventure. It says clearly that when the priest makes an atonement for him, clearly his sins will be forgiven.

But in Exodus chapter 32, Moses does go up to God to get the Israelites' sins forgiven, but he's not sure if he can get those sins forgiven. He doesn't have a sin offering, and he doesn't know what to do, hence Moses was not confident. He said, "Now I go to the Lord to have your sins forgiven, but peradventure, I shall make an atonement for your sins." In verse 31, Moses returned unto the Lord, and said, "Oh, this people have sinned a great sin, and have made them gods of gold."

This is the step of confessing sin. In verse 32, *Yet now, if thou wilt forgive their sin; and if not, blot me, I pray thee, out of thy book which thou has written.* Because Moses does not know how to get his sins forgiven, he does not know how to give the sin offering. Rather, he begs and begs, and asks for forgiveness. But he cannot have the assurance that his sins are forgiven.

The Spiritual Life with the Sin Offering, and Spiritual Life Without the Sin Offering

Everyone, today as well, there are two kinds of spiritual life. There's the spiritual life with the sin offering, and the spiritual life without the sin offering. People who don't have the sin offering, people without the, "thou shalt make an atonement for him and it shall be forgiven him," do as Moses did.

They say, "God, I lied. Please forgive me. I committed adultery. Please forgive me." That's all they can do when they do not know about the sin offering.

When Moses went before God for the sins of Israel, and confessed the sins that they committed, he asked that their sins be forgiven.

And Moses returned unto the Lord, and said, Oh, this people have sinned a great sin, and have made them gods of gold. Yet now, if thou wilt forgive their sin; and if not, blot me, I pray thee, out of thy book which thou hast written. (Exodus 32: 31-32)

He prayed sincerely, but were the sins forgiven? They were not forgiven.

Verse 33. *And the Lord said unto Moses, Whosoever hath sinned against me, him will I blot out of my book.*

Verse 34. *Therefore now go, lead the people unto the place of which I have spoken unto thee: behold, mine Angel shall go before thee: nevertheless in the day when I visit I will visit their sin upon them.*

Everyone, does it say that their sins were forgiven? Or does it say their sins remain and that He will visit their sins upon them? Their sins were not forgiven.

Everyone, there's two paths of forgiveness for us. One is to get our sins forgiven through the sin offering. The other way is to pray, confess our sins, and ask for forgiveness. Our sins are forgiven if it is only through the sin offering. If they are not forgiven through the sin offering, no matter how much you ask for your sins to be forgiven, they cannot be forgiven. Even if 3,000 people were to be put to death, their sin cannot be forgiven. In the last verse of chapter 32 verse 35, what happens?

And the Lord plagued the people, because they made the calf, which Aaron made.

God cursed the people who made the golden calf, the Israelites, and He struck them. It is telling us that their sins were not forgiven. Everyone, until now, we all just confessed sins. But sins were not forgiven.

Judas Iscariot also grieved the fact that he betrayed Jesus and threw the silver into the temple. He confessed and repented, saying, "I have sinned, that I've betrayed innocent blood." But he received destruction. Sin is not washed away through repenting. Repenting is a part of the process to receive the forgiveness of sins. But washing the sins away from the core is only possible through the blood of the sacrificial lamb. To wash our sins away, it's not through anything else but only through the shedding of blood.

What can wash away my sin?
Nothing but the blood of Jesus.

There's nothing else, other than the blood that Jesus shed on the cross, that can wash our sins away.

Oh! I know I'm alive
In the Lord, and I strive
Unto blood with the sin that would damn;
As I walk in the light
There is strength for the fight,
I'm redeemed by the blood of the Lamb.

Whether it be the Old Testament or the New Testament, without giving the sin offering and the shedding of blood and, by it, receiving the forgiveness of sins, there's no other way at all to get your sins forgiven.

Many people today look for ways other than the blood that Jesus shed on the cross. People try to repent, fast, speak in tongues, and try to receive some spirit. Washing your sins away in those ways is all fake. The only thing that can wash our sins away is the blood of Jesus. Because that blood was shed on the cross to wash all of our sins away, now the Ten Commandments are placed in a box and covered with a lid. Because sins are all forgiven and the law can no longer condemn us, the law is no longer necessary.

The tablets of stone and the Ten Commandments are not necessary for people who don't sin. Even a person who has sinned, if he has had his sins washed away, the Ten Commandments are not necessary. That is why, for us whose sins are washed away, they are no longer necessary. That's why they put the two tablets of stone, the Ten Commandments, into the ark, and covered the ark with a lid, which is the mercy seat. On top of it, there are angels spreading their wings, covering it. Why was that so? It means, do not open the Ten Commandments. It's the angels spreading their wings protecting it. Now sin is over with. Through the blood of Jesus, who is the lamb, sin is over with. The law is ended. We're made eternally righteous. We're made holy.

Being saved is believing in that. We're not saved through our works. The last four days, we have been talking about the sin offering. This is the seventh session, and we talked about how the people of Israel were put to death because they did not have the sin offering. Loving folks, don't just learn about the sin offering this time around, but believe it. I hope that you will believe in your hearts that the sin offering of Jesus Christ ended all the sins of your hearts. Everyone, it is not that we need to do something for our sins, but believe that through giving the eternal sin offering, you have been made eternally righteous. Everyone, do you believe it? If you do believe, raise your hand, those of you who believe that yout sins have been washed away through the blood of Jesus. Amen. Hallelujah. I truly hope that you will remain in this faith.

CHAPTER 8
The Power of the Sin Offering Which Has Finished the Judgment

Because people were dying of the curse that came through sin, Moses quickly went to Aaron and told him to give the sin offering. Every second mattered. It is very uncomfortable for the priest to be running around in the clothes of a priest. Usually, he would walk very relaxed. But now, he was running around as quickly as he could. When Aaron completed giving the sin offering, he stood before the dead and the living. The plague came to an end. Why was that? It was because the judgment for that sin was finished through giving the sin offering. Although it was clear that they sinned, the power of sin has disappeared.

Hello everyone. It's good to see you. I hope that the sin offering that you remember in your heart will defeat the guilt of sin or the pain that arises through your mistakes and the sins that you commit. I hope that through this, your heart will no longer remain in the pain of sin, but remain in the peace of Christ. Today we'll read Numbers chapter 16 from verse 41 through 50:

But on the morrow all the congregation of the children of Israel murmured against Moses and against Aaron, saying, Ye have killed the people of the Lord. And it came to pass, when the congregation was gathered against Moses and against Aaron, that they looked toward the tabernacle of the congregation: and, behold, the cloud covered it, and the glory of the Lord appeared. And Moses and Aaron came before the tabernacle of the congregation. And the Lord spake unto Moses, saying, Get you up from among this congregation, that I may consume them as in a moment. And they fell upon their faces. And Moses said unto Aaron, Take a censer, and put fire therein from off the altar, and put on incense, and go quickly unto the congregation, and make an atonement for them: for there is wrath gone out from the Lord; the plague is begun. And Aaron took as Moses commanded, and ran into the midst of the congregation; and, behold, the plague was begun among the people: and he put on incense, and made an atonement for the people. And he stood between the dead and the living; and the plague was stayed. Now they that died in the plague were fourteen thousand and seven hundred, beside them that died about the matter of Korah. And Aaron returned unto Moses unto the door of the tabernacle of the congregation: and the plague was stayed. (Numbers 16: 41-50)

You Can See the Heart of God if You Read It Closely

When I read the Bible, it is so amazing to see how the Scriptures work in my heart. People who do not believe the Bible, but just learn theories at seminary, don't know what God is trying to teach them from the Bible because they are unable to reach the heart of God that's flowing in the Bible. Often times they end up saying that the Bible is not the Word of God.

My daughter plays the piano. Nowadays, she's very busy and she doesn't have much time. But before, from time to time, she would come to me and talk to me about music. A while ago, she spoke to me about the hymn, "Alas, and Did My Savior Bleed."

"Father, the person who made this song, wanted to make this song quite special."

"Really? How is that so?"

"The basic melody is Do Mi Sol, Fa La Do, Sol Ti Re. There are these three types of harmony. In each harmony, it is when these notes mix that the song becomes tender and soft."

"Yeah, I knew that."

"But this composer wanted to express the pain of Jesus hanging on the cross. Because the pain of Jesus being crucified was too extreme, violent, and agonizing, he did not use the consonant chords, but dissonant chords by mixing in Do and Re, and made the music rugged to strongly express the pain.

"Father, when you make music with the consonant chord, it's kind of easy for the choir to sing. Even though they don't sing quite well, they can still harmonize. But songs that are made with dissonant chords are very difficult to sing because, if you don't make the exact right sound when singing in dissonance, the music begins to sound very sharp and strange. That's why the choir practiced many songs that could express the suffering of Jesus through dissonant chords. The choir tried to have the dissonant harmony come out beautifully to express the pain that the composer intended to. That's why I think the song we sang this time was really wonderful."

"Oh, really? I had no idea. At first, I thought that there was something wrong with the music, but that's what it was."

"Father, listen to that song one more time very closely. Moreover, it touches the people's hearts in a much deeper way and draws out the pain in people's hearts much more than the songs that are sung softly with consonant chords."

I asked my daughter, "How do you know the heart of that composer?"

"You cannot tell when you only look at the score and sing the songs. But when you look at the song over and over again and study it, you get to see that the song is not playing out exactly the way it should. But when you examine the music even more closely, then you can fall into that feeling the composer felt when he was making the song.

"The choir director who conducts knows much about music history, knows about the lives of the composers, and also about the background of the composers at the time when they composed the songs.

"Those things come together to create the background to help you discover the heart of the composer when you read the music. When you discover the heart of the composer then you can try to express that heart. The person who performs that song can then involve himself more deeply with the music, and the music becomes very beautiful."

"Wow, if I hang out with you, I think I am going to become a musician, too."

I speak with my daughter about music from time to time. I used to like piano performances very much when I was young. I thought, "If I, later on, get married and have a daughter, I'm going to teach her the piano. When I would get tired, I'll tell my daughter, 'Play a song on the piano.'" I would imagine myself sitting on a chair with my eyes closed, just listening to my daughter play the piano. But I was very busy after getting married. I did not know how my daughter was growing or what she was doing. I was quite busy running around, and I forgot about teaching my daughter the piano.

My daughter is not a very good piano player. My daughter learned the piano quite late. She learned through playing the piano at church. I'm busy and so is my daughter, so I cannot make much time to be with her. But once in a while, I would tell my daughter, "Eunsook, play the piano." I would listen to her playing the piano. I enjoy meeting my daughter at the piano and speaking with her.

Music is an expression of the heart. One may simply perform a song. But if you perform that song knowing the situation and the heart of the composer at the time of the composition, that performance will also include the heart of that composer. That's what makes it really good. I told my daughter, "Eunsook, that's not only true with music. If you read the Bible closely, as well, you can see the heart of God, who speaks through the Bible."

Everyone, spiritual life is most strong, most powerful, and most happy when you discover the heart of God inside the Bible. When that heart of God becomes one with your heart, that moment, your heart becomes extremely joyful and happy.

God Is Going to Help Us

When I first started preaching the Gospel in Gimcheon, I planned to do a children's summer camp. There is a temple called Jikji temple, which is not too far from Gimcheon. Right underneath it was the Jikji Orphanage. By chance, I met the person in charge of that orphanage. I told him, "We are trying to gather young children to have a camp, but we don't have a place," and he let's borrow the orphanage. We decided to have a week of children's camp during the vacation period at that orphanage.

I made the schedule for the camp. I figured out when the kids would come in, the time for the sermon, the time for singing, the time for crafts, the time for dances, and the time for recreation. I made the menu and everything, but the problem was, we didn't have any money. We advertised to different places, saying that we are going to hold a camp and we received calls that many children will be coming from different places. But we didn't have any money to prepare with. The brothers and sisters got together every evening and prayed. Among the brothers, we had a brother who sold macro pikes.

In the morning, he would load his bicycle with macro pikes and visit different villages in the countryside, yelling out, "Buy mackerels, buy mackerels." There was another brother who sold vegetables. All the brothers were quite poor and they would spend all day long, selling these things. Then they would come to the prayer meeting and bow down to pray. During that time, the brothers are happier than when listening to the Word because they can fall asleep during the prayer meetings. It's about ten of us, going around taking turns praying. But the amazing thing is that when it's their own turn, somehow they wake up and pray and then go back to sleep. Once the prayer meeting is over, there are two, three brothers who still haven't woken up yet.

We were tired and in our hearts we were so exhausted. We needed to prepare the camp but we had no money. We didn't know what to do. I thought, "Will we be able to hold this camp? So many kids are coming and what if we're not ready?" Those kinds of worries pushed down on my heart. But I could not go out and say, "Oh, I cannot do this." So, I purposely tried to make myself smile and laugh. Truly, all I could do was pray, but it didn't seem like just praying would take care of things. There was no place where we could get any money. Every evening we prayed. But the amazing thing is, after about ten days of prayer, our prayers came to life. Our hearts began to rise, little by little. The heart that, "It doesn't seem possible now, but if God helps us, it can be done," began to rise in us, little by little.

After praying for about two weeks, nothing about the circumstances changed at all, but our hearts became very close with God. Still there was nothing prepared. We felt, "If God does it, why can't this be done?" God became greater than the circumstances in our hearts. After praying for about twenty days, I felt, "This is a work to preach the Gospel and God is pleased of this. Why wouldn't God help us with this? He will help us. Even if I were God, I would help with this. This will be done." That was the heart that we had.

The circumstances remained the same, but our hearts had changed.

As we prayed, we were happy. We were still the same tired brothers and sisters. But less and less, people would fall asleep during the prayer meetings. When we got up from praying, our faces were filled with joy.

"Yes, God will help us with this. He will do this for us. This is not our work, this is God's work. If God helps there's nothing that cannot be done. There's nothing for us to worry about."

After praying about a month, we were so happy. We felt, "Amen, Hallelujah, we believe that God will help us with the work."

From then on, we no longer prayed, saying, "God help us, give us money." In all of our hearts, we prayed, "God will surely give to us. God will work." We were filled with that kind of a heart. We were so, so thankful. God began to work from that point on. It was so amazing. I cannot tell you everything about that time, but I have so many experiences like that in my life.

As we just go through life, only the difficult circumstances remain in our hearts. But if we pray, read the Bible, and come close to God from our hearts, although it's the same circumstances, our hearts become closer with God. We begin to have the heart, "God will help us with this, God will bless this. If God helps us, why can't it be done?" From then on, we begin to discover the fun in prayer. I realized, "So this is how you are supposed to pray. If I pray like this, then God works. This is how God helps us."

Finally, it was the first day of the camp. I cried so much under the pine trees in the mountain valley. I was so touched to see many children crowding to come. I saw these kids changing. The works that God has done are so great in my heart.

When God made us man, He made the heart. God doesn't have a body and we cannot see God with our eyes. He made the heart for us so that if we go out searching for God in our hearts, we can meet Him. When you get to discover the heart of God and get to know the will of God through the Bible, then that heart and the will of God will be accepted into your heart. When you feel how God's heart and your heart has become one, you become so happy. This is just like a music performance becoming amazingly beautiful when it is performed with the same heart of the composer.

Everyone, you do not have to know a lot about the Bible to be able to give sermons. Giving sermons is not about being able to speak well. It's not by making the audience laugh that you can give a good sermon. Even though the preacher cannot speak well and does not know much, if he knows the heart of God hidden in the Bible and relays that heart, he is a true servant of God, the prophet of God.

The Happy Times that I Had Meeting with the Amazing Pentateuch of Moses

When I used to live in Pa-dong, in Daegu, I was so happy. At that time, we lived on the second floor of a Chinese restaurant. Because the structure of the building was not good, from the second floor you could smell the Chinese food cooking from down below. I love Chinese noodles. It was from that time I started liking them. Back then, we went hungry often. There are two kinds of fasting: the fasting done through your will and the fasting done through God's will. The fasting done through your will is to not eat even though there is food. The fasting done through the will of God is having no choice but to fast because you have no food. Because of fasting we were so hungry. From down below, you could smell the stir fry of the Chinese food. At that time, we started a Bible study at the currency press in Gyeong-san. I went there every Thursday evening.

From Pa-dong to Banwol-dong, I would take the bus, and from Banwol-dong, I would take a different bus and get off at its final stop in Gyeong-san. I would have to walk several kilometers from there to get to the currency press. There were many female employees at the currency press. At almost every meeting, many people received salvation and that brought me so much joy. I was so joyful while walking to the Youngnam University bus station through the deep woods after the Bible study.

The Power of the Sin Offering Which Has Finished the Judgment

"Ock-hee got saved today. Ah, by next Thursday, So-yeong will get saved." I was so happy thinking about those things.

When I returned home, it would be like midnight. My wife would be in front of the door dozing off, falling asleep. I would think, "Ah, I wonder if she knows what this joy is like? Would she know what this happiness is like?" I would think about that at times.

This was before I started the missionary school in 1976, so I had a lot of time. I was so happy while I was in Pa-dong. At that time, I read Genesis, Exodus, Leviticus, Numbers, Deuteronomy - the Pentateuch. I continuously read and studied. These five, the Pentateuch of Moses, which seemed very difficult, were very amazing. Because I enjoyed Genesis so much, I started the Lectures on Genesis broadcast with the Far East Broadcasting and now, we have them being broadcast in L.A. and in New York on TV. They also run in South America and on Africa TV broadcasts. Genesis chapters one through fifty were clearly illustrated in my heart. After that, when I read Exodus, it was not so fun at all. Moses would meet God in the wilderness. God would send Moses to Egypt and send the ten plagues. Once the plagues were over, the Israelites would come out from Egypt.

From chapter 25, it talks about building the tabernacle. The length is how many cubits, the width is how many cubits, the height is how many cubits, until chapter 40, which is the end of Exodus, that's all it talked about. One day, I was bored so I opened to Exodus chapter 25 and began to draw the tabernacle on paper. I measured with a ruler five cubits in length. Using the same proportions, I drew a line of five cubits, on a smaller scale. The width 5 cubits, the height 3 cubits. And as I drew that, I could see there was hidden in the Word the salvation of Jesus. If it's not God, there's nobody else who can draw like that.

From then on, I gave many lectures on the tabernacle. They were very popular.

People don't talk much about the tabernacle. When I talked about the tabernacle, pastors would come and would love listening to it. There were pastors who thanked me, saying that they were getting their Ph.D's and they wrote their thesis based on the tabernacle that they had learned from me.

Then I started to read Leviticus. Leviticus so strongly expresses the holiness of God. Because we're so dirty, we cannot dare to reach the holiness of God. But through offerings, Leviticus works to lay the bridge between our filth and the holiness of God. Laying that bridge between the filthy man and the holy God, to connect the two different cliffs, was what Leviticus did.

Then I moved on to Numbers. The amazing thing about Numbers is that it has laid out all of the things that could arise in the heart of man: complaints, bitterness, the dirty heart, lustful heart, and ambitions. All I did was read Numbers. But I had the heart, "Wow, this is as accurate as looking through the human heart with an x-ray." That's how I felt in my heart.

Just as a doctor can see and say, "This person has this sickness here," God, who can see right through the heart of man, in the book of Numbers clearly and accurately expressed the evil heart of man. He expressed the heart of man that is often filled with complaints, bitterness, lust, and filthy and dirty things. As I saw that, I was very thankful because the heart of man expressed in the book of Numbers was exactly like my heart. If there was no cross of Jesus, I should have also received the curse that the people in the book of Numbers received. As I thought about that, I was so thankful to the Lord and so moved.

Deuteronomy tells us about the posture of the heart we need to have to live life.

Even now, I miss Pa-dong, I miss those times. I'm not so good at English. Because the Korean Bible was not enough, I often bought English Bibles and read them. I read the Amplified Bible, King James Version, Standard Version, the Living Bible. I also opened up a Japanese Bible and searched to see how things were expressed in the Japanese Bible. Because I didn't have enough English vocabulary, I had a small dictionary and I would search the words and read the English Bible every day. Occasionally, I would read an expression you could not find from the Korean Bible. The parts that I could not understand from the Korean Bible, I would read them sometimes from the Amplified Bible or from the King James Bible. As I did that, the eyes of the heart to see the Bible became bigger and bigger. I was able to see the heart of God. From then on, I started to become bold.

I would think, "If God and I are of the same heart, then this would be done, no matter what the circumstances, no matter what the problems." From then on, I began to work with boldness. Whenever I stood in front of a situation or in front of a problem or some work, I often searched out my heart. "Is this of my own ambition? Is this something from me? Or is it clear that this is the will of God?" It took me some time to figure out these things.

But once I believed in my heart that this was the clear will of God, I started the work with boldness. Then those works became beautifully fulfilled through God. From then on, no matter what work I've done, I've never once failed. It is because it is done with the same heart as God.

Time to time, I miss that chapel in Pa-dong, Daegu. After the early morning service and after breakfast, people barely ever came to see me. All morning long, I would fall deep into the Bible. That's when I realized the words about the sin offering. About killing the lamb, about the laying on of hands, how the sin is moved over, how it's connected to Hebrews. From then on, I got to know how sins are forgiven. I was so thankful. Around that time, I started the missionary school. The time that I used to spend in the mornings reading the Bible, I lost all that time lecturing at the missionary school.

The Tank Landmines at Bibong Mountain

A while ago, the walls of our home in the countryside collapsed because of the rain. My nephew was rebuilding that wall and found a landmine under the wall. He was so shocked, he contacted the military. The military came and cleaned it up. After I heard that, I remembered how my father buried that landmine under that wall.

After the Korean War was over, my hometown, Seonsan, was completely filled with weapons from war. We could not even tell whether those weapons were American or North Korean weapons. In Seonsan, there is a mountain named Bibong and in the caves of that mountain, there were many landmines: tank landmines, landmines for people. There were landmines at each home. In some houses, the owner of the home would put a nail on the wall and would hang the landmine on the wall.

People used to do that back then.

My father at that time, cleaned up all the landmines at our home, but there was no way to get rid of them all. My father thought long and hard and decided to bury that landmine in the ground, but even that was a little dangerous. Because, what if you're digging the ground or plowing the field, and what if the landmine explodes? He buried the landmine between the walls and built another wall on top of it thinking there would be no need to reconstruct that wall. But recently, as people were rebuilding that wall, they found the landmine.

When the war was over and when we came to our hometown, we didn't have toys like people do today. All of the things that we played with were weapons of war. Do you know the caliber of a semi-automatic pistol? A 50-caliber gun is used to shoot down airplanes. A 30-caliber, is a semi-automatic pistol with a more slim and longer bullet. When you shoot that gun, the head of the bullets shoot forward, while the shells release through the side of the rifle. We would tie up those shells with rubber bands and drag them around with our foot.

We would make slippers with M1 rifle bullet clips. If you have a bullet and you bend left and right, the tip of the bullet falls off and inside of it is the gun powder. On a bicycle, there are those little things that look like nails that connect the spokes to the wheel. When you remove that and fill the front part of the hole with candle wax, and fill the other side with gun power and hit it, it goes, "Bang!" and makes a huge sound. That was how we played with weapons of war.

Kids who were a bit older than us, used more advanced weapons for fun. They would play with tank landmines. Because the tank landmines are made to explode when a tank moves over or on top of it, it won't explode when a person jumps on it. The tank landmine has a ring, a big ring. My older brother's friends, they would go to Bibong Mountain and would bring back the big heavy tank landmines. Then under a bridge, they would disassemble it and remove the ring. They don't have screw drivers or wrenches or hammers to remove them. They just tap on it with a stone to remove it. Back then, if you made a hoop out of the rings from the tank landmines and roll it around, you had the most popular toy. But many kids died trying to remove the rings. If it were like today, you would see the army or the police cleaning up the landmines or burying them or taking care of them somehow. But back then, nobody knew about any of these things. At that time, I was about 10 years old.

Every morning, my dad would look at me and say, "Ock Soo, you're going to be in big trouble if you go where the landmines are. If you go there, you're going to die." But still, I didn't listen to my father at all. I, too, wanted to follow the older kids of my neighborhood and go to Bibong Mountain. In my neighborhood, there was an older kid named Tagwan. One day, he and his friends decided to go to Bibong Mountain and so I decided to follow along. But the older kids told me that I was too young and they threw rocks at me telling me not to come. Ultimately, I didn't get to follow them and I came home crying. That day, those older kids brought down a tank landmine and were removing the rings under the bridge when it exploded, killing three of them. Tagwan was badly injured. He still lives in our hometown right now, and even now, he is very unwell.

The Landmine Without the Detonator and Gun Powder Is Nothing but a Piece of Metal

I'm sure you also know much about landmines or grenades. But I want to tell you a little bit more about them. Landmines or grenades are made with iron on the outside. Inside of them are the explosives. Also, there's the detonator. The human landmine doesn't blow up when a person just steps on it. It blows up when a person steps on it and then removes his foot. That's when it explodes. Once the detonator goes off, the detonator triggers the gun powder within the landmine. Then the metal is broken into many little pieces and the shrapnel flies and strikes the people. That's how it kills people. When landmine experts are clearing an area, and they step on a landmine, they can feel it immediately.

"Ah, I've stepped on a landmine."

Now, if he removes his foot, he dies. Now what does he do? He screams and calls out to other people. They dig around the place where the landmine is buried. After pulling out the landmine, they get rid of the detonator. The landmine doesn't explode without the detonator. It's when the detonator is triggered and ignites the gun powder inside, that causes the landmines to explode.

When I was young, it was still not yet safe. Many kids died because of the landmines. Several times a day, you could hear the blast of landmines exploding. Adults would set up barbed wire to keep the kids from going up Bibong Mountain. But still, the kids would go up there. They loved that hoop so much, just to roll that hoop around. Because they are still alive, they don't know what it's like to die, and all they've seen are the people playing with the hoops. The kids don't worry about dying and all of their hearts are fallen into just having the hoop. They completely lose their heart to that.

In those days, people did not know better and would say bullets cannot penetrate cotton. Some mothers took out the cotton from their blankets and put the cotton all over their kids' bodies, here and there, like Santa Claus. The mothers would tell them, "Here you go. Now, the bullets will not be able to penetrate you." They would tell the kids that if a plane flies by, they should get on their stomachs, cover their ears, and open their mouths.

Landmines and grenades have detonators. If the detonator is removed or if the detonator is disabled, the landmine or the grenade itself does not have any power. It's nothing but a piece of metal.

But the landmine or the grenade with the detonator is not just a piece of metal, but it's a bomb. That is something to be feared. That is something to be scared of. That is something we should not touch and should avoid. But a landmine or a grenade without the detonator is nothing but a piece of metal. It cannot do anything.

If the detonator of a grenade has gone off, it cannot explode again. A landmine, without a detonator will not blow up no matter how much it's struck. It is the same with sin. When a person has committed a certain sin, that sin always summons death. That is why that person must be put to death. But once that sin is judged, once the sin has gone through the judgment, it is sin, but it cannot bring us destruction. The sin that has been judged, although it is sin, cannot curse us nor bring us pain. That is why God passed his judgment upon sin.

There is love, there is mercy, there is peace, and there is blessing in the storage of God. God wanted to take mercy from there to give it to us. God wants to bring love and pour love upon us. But in the storage of God, there is not only kindness, mercy, love, and things like that, but there is also the judgment. Why would this good God give the judgment? Judgment brings pain and fear. Nobody likes it. But God has to do this because if the judgment is not given for the sins that we committed, then one day, it will summon the curse and, one day, it will summon destruction upon us.

Sin is similar to a landmine. Once the detonator is pulled and it explodes, the landmine can no longer function as a bomb. The landmine with the detonator is very scary because it will one day explode. When we were young, some homes would have boxes of bullets. The bullets in those boxes were very smooth with oil on them, so that they could easily fit into guns. These bullets also cannot explode without the detonator.

God judges our sin. If the sin is not punished but just left alone, then that sin, one day, will receive the judgment. Then the sin becomes a wall to block us from God, and becomes a problem and a difficulty. But the sin that is punished is just like a grenade or a landmine with a detonator or gun powder that has been removed. On the outside, it's a landmine or a grenade. But because it's missing the detonator and the gun powder, it can never explode. It's just a piece of metal. No matter what sin we've committed, once the punishment for that sin has been received, that sin can never make us afraid. It cannot give us pain, it cannot give us hardship, it cannot bring us the curse. For this, God punished sin.

The Culprit of All Fights in This World: Rightness

In Numbers chapter 16 which we read today, the people of Israel complained against God, complained against Moses, complained against Aaron, and they sinned. In verse 41, it says, *But on the morrow all the congregation of the children of Israel murmured against Moses and against Aaron, saying, Ye have killed the people of the Lord.* That's what they said. The children of Israel came out of Egypt through the grace of God. Through the power of God, the Red Sea split. The pillar of cloud and the pillar of fire guided them. They drank the water that came from the rock. They ate the manna and they ate the quails. In this way, they received the guidance of God. But the devil is still relentless. The devil continues to strike up conditions inside of us to murmur, complain, and fall into trial even though we receive the grace and blessings of God. If you are close to Satan, no matter how much grace or blessings you receive from God, you will complain, you will murmur, and fall into trial. And you will go against

God. On the other hand, if you are close with God, no matter how difficult, you will be thankful and joyful.

It's not so good, biblically, for husband and wife to live separately from each other. If the husband and wife live separately from each other, there are many problems and discomforts. The most serious problem is that the husband and the wife's hearts grow further and further apart. Actually, even though their hearts may be apart, you just have to bring them back closer together. If the husband is in Seoul and the wife is in Daejeon, they only need to say, "Honey, hurry up and come here, or should I come to you?" That's all they need to say. But people don't like to do that. If the husband calls and says, "Come on over," the wife says, "No, you come."

That's why once the hearts become distant, the problem becomes serious. From time to time, among our church members, the husband and wife get into a fight and I go to their home. When I go over there, they tell me this and that and all these reasons for the fighting. I tell them, "I don't know about that. I don't understand. Fight in front of me and show me why you fought. I'll watch and be the judge." When the husband and wife fight, it's because there's a problem between the couple.

Husbands and wives usually fight about their relationship, and also about the relationship between the wife and the mother-in-law. The mother-in-law and daughter-in-law have different personalities. Since the son has lived with his mother for a long time, even if the mother may be wrong, it's not much of a problem to him. He can say, "That's how my mother usually is," and just let it by. But the daughter-in-law after marrying into the family, sees so clearly that the mother-in-law is wrong. She also sees that the husband just lets it by. That's why the husband and wife begin to fight. The wife says, "Honey, what Mother did was wrong."

But the husband does not feel so. He says, "What? That can happen."

"No, honey, your mother was wrong in what she did. How can you say that it can just happen? What's wrong is wrong."

Because the husband has lived with his mother for a long time, he is very generous concerning his mother's wrong-doings. He thinks, "Even if my mother did do that, she's still a nice person. What's wrong?" Who's mother would not have any weaknesses or mistakes? Not just the mother-in-law, but so are daughter-in-laws. That's how all people are.

But when the daughter-in-law looks at the mother-in-law with the standard of good and evil, she sees her mother-in-law to be wrong. She is able to say to her husband, "Honey, what Mother did was wrong. How come you're not saying anything?"

"What? What do you want me to do?"

"You just say something."

"What do you want me to say? What was so wrong about what she did?"

"How was that not wrong? Just because she's your mother, you take her side."

There's this kind of conflict between the mother and daughter in law. In that situation, the husband's position becomes quite awkward. Although he loves his wife, he feels upset. He thinks, "Why must she pick on my mother's weakness like that? Fine, then, are you perfect?" Then that's how the husband and wife begin to fight.

As the husband and wife fight and the problem becomes serious, I get called into it. I go there at night, or during the day. I would talk to the sister, who is the wife, "Sister, there's one thing I hate the most in this world."

"What is it?"

"I hate rightness, the most in this whole world."

Then she becomes wide-eyed, saying, "Pastors are supposed to teach what's right and have them do it, but you say that you hate rightness?"

I would explain to them, "Did you know that all fights in the world come about from being right? If there's no rightness, then there's nothing to fight about."

Please think about this, everyone. People fight because they believe themselves to be right.

Does anyone fight, saying, "I'm wrong?" There's nobody like that in this world. Because the daughter-in-law does not want to give in to the mother-in-law, she brings forth the right things, saying, "This is right, see?" Because of such rightness there is division, there are fights, and there are arguments. So I call those right things, "rightness, good for nothing."

I said, "Sister."

"Yes?"

"Why can't you just throw away your rightness? That rightness, it's good for nothing. Just throw it away. Then you have nothing to fight about. The mother-in-law is old. She has lived in that family 30 years longer than you and her habits have been hardened and you're trying to fix her hardened habits?"

Our Brother Douglas, his fingers have been hardened for 20 years and the orthopedic surgeon said that they cannot be unfolded. It would be so nice to open his hand. But, he said his hand cannot be opened. But unfolding the heart of the mother-in-law is much more difficult than unfolding bones. Isn't this true? You can forcefully open up and unfold bones, but you cannot do that with the heart.

Everyone, we all have crooked aspects, wrong aspects, weak aspects, and evil aspects. That's why even though you're wrong in your own many ways, if you have one rightness, you will hold on to that and push forward. Actually, what rightness does man have anyway?

When I used to fight with my wife... If I say this people may think that my wife and I fight every day, but that's not true. We argue once in a while. What upsets me is that women are so good at talking.

I don't know where they get all those words. They talk, connecting these words that I can't even think of.

There's no way I can keep up with my wife. This is what men have to know. The women are quite spontaneous. For example, if you tell a man to come to church, he begins to think, "If I believe in Jesus, what will my father say? What will my younger brother say? How are we going to do our family offerings? What will my wife say? And what will they say at my job?" It gets complicated because he thinks about all of that. But if a woman is told it's good to believe in Jesus, then she just believes. That's the difference between men and women. That's why during an argument, a man's weapon comes out a little late because he's thinking, "Should I say it like this, or should I say it like that?" But the women pull out their weapon very quickly. That's why even though surely I'm right, I've never once fought with my wife and won. When we go at it with words, my wife always wins. I say, "Oh, no" and become upset.

Humans are not machines nor gods. Humans are not perfect, and that's why the human life is fun. We're not perfect.

That's why we must also accept that our mother-in-law is not perfect. When she herself becomes a mother-in-law, she will be the same, too. It is because her mother-in-law has weaknesses, that she is fun.

"Hey, this is my mistake."

"Mother, how is that a mistake, we're family."

Because of the mistakes you can have a good relationship.

It's the same thing when a husband is dealing with his wife. The wife burned a brand new suit, that the husband bought, with an iron.

The husband said, "Do you know how much this is? What's wrong with you?"

But is acting like that going to repair the suit?

"Honey, maybe the temperature of the iron is not right. I think the iron is broken. We should buy a new one."

That is the way to go.

At times, my wife looks very pretty to me. When we were first married and living in Gimcheon, we lived on a second floor hall. We didn't have a kitchen. It was somebody else's house and we couldn't make a kitchen. My wife had put a little charcoal furnace in front of the bathroom on the first floor. She put our pot there to make rice. She would bring that back upstairs. I felt so bad to see my wife cooking food like that. I told my wife, "Honey, I'm sorry."

My wife answered, "So what if it's like this? We're living for the Gospel." How beautiful she looked when she said that!

Not long after we got married, I went to a conference. After the conference, they gave me some travel money. I was thinking of my wife and, for the first time, I bought a women's blouse and brought it home. I was so happy to bring it home and I said, "Honey," called her over and gave her the blouse.

She looked at me and became wide-eyed. Then, she immediately asked me, "How much did you pay for this?"

For a moment I thought to discount the price and tell her, but I just told her honestly.

She got angry and said, "You paid that much for this?"

Right then, I thought in my heart, "I'm never going to buy you a gift again. This is my last one!"

Life is not fun if it's perfect. It has to have shortcomings. If you love, even with shortcomings, you can still love. The mothers love their kids even though they poop. They're lovable even if they pee. They're lovable even if they drool. That's why I tell the people who fight with their spouses, "Gee, I guess you really have nothing better to fight about. You guys fight over that?"

The Only Way to Rid the Function of Sin: Judgment

God gives the judgment. No matter what sin you've committed, unless it goes through the judgment, it can never be taken care of. It will just remain as sin. This is exactly how a landmine has the potential to explode, unless its detonator and gun powder are removed. But once the detonator and the gun powder are removed from the landmine, on the outside, it's a landmine, but on the inside it's not a landmine. It's just a piece of metal.

Sin must absolutely receive the judgment. Sin summons curse, it summons destruction, it summons the guilt of the conscience, and works to build a wall between God and us. Just as you separate the detonator from the landmine and remove its gun powder, there is only one way to get rid of the function of sin, and that is through the judgment. Only through the judgment, sin can lose its power, no matter what the sin may be. No matter the sin, no matter how small it is, if it has not received the punishment, its function of sin is alive. It brings us to be cursed, to destruction, to judgment, and to pain. On the other hand, no matter what the sin, once the judgement is received, it has lost its function as sin. Although one has clearly committed adultery, committed murder, committed theft, the sin is no longer effective. Sin, which has ended through judgment, is not sin anymore. That's why God was pleased of giving the judgment.

Because God loves us, he bestows mercy on us, and bestows kindness upon us. But He also wants to give us the judgment. It is through that judgment that sin is destroyed. It destroys the function of sin. Although it is sin, it cannot give us the curse. The judgment makes the sin unable to lead us to destruction. The Bible is trying to teach us about these things.

Numbers chapter 16 speaks about these things. In Numbers chapter 16, the children of Israel committed sin by murmuring against God. As soon as they sinned, a plague began to go around and people began to die. biblical scholars, nowadays, studied this plague saying, "We wonder what that plague is. Was it a pest? Was it typhoid?" But we don't have to know about these things. As long as we know it was a plague. All we have to know is that people died because of this plague. Because the biblical scholars cannot discover the heart of God inside of the Bible, they lead people's hearts to knowledge, and try to make them understand their hearts through that.

Before getting saved, I also knew many useless things. I would sit around with the youths of the church and ask, "Did Adam have a bellybutton or not?" That was what we discussed. Because the bellybutton is the tip of the umbilicus, we discussed, "Because Adam was not born from a mother, he must not have had a bellybutton."

"No, he must have had one."

Those were the kinds of things we talked about. We would talk about how many angels could stand on a tip of a needle.

The church would also make us debate to see whether the growth of the church depended on witnessing or on prayer. We would debate, "Does the well being of a child depend on the role of a father or the role of a mother?" Without knowing the heart of God that's hidden in the Bible, our hearts were led to stray paths.

Many pastors teach that if you do good things and live faithfully according to the Word that things will be well. But in reality, even they themselves are unable to live according to the Word.

There was a couple where the husband was a soldier and attended our church, while the wife attended a different church. One day, the couple was watching TV together. Because it was Family Day, the pastor on television was preaching on the topic of family. The pastor said, "Everyone, do not make your children angry. Do not speak rudely to your wife. I have never once did anything upsetting to my wife, in my whole life."

Upon hearing that, the wife said to the husband, "Honey, see? You heard what he said, right?" It meant that the husband has said things upsetting to her.

Right then, the husband said, "That pastor, he's a liar. The Bible said that if you do not make mistakes with words, you are perfect. That guy, he's speaking as if he never makes mistakes with his words. If so, what sin would that person ever commit? Does that mean he has not stolen, not had covetousness, and not had lust in his heart? Then why would he need to believe in Jesus?"

Many pastors say that you have to do good things. People are deceived by this.

Once, I went to a conference in Los Angeles. After the sermon, two pastors and their wives sat down and spoke with me. One of them said to me, "Pastor, I commit fraud every day. After every sermon I give, I call my friend, another pastor, and I ask him, 'So, how did you cheat your people today?'" He was saying that he was telling the church members to do things even he cannot do. He was saying that is exactly what fraud is. He said that he cannot live according to the words of the Bible. That day, he and the rest of them received salvation and they were so happy. They wanted to come to our missionary school. But they could not come because the people around them would not let them.

Truly, everyone, we are not perfect. We can never reach the standard of God. Trying to do well, on its own, is arrogant in front of God. In front of God, we must say, "God, we cannot do it. There is no way. God, you have to do it. How can we be good?" That is the true word that comes from our lips. Even though we are dirty inside, acting like we are doing good, acting like we are well, acting like we are kind and such, are what God deems to be fake and hypocritical.

Aaron, Quickly Go and Give the Sin Offering

The plague started because the people murmured against God. They were dying. What should they do? Should they not murmur? Should they do good things? Should they be faithful? Should they give offering? Should they pray? No. Since the plague started because of sin, they must stop the function of sin. Without that, there's no power to stop the plague. If so, then the function of sin is stopped through what method? It is through the judgment, that you can stop the function of sin. No matter how black the charcoal is, once it's burnt, it's nothing but ashes. That burnt charcoal may look like charcoal but it cannot burn again. No matter how much you try to light the burnt charcoal, it cannot light on fire, because it's already all burnt.

The sin that has gone through the judgment, no matter how much one tries to punish it, cannot be punished. It cannot be punished because it has already gone through the judgment.

The Power of the Sin Offering Which Has Finished the Judgment

Sin must go through the judgment. What is the sin offering? It is the judgment. When you have stolen, committed adultery, or told a lie, the judgment of that sin is received by the goat or the lamb, instead of you. But ultimately, the lamb or the goat has to be put to death for the punishment of sin to be received. The sin offering, in other words, represents the judgment. If a sin offering was given for a sin, it means that the judgment has already been received. Hence, there can be no more judgment for that sin, no more curse and no more destruction.

The people of Israel committed sin and they were dying of the plague. So what must they do? Doing good will not solve the problem. It is not about giving service, praying, or realizing their sin. But they must quickly give the sin offering to stop the effectiveness of the sin. The only way to destroy that power of sin is through the sin offering.

When Moses realized that there was a plague, he quickly told Aaron, "Aaron, Aaron! Quickly go and give the sin offering."

And Moses said unto Aaorn, Take a censer, and put fire therein from off the altar, and put on incense, and go quickly unto the congregation, and make an atonement for them: for there is wrath gone out from the Lord: the plague is begun. And Aaron took as Moses commanded, and ran into the midst of the congregation; and, behold, the plague was begun among the people: and he put on incense, and made an atonement for the people. And he stood between the dead and the living; and the plague was stayed. (Numbers 16: 46-48)

Aaron didn't walk over, but he ran. Because the plague was going around the congregation of Israel, the camp of Israel quickly became a huge mess. One would fall over, another would be having terrible fever while people would try to cool them off with water. Another person would die, there would be people crying, weeping, "My son is dead," and some crying, "My husband is dead." Because the curse of sin came upon the people and they were dying, Moses quickly went to Aaron and told him to give the sin offering. Aaron ran over. There were many people dying every second, so each second counted. It's very difficult to run wearing the priest's clothing. Usually, he would be able to walk slowly wearing those clothes. But in this situation, things were too urgent. There's no way for him to check whether his hat was on the right way, whether he was buttoned up. He was just running around as quickly as he could. When Aaron went and completed giving the sin offering, he stood before the living and the dead, the plague had completely ended. Why was that so? It was because the sin offering had been given and the judgment for sin had been finished, even though sin was definitely committed. The power of that sin was no more.

The Cross of Jesus Which Stopped the Curse and Ended the Judgment

Everyone, this is what you must know. Jesus being crucified on the cross means that He received the judgment of sin that you should have received. Whether you committed adultery, theft, or murder, Jesus received the judgment for that sin. Yes, this is something you should know. This judgment He received, He received in front of God. If you steal, then you must be punished according to the laws of the world. If you committed murder, you need to be punished by the laws of the world, but also you need to be punished according to the laws of God. Jesus, in order to receive the punishment according to the law, died and was crucified on the cross. He did that so the judgment would be passed according to the law of God. In the courts of the world, if you say, "I have sinned, but because Jesus died on the cross for me, I have no sin," they will consider you to be mentally ill. Jesus did not save us according to the laws of this world. But He saved us according to the laws of God. To fulfill this, He received the judgment, instead of us. Now, because the judgment for our sins is over with, the sin is also finished. Amen? This is what we should believe.

In Numbers 16, the people of Israel committed sin and there was a plague going around. It is not that they should pray; it is not that they should do good things; it is not that they should be determined to not sin, and repent. But they should quickly give the sin offering to receive the judgment. Look at the Bible. When the sin offering was clearly given, the plague ended. The cross of Jesus put an end to the curse that was to come upon you and finished the judgment. If not, then there would be many people among you here who should be put to death.

In the Old Testament, through murmuring, people died; through committing adultery, people died; and through committing such sins, people died. It is not just one or two people here who would be murmuring. Don't you think there are people here who committed adultery? Don't you think there are people here who committed theft? They are all people who should be dead, but are alive because of the cross.

In the book of Numbers, the people of Israel continually faced death. They died because of this, they died because of that. It continually talks about them dying. That is our fate also. But through Jesus Christ dying on the cross, He ended that fate. But people who don't accept this into their hearts, this grace cannot be upon their hearts. When they accept this by faith in their hearts, saying, "Yeah, even though I committed these sins, they cannot lead me to destruction. Jesus already received the destruction and the judgment for this sin, instead of me," then they can rejoice. They can say, "I should have received the curse, I should have received the destruction, but Jesus, instead, received the judgment for me and was cursed instead of me." With that, we overflow with thankfulness.

When we read Leviticus or Numbers, it is so amazing that it shows how all the ways to take care of all the problems that arise in our hearts. That is why, whenever I stand before you, there are so many things for me to say. Everyone, go ahead and read the Bible. At first, it may feel difficult. But as you keep on reading it, you can see the heart of God inside of the Bible. Through that, when your heart becomes like the heart of God, and the things you want to do come in line with the things that God wants to do, you can do anything. That is why we are happy and there's nothing for us to worry about.

CHAPTER 9
The Eternal Sin Offering Given at the Temple of Heaven

There is nothing eternal on earth. But heaven is eternal. That is why even if a sin offering is given here on earth, it cannot become an eternal offering. The offering must be given in the temple in heaven in order for our sins to be washed away forever. Jesus, with His blood, went to the greater and more perfect tabernacle that does not belong on this creation and entered the temple in heaven. He put His blood on the horns of the altar and sprinkled it on the mercy seat to wash away our sins forever. The offerings given on this earth only washed away the sins of that time, but the offering that is given in heaven can forgive us our sins forever.

Hello everyone. Tonight we will also speak about forgiveness. We'll read from Hebrews chapter 9 verses 11 through 14:

But Christ being come an high priest of good things to come, by a greater and more perfect tabernacle, not made with hands, that is to say, not of this building; Neither by the blood of goats and calves, but by his own blood he entered in once into the holy place, having obtained eternal redemption for us. For if the blood of bulls and of goats, and the ashes of an heifer sprinkling the unclean, sanctifieth to the purifying of the flesh: How much more shall the blood of Christ, who through the eternal Spirit offered himself without spot to God, purge your conscience from dead works to serve the living God? (Hebrews 9:11-14)

Spiritual Life Is Fitting Our Heart With the Heart of God

I once took a witnessing team on a bus to the countryside. One of the sisters was sitting in the front most seat on the right-hand side of the driver. Because it was a transit bus in the countryside, people would get on and off along the way. Yet, every time a person would get on, the driver would look at that sister. Seeing this, I went to that sister and said, "Hey, Sister."

"Yes Pastor?"

"I think that driver really likes you. He looks at you every time the bus stops." At first this sister didn't think much of it, but when she looked at the driver she saw that he would look at her every time the bus stopped and went. As this continued on, her face began to turn red. I like to be a bit goofy at times, so I said, "See? He's looking at you again!" As this went on, this sister just wanted to die.

After a long while, I went and told her, "Hey, you don't need to worry about it. The driver isn't looking at you; he's looking at the rearview mirror." Because the driver's seat is on the left side and the doors are on the right side, the driver has to make sure people get on and off safely when he stops the bus. To check this, he has to look at the rearview mirror. Since the sister was sitting right next to the rearview mirror, she thought that he was looking at her. When I made fun of her, saying, "Hey, I think that driver really likes you," her face turned as red as an apple.

The Gracias Choir performed tonight as well. The people who are performing often look at the first violinist. They tune according to the piano, but they set their tempo with the first violin. The person furthest away from the first violinist has a receiver in her ear; this is so that she can hear the sound. Trying to hear the first violin herself would be difficult, so she wouldn't be able to set the tempo. When we look at the choir performing, whether the person is playing the clarinet or the flute, she continually looks at the first violinist. That's why the sisters who play the instruments always have a sharp look in their eyes.

There are many people who are unclear about spiritual life. To live proper spiritual life is to tune our hearts with the heart of God. When your spiritual life fits with the heart of God and tunes with the Word of the Bible, then you are able to have tremendous boldness in your heart. For those of you who have received the forgiveness of sins through this conference, I hope that you will be able to begin such a life.

God, Even if I Get Beaten, I Will Not Steal

In 1965, I entered the army. I was trained for six weeks as a new soldier at the 54th Division in Daegu. When I went to lie down and sleep on the night of my first day, I could hear curse words echoing throughout my ears. At the training center, people begin speaking with curses and end with curses. They say all kinds of curse words. I want to talk to you about the first hardship I faced while I was in the army.

When I entered the army, they stripped me of all that I was wearing. So, I had to use only the supplies that the army gave me: a helmet, gun, ammo belt, army boots, sneakers, work clothes, fighting clothes, etc. In the evenings, I would put my helmet and ammo belt on top of the cabinet, and on top of that I would put my woolen gloves. It was winter at the time, so they had given us woolen gloves made out of yarn. However, when I woke up one morning my woolen gloves were gone. I had surely placed them on top of my helmet the night before, but when I woke up in the morning they were gone. I didn't know what to do.

In those days, they would beat you very badly in the army. If you did not obey, the captain of the barracks would take a hoe and beat you with it. I had never been beaten before, so when I thought about being beaten by the barracks captain for having lost my gloves, I became afraid and worried. "Hey! What did you do with your gloves? Who did you sell them to?" That's what they usually say in the army.

That morning I took my gun and joined in singing the army song, "I Was Born a Man!" Then I headed off to training. Every other person had their government issued gloves on, so when they lifted their hands it showed blue. I was the only one who showed the color of red with my cold bare hands. I wasn't worried about my hands being cold, but I was so worried about getting caught by the barracks captain.

In the army, they don't call stealing, theft. No matter how much you steal, the equipment remains within the defense department so it still belongs to them. Thus, stealing is just simply called "relocation." Actually, in the same way that somebody stole my gloves, I could just as quietly steal someone else's gloves and they would become mine. I had no other way. Plus, since they're all the same, no one would be able to tell who stole them. But then, I began to worry deeply about this.

"I should steal them, but I believe in Jesus. How can I steal? No, this isn't stealing. It's relocation. It all remains within the Department of Defense." I thought long and hard for three days about whether I should steal or not. "This is the army! You're no different! You need to steal. If you don't, then the captain of the barracks will beat you with a stick. It's going to be painful and difficult." While I was conflicting like this, God showed me a reason why I could not steal. "If I get caught stealing, then how will I witness afterwards? Sure, I may not get caught, but if I do, then how will I witness in my barracks?" When I felt that in my heart, there was no way I could steal.

On the night of the third day, I laid down on my bed and began to pray, "God, please give me a pair of gloves. I had been in doubt until now, but I will not steal gloves. If I get beaten for having lost my gloves then I will get beaten by the barracks captain. If I'm given hardship then I will suffer hardship. If pain comes to me then I will suffer the pain, but I will not steal. God, please help me."

The next day I went out to receive training again. That day, we were learning how to throw grenades. "This is how the grenade works. If you remove the safety pin and release the handle, it will strike the detonator and blow up in three seconds." After receiving the instruction we practiced throwing the grenades. After removing the safety pin, we would shout "One! Two!" and then throw the grenade. The grenade blows up at a 45-degree angle, so you have to quickly get down on the ground.

In the army, you have a 50-minute training session and then a 10-minute break. During the break time, a friend came to me. We had not yet been in the army that long so I didn't really know anybody. I only knew this friend by his nametag. "Hey, Ock Soo Park!"

"What?"
"Don't you have gloves?"
"You know what? I'm in big trouble."
"Why?"
"I woke up in the morning and someone had stolen my gloves."
"Hey! You should've told me!"
"What? You got two pairs of gloves?"
"Yup. I have two pairs."
"Where did you steal them from?"
"Steal?"
"How can you have two pairs if you didn't steal one pair?"
"My older brother is a company commander."
"Really?"
"I get frostbite, so my older brother gave me another pair."
"Oh, really?"
"Hey that's what friends are for. I'll share these with you." That friend took off a pair of gloves and gave them to me. I put them on my hands and looked at them; I was amazed.

"That's right! I have God! God is living and He is with me."

How Could God Be With Me Who Is So Pitiful?

Although I'm a pastor, I often do wrong. At times, I scream; at times, I get upset; and at times, I get angry. At times, I'm lazy; and often times, I'm lacking. At times, when I think about it, "Maybe God will not love me. Why would He love someone like me? God may throw me away. I'm so lacking in the eyes of God. I'm so weak." Those kinds of thoughts come to me. Often times, I feel ashamed in front of God. Some people tell me that I'm very generous-looking. I know they just say that to be nice, but I had never once thought of myself to be that way.

Once, when I went on a home visit, the grandmother of that home said to her grandson, "Hey, Pastor is here. Why don't you sing a song for Pastor?" So that child sang a song. It was my first time hearing that song, but I memorized it right there on the spot.

The pastor of the church I go to, he's the happy smiley pastor, He's so kind, He's so virtuous, Our happy smiley pastor, La la la, la la la, la la la Our kind, our virtuous, our happy smiley pastor.

As I heard that song, I thought, "That is not me. Maybe there are pastors like that, but that is not me." Everyone, although I'm a pastor, I'm a person who has so many shameful things in front of God. We're all the same humans bundled up into the same pile of flesh; that's why we have ambitions.

Whenever I see some pastors on TV boasting of themselves, I would feel in my heart, "Wow. How can he come out and say such a thing? I'm so lacking and I have so many shortcomings." I feel that way in my heart. Even when I look at myself, I feel in my heart that God's not going to love a person like me. Rather, it feels like He will throw me away. However, everyone, the amazing thing is that even though I am lacking, I am weak, at times I make mistakes, and I commit sins; yet, the fact is that God is always with me.

God is not with me because I am perfect. It is not that I am so faithful that God loves me and cares for me. It's not because I read the Bible, prayed much, gave good sermons, or was more kind and truthful than others; God is not with me for those reasons. I still continue to be weak and I still continue to lack. I often throw fits at my wife and talk obnoxiously. I'm very small-minded and always change my mind. Sometimes when the church members look at me and call, "Pastor," I feel so ashamed and I say in my heart, "How could I be a pastor?" Yet, just because of that I can't just go and tell them, "I'm pitiful in this, and this, and that way." Really, I'm such a lacking person. I have so many blemishes and I'm so filthy. Everyone, I have so many flaws, I'm so lacking, so filthy, and so weak. So how could God be with me? How can God walk together with me? The reason is very simple.

Although I am weak, filthy, dirty, lacking, and a person who is always changing his mind, the blood that Jesus shed on the cross has perfectly washed my sins away. Thus, I am clean in the eyes of God. I'm righteous in the eyes of God. I am holy in the eyes of God. Hallelujah! I praise the Lord.

Salvation Was Based on the Standard of a Dirty Sinner

You may think from time to time, "Since Pastor doesn't have to go around trying to make money or run a business, he probably doesn't lie. All

Pastor does is pray and read the Bible every day so he probably doesn't have evil thoughts. He must be holy." That is not so! Pastors are all the same humans.

Suppose I don't eat for one day. I'd go crazy, being so hungry. If I don't drink water for a day, I'd almost die of thirst. Even after one difficult day I complain and become bitter. We're all the same humans, the same descendants of Adam and the same filthy, dirty human beings. That is why thinking, "Oh, when I'm done making money and I finish my business, then just like the pastor, I'm not going to lie. I'll become good. Then I'll get some faith. Then God will wash my sins away," is absolutely wrong.

When God saved us, He did not set the standard on clean and good people. Rather, He set the standard according to filthy and dirty people. So, if you are a filthy and dirty sinner, then you are a person who has the fitting conditions to be saved. Where does the sin offering begin? *If a common person sins and does something against any of the commandments of the Lord…* It starts with the sin being committed.

A long time ago, when the chapel of our church was small, it was the cold winter but the students would keep the door open. So, a lot of cold wind would blow in. I would yell at them saying, "Hey kids! Just because the chicken walks around bare footed, did you think it was summer? Why did you leave the door open?" No matter how much I told them, they would just reply, "Yes, Pastor," but the next time the doors would be open again. I told a brother about this and had him work on the door so that it would close automatically. So that brother went out, bought a door closer, and quickly installed it. It made the door close automatically, and it was so nice to have that installed. Even if the students left the door open it would close on its own.

Once, we were having service, there was this very quiet sister in our church who arrived late. At that time, the chapel was so small that I could clearly see the sister walking in. She was walking in very carefully and started to close the door. All she needed to do was just leave it alone, but doors that close automatically don't close when someone pulls on them. Seeing it wasn't closing, she pulled on it harder. As she pulled, it suddenly made a loud noise, "Snap!" and then it closed. Everybody turned around and looked back.

The door closer was installed on the door for those kids who would leave the door open. So, these married sisters who were very quiet and calm needed to fit their standards to these little kids. If these married sisters would just leave the door open like the kids, then the door would close automatically.

So where did God set the standard for spiritual life? God did not make spiritual life by setting the standard upon the calm, loyal, clean, honest, people who read the Bible, pray well, and who do not sin. Rather, He set the standard based on those who commit sin, fight, murder, commit adultery, steal, and commit fraud. He set the standard on people who commit all kinds of sins so that it would be easy to receive salvation. That's why, when we read the Bible, it can be seen that these kinds of people much more easily received the grace of God, rather than the kind and gentle people. Take for example, the woman taken in the act of adultery, the Samaritan woman, Zacchaeus the publican, the thief at the cross, or the man with the infirmity for 38 years. It was these people who received the grace of God. But those kind, gentle people who lived spiritual life well, those Pharisees, those priests, those scribes who claimed to have no blemishes and claimed to believe so well; those kinds of people were far from grace.

You Must Become an Evil Person to Receive Salvation

People who want to unite their hearts with Jesus must arrive at the point of salvation. The point of salvation was not made to be arrived at by the good, the truthful, the honest, or the people who do no evil. The way of salvation was made so that it would be easy for the filthy, the evil, the deceitful, the lustful, and the hypocritical human being to receive salvation. That is why, for you to receive the true salvation, you should not become good people. You must become the evil person.

If you want to receive true salvation, you should not become honest and true people, rather you should become the liar. If you truly want to receive the grace of God, you should not become clean people, but rather filthy people. That is why God made us filthy people. It says that He had just left us over to commit sins.

Now, we have all become filthy people, yet still in our hearts we try not to become filthy people. We have already become evil people, but in our hearts we try not to be evil. We are already dirty people, but in our hearts we strive not to be dirty. We are lustful people, but if we don't become lustful people from the heart, then we remain far from salvation.

If you truly enter into the world of faith, then God makes you into such a dirty, filthy, and evil person, to the point that you wouldn't even be able to lift up your head. That's how it was when I received salvation. Because I went to church ever since I was young, I lived thinking that I didn't do bad things and that I was good. But one day, I received the grace of God and I saw my own image as being so filthy, deceitful, lustful, and dirty. I was so ashamed even when I looked at myself. I would often look at myself in the mirror and say, "Ock Soo Park! You're so dirty. You're so low. You're so evil!" and I would yell. At such a time, I hated people who even looked like me or had big mouths and thick lips like me. That's how it was when Jesus Christ began to work inside of me.

Everyone, the person that Jesus looks for is the sinner and the evil, dirty person. However, because many people today live spiritual life backwards, they are fooled into wanting to become good and honest people. Having been deceived by Satan, they think that if they are kind and good then they can receive grace; but that is absolutely wrong. Who can receive grace? It is the sinner. Think about it.

If there was a person who owed fifty-denari versus a person who owed five hundred-denari, and both of those people got their debt pardoned, then which of the two received the greater grace? Which of them would love their pardoner more? It is the person with many sins that receives grace. The Bible says, "Where sin abounded, grace did much more abound." That's why in order for you to receive grace, you must first realize that you are an unspeakable sinner in front of God and that there is no good in you. You have to know that there's no truth in you. When you say, "Even if I try, I cannot. I'm dirty. I'm bundled in sin," and throw away the thought that your good deeds mean you're doing well, faith towards Jesus begins to arise in your heart. Many people try to become more honest and more holy themselves. They think that if they become more diligent then they can live a good spiritual life, but that is not true.

Man's Perspective, Which Is the Complete Opposite of the Bible, Thinking That You Must Do Good to Be Blessed

When I was young, I read the story of Heungbu. Heungbu was kind-hearted. Once, a swallow had hurt its leg, so Heungbu repaired the leg with a bandage. The swallow gave him a gourd seed in return. A while after, Heungbu planted the gourd seed, and it bore a fruit that following year. When he opened it, it was full of gold, silver, and treasures. Evil-hearted Nolbu saw the prosperity of Heungbu, purposely broke the swallow's leg, and repaired it with a bandage. Then, when the swallow brought him a gourd seed, he planted it and opened the fruit. However, strange things and dung came out, and it was a great big mess.

This is a story that was written by man. The stories written by man pretty much follow this kind of storyline. When my kids were young, there was a movie playing in the theater called *Mazinger Z*. My kids wanted to see it so much, so I took them to the theater. I watched the *Mazinger Z* movie and learned the whole thing. In children's movies like *Mazinger Z*, there's a main character who is the good guy and stands up for what's right. Then there's the villain. In the beginning it looks like the villain is going to win, but in the end *Mazinger Z* is victorious. This is also true with the movies *The Eagle Five* and *Galaxy Express 999*.

We cannot make up stories like we find in the Bible with the brain of man. All other storylines are the same. Nowadays, I don't watch cartoons so I don't really know about children's cartoons. But when I do watch them, the beginning always sees the good guys going through hardships and the villains giving the good guys a hard time. Yet, at the very end, the good guys win. The scriptwriters cannot come up with a script that breaks this box.

A long time ago, I watched a wrestling match on TV. A wrestler named Kim-Il had a match against a Japanese wrestler. The Japanese wrestler committed so many fouls that Kim-Il was half-dead. Even I was thinking, "Man, will he recover from this?" That's how badly he was beaten up. I was thinking, "Oh, no. Kim-Il is defeated." But then Kim-Il got up all weak and wobbly and approached the Japanese wrestler. Then, holding the Japanese wrestler, he did his special move, which was the head-butt. All of a sudden, the Japanese wrestler fell backwards. Kim-Il then gave multiple head-butts to the Japanese wrestler's shins, so he couldn't get up. Now the Korean cheering teams were cheering, applauding, and getting excited. That's when the match ended, and wrestler Kim-Il put on his belt and waved excitedly.

Later, I found out that wrestling is all pre-scripted. In Korea, the wrestling match always followed the storyline. I heard that in Japan it was Kim-Il who committed the fouls and threatened to beat the Japanese wrestler, but at the last second the Japanese wrestler won and made all the audience happy. I don't know if that's true or not. Whatever man makes, whether it be cartoon movies, or novels, or wrestling, it's the good guys who win. If you do good things you get blessed, and if you do bad things you get cursed.

However, when we read the Bible, the very interesting thing is that there is not one story of somebody doing good things and getting blessed. Look for it. There's none. On the other hand, there are so many people who do evil things and get blessed. These are people like Apostle Paul who persecuted and killed so many Christians, and the thief at the cross who also got saved. It is completely different from the perspectives that we hold.

Everyone, the reason behind your spiritual life not working out so well is because you say, "I'm going to church. I'm not going to commit sins. I am going to be good and truthful. If I give offering, read the Bible, and keep the law, then I will be blessed." It is because you hold that kind of perspective. That's how the Bible sounds when you just read it outwardly, but if you enter deeply into the Bible, it looks completely different. When you read the Bible outwardly you cannot see the heart of man.

If I say, "How are you, Brother? How are you, Sister?" and politely greet you, then I appear holy right? And on top of that, my hair is all white. But inside I'm not like that; I'm neither honest nor clean. I'm filthy. That's why I rely on God. Unless God upholds me, I quickly fall into sin. Unless God upholds my heart, there are plenty of chances for me to truly fall into temptation and to become evil and corrupt. That's why, even now, I do not trust myself. I can only trust in God. Even in my eyes, I'm a very terrible, pathetic human being, but I can see that God is always together with me. Why is that? Through the sin offering that Jesus gave, all of my dirty, filthy sins were washed whiter than the snow. That's why.

In the eyes of God, the sins that I've committed are no longer sins. Because the judgment is already finished, the sin has lost its effectiveness. Hallelujah! It's not that I'm perfect that I can stand before God. Although I have blemishes and am lacking, by the grace of the cross of Jesus, even today, I come boldly before God. He hears my prayers and works upon me.

Administration Officer, Remove Him

Everyone, if you receive the forgiveness of sins here, then little by little, you will get to experience this kind of a spiritual life. If you study the Word a little more at our church and if you get to know this world a little more, then you'll learn something very amazing. You will learn that even though you are lacking, God takes care of all the problems that arise in you.

Once, when I was in the army, I was walking back to the barracks with some colleagues of mine. The commander of the training camp was walking towards us, so the three of us saluted him. The commander received our salute, walked a bit, and then called us, "Guys! You guys get over here." We ran back to him and once again saluted him loudly.

"Salute! ROC First Class, Private Ock Soo Park and two others are here reporting to you, sir!"

Behind the commander was the aide-de-camp, and the commander asked the aide-de-camp, "Aide-de-camp, is it possible to award even cadets-in-training?"

"Yes, it is possible, sir."

"Award these guys. They gave a good salute." It's a given that you have to salute the commander, but that day, the commander's heart opened. We returned to our barracks and laughed so much about this. We got to go on a four-day vacation and at a meeting in front of all of the soldiers we received an award.

"Private Ock Soo Park, the above-mentioned person, has demonstrated an excellent mindset of an excellent soldier, etc. and for this he is rewarded." It said all kinds of good things.

The communications training center where I served had neither a chapel nor a military chaplain. So although I was just a soldier in training, I led the church service there. One day, I was giving a sermon when the back door opened and the commander came in. I was so shocked that I stopped for a moment, but the commander told us, "Continue the religion." I felt so nervous with the commander sitting there so I quickly finished my sermon.

The commander then stood up from his seat and began to speak to us: "I don't know since when you guys have been doing this religion but, neither the night-duty officers nor day-duty officers have reported to me that this was going on. It was very heartbreaking to me, upon coming to this base, that there was no church here. This is great! Let's build a chapel together!"

The commander and I began to build a chapel together, but there were no construction materials at the base at all. So, every day we would take five trucks and go to Munmak, which is 18 miles away from Wonju. We'd get truckloads of sand, deliver them to the brick factory, and they would give us 20 bricks for that. That's how we gathered the bricks and built the chapel. As we built the chapel, the commander and I became very close.

At that time, it was the middle of the Vietnam War, so many soldiers who specialized in communications were killed in combat. Because I was a part of the first class trained at the communications training center, I was always selected as one of the soldiers to be sent to Vietnam. Once, I was selected to be sent to Vietnam, so I went to report this to the commander. "Now I've been dispatched to Vietnam."

"Oh, you're going to go to Vietnam?" he asked.

"Yes, sir!" I replied.

"Hey! Administration Officer, remove him." I then returned to my company.

The company commander asked me, "Hey! Why are you back here?"

"The commander told me not to go," I replied.

"Do you know the commander? Are you related to the commander somehow?"

"Yes. He is the commander and I am the subordinate."

"Hey, don't say that. Tell me what relationship you have with him." From then on, the way the company commander looked at me completely changed. He must have thought, "Ah, because he has the commander behind him he's acting sly and not telling me." Perhaps that's what he thought. From then on the commander was good to me, the company commander was good to me, and the training officers at the training department where I worked were also good to me. My military life was very comfortable.

During the three years that I served at the communication training center, we would receive new soldiers every Saturday. Every weekend, new trainees would come and old trainees would go. For those three years, God allowed me to gather the recruits there, lead services, and preach the Gospel to them.

The Reason Your Spiritual Life Does Not Work Out Is Because You Do So Well

Everyone, it's not that we must try hard to do something well. It's not that we have to be faithful. It's not that we have to be truthful. Even though we're just a disaster, the blood of Christ has made us perfect so that we may lack nothing. That's the fact that we must believe in. No matter how faithful we are, it's not as good as the blood of Jesus.

My loyalty, my effort, my diligence, my offering, and no matter what else I bring forward cannot even compare to one drop of the blood of Jesus. On the other hand, even though I'm filthy and dirty, and even if I'm the most wicked villain in the world, when I rely on the blood of Jesus, I am clean. When you rely on the blood of Jesus, you are also clean. Our holiness is in the blood of Jesus, it's not in our works.

The Lord was always together with me. When I lived in the army, I felt in my heart that, "If this is going to be my army life, then I wouldn't mind living the rest of my life as a private in the army."

Other people say, "I'm so sick and tired of this army," and they frown, get together, and share their complaints and grief about the army. However, I was happy every day. One day, I was beaten by a senior recruit six times on my bottom with a hoe. It was New Years Day and almost everyone had gone out on vacation. Only a few of us had remained in the barracks, but among us, a private had gotten drunk and had beaten up a corporal.

The senior officers came and said, "What's happened to the order here at the communications training camp? On your stomachs!" Then they lined us up and did what was called a "chain beating." A "chain beating" is where they'd make you stand up according to your rank while the most senior recruit takes the stick part of the hoe and strikes each person once. Then the next highest senior recruit takes his turn hitting everybody, and then the next senior takes his turn, and so on. So, the lowest ranking recruit has to stay there and get hit by everybody. That day, as I got hit three times, I thought that three times was just about right. It hurt so badly. After the fourth time I thought, "If this continues, I may go unconscious. Should I keep getting hit like this or should I run away? Should I stand up to my seniors and ask them why are they doing this?"

It hurt so bad that all kinds of thoughts went through my mind. But the amazing thing is that, right then, I thought about the suffering of Jesus as He hung on the cross. So without me even knowing it, I just simply smiled. As my senior was about to hit me, he saw me smiling. "You punk!" he shouted, "Are you smiling? Are you messing with me?"

"No, no!" I replied. Without me even realizing it, I had a smile on my face, and it almost cost me more strikes. Luckily, however, he only hit me once and passed by. After getting hit the sixth time I thought, "I can't take this anymore," but fortunately that was the end for me. The guys who were of lesser rank than I, were hit seven times, eight times, and even nine times.

I was so joyful as I lived in the army because I spent my time there together with Jesus. While I was in the army for three years, I not once went out or slept outside of the base. So, I never had any reason to spend any money. Plus, every Saturday the new recruits would come in. I would find out which of them were Christians, make a list, and prepare service. Then on Sundays I would have to lead the service and give a sermon. So, I was always on the base. It was so joyful. After service, I would ask the recruits who wanted counseling to raise their hands. And every week about ten people or so would remain, and I would preach the Gospel to them.

I didn't live a life that was fitting of me, but through the grace of God, the Lord led me to live a Jesus-like life. My life was so amazing. Who gets to live that kind of a spiritual life? A person who does not do well gets to live that kind of spiritual life. The reason you're unable to live a spiritual life is because you do too well. Remember the door of the chapel that I talked about earlier? All you need to do is just leave that door open wide. However, the calm, polite people want to forcefully close it, so it makes the, "Slam!" sound. The problem is that they're trying too hard to be quiet.

When God saved us, we were filthy, lustful, riotous, and evil people. That's the kind of person who God set his standard on. Yet, you're trying to not become the villain. Instead you're trying to be good people. You're unable to become good, your spiritual life doesn't work out, you're not this, you're not that, and you're in pain. It's difficult and you become ashamed.

I meet people and I ask them, "Are you good at tennis?"

"I'm not that bad," they say.

"Are you good at soccer?"

"Sure. When I was younger I used to play soccer for my school."

"Are you good at golf?"

"Yeah, I golf pretty well." When I ask about those kinds of things they confidently answer that they're good. But they don't feel that way about spiritual life.

"How is your spiritual life?"

"Sigh."

Whenever I asked about how one's spiritual life was, I never met one person who said, "Oh, it's not that bad."

I haven't even met anybody who says, "Well, I'm not that great, but I'm not that bad either." I've met people who are good at golf. There are many people who are good at tennis. There are many people who are good at swimming. There are many people who are good at soccer. Yet, they all answer that they are short in spiritual life. Why is that? It's because they don't know the principle of spiritual life.

Salvation was not made for the good, the clean, the honest, the holy, or the truthful person. The path of salvation is open for the evil, the filthy, the dirty, the lustful, the deceitful, and the wicked. That's why good people cannot enter through the doors of salvation. Even the truthful, clean people cannot enter through it. One must be evil, must be dirty, must be filthy, and must be lustful to enter into the doors of salvation. Many churches today teach spiritual life backwards. Even though people believe for 10, 20, 30, or even 40 years, they're still unable to live the upright and proper spiritual life. They are confident about everything else, yet they always say that they lack in spiritual life. It is because they look at themselves.

Older Brother, I Am a Good Son

When my father was close to passing away, my older brother was in Japan when he heard that our father's life was in danger. He wanted to get on a plane and come, but there weren't any seats available on the flights.

So instead, he took a boat to come. However, when he arrived, Father had already passed away. After the funeral was over I told my older brother, "Older brother, I'm a good son," and he was very shocked.

I guess he must have been so stunned, as he asked me, "You're a good son?"

"Yes, older brother. I'm a good son." As my older brother was the eldest son, he so sincerely served our father. I've never seen as good a son as my older brother was; he was really good to my father. Nowadays, people don't set up a special room for the coffin, but my older brother insisted that we do it.

I told my older brother, "Older brother, when Father was passing away he received salvation first and then passed away. Father went to heaven. Must we set up that room for the coffin?" Do you know what my older brother said to me?

"Little brother, listen. I understand that this is really useless. And I know that even if I set up the food there and pray there, that Father is not going to come and eat it. But I was such a bad son to our father. So, if I at least do this, maybe my guilt of being a bad son will disappear a little bit. So please understand me." When my older brother said that, I couldn't say anything. So, he set up the room for the coffin. Afterwards, on the first day of the month, and also on the mornings of the days with the full moon, he would go to mourn and grieve. That was the kind of good son my older brother was and that was how he served our father.

I was young, and all I did was make my father worry. Also, after receiving salvation, I was always away from the family. However, since my older brother was in Japan, our father stayed with me at my house before he passed away. It was at that time that he received salvation. So, I boasted saying I'm a good son because I had guided Father to heaven.

More than my older brother serving our father his whole life, how I served my father for one month was much more precious and better served because my father got to receive salvation and go to heaven. God had made me into a good son. Even in front of my family I say that I'm a good son. I guided him into eternal heaven. "Father received salvation and went to heaven," I say. I am like this in all things; it didn't work out through me doing it, but God made me into the good son. God made me into a pastor.

God made me work for the Gospel.

Although I'm just a pathetic human being, all of this was done through God. None of it was done through me. If it weren't for God, I would just be living in darkness, as a complete lowlife, a person who would fall deep into sin.

Jesus Is the Only One that God Accepts

In the world, they give scholarships to students who study well and awards to people who do good. There's no place that gives blessings and grace to people who are evil, filthy and dirty. However, the world of God is different from this world. God takes the filthy, dirty, deceitful, evil, lustful, pitiful human beings, and He makes them clean and pure. He then has them to sit in the holy heaven with Him. That is why we don't need to do anything well to come before the throne of God.

Everyone, do not try to do well. Even though you have tried, didn't you fail?

Everyone, did you keep all the laws? Did you consistently tithe? Is the core of your heart really clean? Do you not have evil, filth, deceit, and lust in your heart?

What I'm saying is, that's how you are, so do not act like you're clean. Do not act like you're living truthfully, but rather throw this fake, hypocritical life away.

You must come before God, saying, "God, I am dirty, filthy, lustful, and deceitful. I am unable. God, you must do it. The only way is in your hands, God."

Then God can work.

I came to clearly know that I was unable. When I preach sermons at my church, I have never once preached that people should be loyal, because that is not something you can become by trying. In the same way, you cannot love just by trying to love.

Once, when I was in Daejeon, a sister got remarried. The man, who was to be her husband, had a daughter from a previous marriage. I was with their family, talking with them when that sister said to that daughter, "I will treat you as if you're my real daughter."

I told that sister, "Stop lying." That sister was a bit startled. I said to that sister, "How can a stepmother treat her stepdaughter as if she was the real mother. That is impossible, that would be a lie."

That sister was startled, and she asked, "What am I supposed to say?"

"What are you supposed to say? Say, 'Haven't you seen Cinderella? In it there is a stepmother. I am that stepmother. I cannot treat you like I'm your real mother, so don't even expect that from me. I don't know how I ended up raising somebody else's child and I don't know how you ended up not getting raised by your real mother. But anyhow, don't ever expect me to be like a real mother. I can never, ever do that. I can try, but don't expect me to be like your real mother. Is that clear?'"

I told her to just be straight forward and honest. People have no idea how difficult it is to raise somebody else's child. Even if the stepmother treats the child well in 100 or even 1,000 things, if the child feels mistreated with just one thing, the child will not open his heart. The child will think, "She treats me like that because she's not my real mother."

Even if the real mother says all kinds of harsh words like, "You little punk! You little rascals, listen! What's wrong with you?" The child at the end of the day will still say, "Mommy," and run to her.

However, that's not the case with somebody else's child. No matter how good that stepmother is to that child, if the child does not open his heart, it just exhausts that mother.

One day, after my children were all grown, my wife said to me, "Honey, how about if we adopt maybe two kids from the orphanage and raise them?"

I said to her, "You, raise somebody else's child? Even with your own children, all you ever did was spank them day and night and yell at them." Ever since I said that, she would stop talking about it whenever I brought it up.

I really have so much respect for people who raise other people's children. Some people may say this and that about them, but it really is a tremendously difficult thing to do to raise somebody else's child. We must all be honest.

Everyone, a stepmother can never do as a real mother does. The stepmothers that we hear about in folk tales did not act the way they did because they wanted to. They also wanted to be good people in their second marriage, but that was just how they ended up becoming. That is how we humans truly are.

God knew that humans could not do any good. God knew that through man's power, man could not overcome evil and temptation. God knew that sin could not be washed away through the efforts of man. That's why God sent Jesus! You must completely rely upon Jesus for you to become good, for you to become holy, for you to become righteous, for you to become powerful, and for you to be blessed. All of that must be done only through Jesus.

If there is anyone of you who thinks, "I fasted for 40 days. I went to early morning prayer service every day. I did overnight prayers. I sold my house to build the chapel. I cared for the orphans. God loves me because I did all of these things," you will be thrown away. God does not love us because we did those kinds of things.

Man is dirty and evil to begin with. God does not care for prayer, hymns, and offerings that come from man. He only cares if it is something that's done through the inspiration of God in your heart, and if it is done not through you, but through Jesus. God receives it when it is done only though Jesus.

The Bible says that in the judgment, on the last day, certain people will say to Jesus, "Lord, Lord, in thy name we have prophesied, and in your name we have cast out devils and we have spoken in tongues in your name."

Right then, Jesus will not even look at them, and He will say, "I never knew you." Why is this? The reason is because it was they, who acted as prophets, cast out devils and spoke in tongues. Jesus does not care for these wonderful things that they did. When we come before God there is only one thing that God accepts. God only accepts Jesus. And the only offering without blemish in front of God is Jesus. That is why we must bring forth what Jesus did.

"Hey, how did you come to heaven?"

"I did these good things, I acted as a prophet, I cast out devils and I did many wonderful works." Then that person will go to hell.

"Hey, how did you go to heaven?"

"Well I'm just a bundle of sin, but didn't Jesus make me clean through His blood on the cross?" That person can surely go to heaven.

"You received a reward, so how did you receive that reward?"

"God, I'm nothing but a fraud, a drug addict, a thief, but Jesus changed me and He did all the work and He had me receive the golden crown. I am so thankful." That is the correct spiritual life.

People who say, "Because I did well, because I became a pastor, because I held revivals, and gave sermons, and led many people to believe Jesus, because I ministered well, and the congregation grew..." Such people must enter into the pits of hell. Read the Bible everyone.

Where does it say, "I" the most in the Bible? It is Romans chapter 7 verse 18. It continuously says, "I and my, I and my." That is why, what does it say at the end?

Romans chapter 7 verse 24. If it continually says, "I" then it heads towards emptiness and towards destruction.

Even in the story of the prodigal son, the end result of all the work the younger son did was heading towards death and destruction. But the result of the work that the father did was glory. These two are clearly divided. Look at the work that the younger son did: eating and hanging out with the harlots and living riotously, and then going to the pig pen and eating of the husks that the swine fed on. But, when the father begins to work, the younger son is made clean and becomes blessed.

"Bring forth the best robe and put it on him. Put a ring on his hand, put shoes on his feet, and kill the fatted calf." So are the works of the father.

Lord, I Was Terribly Wrong. I Have No Confidence in Raising My Daughter Well

Everyone, do not try to do well. Allow the Lord to do the work. I am a pastor. I thought about how I can minister well at the Good News Gangnam Church, where I serve. Today, I had an interview with a newspaper. They told me to say something about the churches in Korea today. Do you know what I said? There is no room for Jesus in Korean churches today. There is room for the chairman of the association. There is room for the chairman of the elderly association. There is room for the pastor. But because everyone just uses their own methods, there is no room for Jesus to stand. When we listen to what the Korean churches talk about, there is no Word about what Jesus did, but it's all about who did what and how well they did it. That's all they talk about. As I see these things, I don't want Pastor Ock Soo Park to stand in this church; I want Jesus to work, so that I can rest. That is why I can truly rest.

Once I went for a health check-up and the doctor asked me what my occupation was. I told him that I was a pastor.

"Oh, Pastor, it must be so difficult the work you do. It must be so difficult for you to prepare sermons."

"No, it's not hard at all."

"No, I'm sure it is. It must be so difficult and hard work for you to care for all of your church members."

"No, well, it's not hard at all."

"But still, I'm sure it must be very, very difficult."

Really, everyone, it's not hard for me at all. I don't try hard to prepare my sermons well. What do I do well? There's nothing I can do well.

Once, I went on a visit to the home of one of our church members. I don't even know our church members' names or where they all live. Now, the number of church members has increased so much, I know even fewer now than I did before. When I say hello to them, I often get confused who's who. I often feel so guilty about this. I once went on a home visit and it was very graceful. I thought, "From now on, I should go on home visits more often," but it didn't go as planned.

Once, I read the Bible all day long and I thought, "Wow, this Bible is amazing. From now on, I should put everything aside and just read the Bible." But after one day, it didn't go so well. Another time, I got together with the elders of our church and we fasted and prayed together. It was so graceful to get together and pray. I thought, "Wow, we should get together and fast more often," but that also didn't go so well. There's nothing I can do well.

Because I know that I am lacking, I hand over the position of pastor to Jesus. The shepherd of this church is not Pastor Ock Soo Park, but Jesus. People do not understand this very well, so they call Pastor Ock Soo Park the pastor. But actually, it's not me who is at work, but Jesus.

When I was young, I thought about the aspect of raising my kids. When I would visit other people's homes and see kids acting rude, I would think, "Gee, why did they raise their kids like that? They should have raised them upright." I made up my mind that after I get married and have kids, I would raise my kids to be upright. Not long after getting married, my wife gave birth to a very beautiful daughter. She was so cute and so pretty.

One day, after I came home from witnessing, I saw that my lovely daughter's hand was wrapped in a bandage. I asked my wife, "Honey, what happened to Eunsook?" That day, my daughter was playing at the neighbor's house and the kids pushed my daughter. In the countryside, houses have doors that connect the rooms to the kitchen. That door swung open and my daughter fell on top of the furnace and was burnt. That night I held my daughter and I prayed, "God, please let Eunsook be quickly healed and do not allow any scars to remain." While I prayed, there was a heart that came to me.

"You think you can raise your kids upright? What were you doing when your daughter fell on top of the charcoal furnace?"

I was completely shocked. I could not protect my daughter from falling on top of the charcoal furnace. But I had thought that I could raise my daughter well. Right then and there, I turned from the heart that I had. I said, "Lord, I was truly wrong, I have no confidence in protecting my daughter well. Lord, may you raise her." From then on, I trusted my kids to the Lord. My wife and I were really busy running around over the years and now our kids are all grown. Whether it is raising kids or the works of the church, I did not do anything at all. The Lord did them all.

Everyone, once you get to know the Lord, and once you get to know who you are, you will change. If you get to know how pitiful you are, you will be unable to think that you did something well. Thinking that you did well is exactly like Peter thinking that he will not deny Jesus, even if he were to be put to death. Peter said that he would not deny Jesus even unto death, but that very night, he denied Jesus three times. That is the result of the determination and the effort of man. If you know you're weak, then you have no choice but to rely on our Lord. Then the grace of God comes upon you. You realize that the grace of God is upon you when you truly realize how powerless and unable you are.

Gave the Eternal Offering at the Temple in Heaven

Today, in Hebrews chapter 9 verse 11 we read, *But Christ being come an high priest of good things to come, by a greater and more perfect tabernacle, not made with hands.* Here, what does this tabernacle that is not made with hands represent? The priests of the old days gave offerings at the altar made with hands, and at the holy place made with hands, and at the ark made with hands. But Jesus gave the offering at the temple in heaven, which was not made from the hands of man. When God created the world, he set a limit to the earth so that it would not last forever.

The earth is limited by time and limited by temperature. That's why this earth belongs to the realm of time, whereas God is eternal. There is nothing eternal on earth. Gold changes and diamonds also change. If you go to the Gyeongju Museum, you can see that all of the golden crowns, all of the golden furnishings from the Shilah Dynasty are rusted. People say that gold does not change.

What that actually means, is that it does not change relative to other things. There is nothing on earth that does not change. If something changes, that means it, too, will ultimately disappear.

On the other hand, heaven is eternal. That is why when you give an offering on earth to wash away sins, it cannot be an eternal offering. But the offering must be given at the temple of heaven in order to wash away sins eternally.

Jesus gave His own blood and did not enter the tabernacle on earth, but rather into the greater and more perfect tabernacle which is the temple in heaven. He put the blood on the horns of the altar at that temple and he sprinkled his blood at the mercy seat to redeem us of our sins forever. The offerings given on this earth forgive the sins for that moment. But the offering that is given in heaven forgives sins eternally. Let's read from Hebrews chapter 10 verses 10 and 11. *By the which will we are sanctified through the offering of the body of Jesus Christ once for all. And every priest standeth daily ministering and offering oftentimes the same sacrifices, which can never take away sins.*

In the Old Testament, the offerings given at the altar made with hands could never take away sins, but rather only wash away their sins for that moment. In verse 12, *But this man, after he had offered one sacrifice for sins for ever, sat down on the right hand of God.*

There is no eternal redemption on this earth. It is because this earth belongs to the realm of time. To wash sins away forever, it must be done in heaven. That is why Jesus took His blood and went to the temple in heaven to wash away our sins forever. There, He put His blood on the altar and sprinkled His blood on the mercy seat.

But Christ being come an high priest of good things to come, by a greater and more perfect tabernacle, not made with hands; that is to say, not of this building. (Hebrews 9:11)

This chapel that we're gathered in is built with hands, the temple of Jerusalem was built with hands, the temple of Solomon was also built with hands. The temple that is not built with hands is the temple in heaven. The blood of goats and calves or lambs redeemed sins of this earth, but in that temple it was Jesus' own blood that fulfilled the eternal redemption. That redemption is everlasting. If redemption is not eternal, it's meaningless. Why?

Because people sin again even if their sins are forgiven. Unless the redemption is eternal, people will always become sinners again and go to hell. That is why the only true redemption is eternal redemption. All redemption, other than the true redemption, is meaningless. Even if sins were washed every day, people still sin every day and become sinners again. If so, then they must go to hell. That is why we can only be saved if eternal redemption is fulfilled. People say whatever they want, saying, "Jesus washed my original sins, but our daily sins, we have to wash them away." There are also people who say, "Jesus washed my past sins, but the future sins I must wash away." That is complete nonsense. How could we, who are so dirty, wash sins away? It is Jesus who must wash sins away.

Your sins are eternally washed! All of your sins! Do you understand? Now, stop trying to do this yourself. Just believe that Jesus achieved the eternal redemption for you. Believe that in your heart. If that faith comes upon your heart, God is with you. Not because you did something, but because the blood of the cross washed your sins away. If in this week, you receive the forgiveness of sins, there is nothing that can come between you and God. You will be forever together with Jesus Christ, and all the problems and hardships that you go through will become, not yours, but Jesus' problems. That is why we praise the Lord and glorify God.

CHAPTER 10
For the Law Maketh Men High Priests, Which Have Infirmity

The priests of the Old Testament gave offerings every day. Those offerings had to be given continually because they only washed the sins away that were committed right then, right there. But Jesus does not need to do that because He achieved eternal redemption. He completed the sin offering once and for all. That is why we no longer need to give the sin offering. The effect of the offering that Jesus gave is eternal. The blood that He shed 2,000 years ago is powerful and alive today. It will continue to be forever, whether thousands or tens of thousands of years pass.

Today, we will read from Hebrews chapter 7 verse 22.

By so much was Jesus made a surety of a better testament. And they truly were many priests, because they were not suffered to continue by reason of death: But this man, because he continueth ever, hath an unchangeable priesthood. Wherefore he is able also to save them to the uttermost that come unto God by him, seeing he ever liveth to make intercession for them. For such an high priest became us, who is holy, harmless, undefiled, separate from sinners, and made higher than the heavens; Who needeth not daily, as those high priests, to offer up sacrifice, first for his own sins, and then for the people's: for this he did once, when he offered up himself. For the law maketh men high priests which have infirmity; but the word of the oath, which was since the law, maketh the Son, who is consecrated for evermore. (Hebrews 7:22-28)

The Discovery of the Fuse

There was an inventor in the United States. When he died, he left behind assets worth about 2 billion dollars. At that time, President Junghee Park of Korea was trying to reform the economy, but there was no money. The United States sponsored Korea with one hundred million dollars each year as an economic stimulus. President Park said that if the United States could sponsor three years' worth in one payment, it would be extremely helpful in reviving the economy and he sincerely requested that. Our country was seeking 3 hundred million dollars to revive and strengthen the economy. We can see how rich this man was, because he had a personal wealth of 2 billion dollars. We can see how rich he was.

How did this man make all of his money? He was making an electronic product and plugged it to test it. Then, all of a sudden, there was an burst of electricity and there was a, "POP!" and it began to smoke and smell. He was completely shocked and thought the whole machine was fried. But when he carefully disassembled the machine, it was unexpectedly fine. He thought, "Surely, it popped and had smoke coming out of it. How can this machine still be fine?" When he looked closely at the circuitry of the machine, there was a weak part that has been soldered together. But when there was an overcharge of the electricity, the lead melted and the electricity was blocked out from surging through the rest of the machine. That's why the machine remained protected. He realized that electrical products should not be strong all throughout, but rather one part of it should remain weak so that the part will melt when there is a surge of electricity. The weak part can safely protect the machine.

Through much research, he mixed lead with tin. He made them very thin and installed them into the machines, so whenever there was a surge of the electricity, that part would melt and cut off the electricity from the rest of the machine. He called this invention the fuse and patented it.

It was a very simple concept but nobody else had invented something like this before. All the large electronic companies in the world had to pay this man royalties to install the fuse into their products. Through this one invention, this man became tremendously rich and left behind 2 billion dollars worth of assets when he died.

But he was miserable. He died in solitaire in a hotel room. He had a bad relationship with his family. Because he had so much money, his family wanted to take his money and indulge. Through these kinds of problems, disharmony came about and ultimately his family members broke ties with him. He was found when his employee visited his room after not hearing from him for weeks. This was a very controversial incident at that time.

Everyone, we think that every part of an electrical product should be without blemish and perfect for it to be protected. But that is not the case. The fuse was purposely made weak so that it would melt when there's a surge of electricity. Now, this fuse is used everywhere. Your refrigerator, washers, TV's, and air conditioners all have the fuse. A car has multiple fuses. There is a separate fuse for the headlights, horn, wipers, and radio. It is the fuse that protects the electronic products in the car.

How Spiritual He Would Have Been if He Knew the Bible on Top of His Brilliance

Most people just live spiritual life with the first thought that comes to mind. But if they think deeper, spiritual life becomes very easy and fun. I mentioned cars a little earlier. When Korea first made a sedan, called the Sephia, Korea was unable to build engines. The Kia car company had built factories, but they had to purchase engines from Japan because they could not build their own. They had a contract with a Japanese company that built engines. They said, "We will buy many engines from you, but you must later on teach us the technology to build these engines." That company agreed and Kia bought the Japanese engines to build their cars.

Time passed and they wanted to build their own engines, but they did not have the skill or technology back then to build engines. This was not too long ago. The chairman of the Korean car company asked the chairman of the Japanese car company to teach him the technology to build engines.

He said, "We have bought many engines from you till now, so please, teach us how to build the engines."

"That's not so easy. Your technology is insufficient for you to do it on your own right now."

"Please teach us, we can do it."

"I told you, no. You still have a long way to go."

"So when will you teach us?"

"Just wait a little more."

He had no choice but to have more patience and wait. After some more time passed, he felt that it was time and he once again went to the chairman of the Japanese auto company to ask him to teach him the technology. He said, "Now, we've bought so many engines from you. Won't you teach us how to build the engines?"

"You people are so arrogant! Why do you think that you are able to build the engines? It is not time yet for you to build engines."

The chairman of the Korean company became angry and said, "If that's how you really feel, we will make our own engines."

Right then, the chairman of the Japanese company laughed and said, "If you build your own engines, do you think the cars with those engines are actually going to run?"

The chairman of the Korean auto company got so angry, he said, "What did you just say?" He pulled out his notepad and right there he wrote, "Do you think that the cars with the engines you build are actually going to run?"

He came back to Korea and called all his employees together. He said, "I just spoke with the chairman from Japan, and he said to me, 'Do you think that cars with the engines you build are actually going to run?'—Everyone, take out your notepads and write down those very words, and post it on the front of your desks. Let's build our cars and see if they really do run or not." So, the Sephia is the first car that had the Korean-made engine. And ran very well. Japan was shocked.

Afterwards, the Korean technology to build engines has advanced much and now Mitsubishi, a Japanese car company, uses Korean engines. Mitsubishi builds cars, and they build their own engines that are similar to that of Hyundai. But the Hyundai engines consume less gas and remain strong for a long period of time even if the car is heavily used. But Japan is unable to make the same quality of Korean engines at the same cost. The people of Japan were so shocked to see this. They thought, "These Korean companies are always having disputes with labor unions, but these days, how are they able to produce such good cars?" I heard that nowadays, the Japanese cars really struggle competing with the Korean cars. Even in America, I heard it was the Japanese auto companies that are most afraid of the Korean cars emerging in the American market.

When we see these things, we can see that Koreans are really smart. It is almost a problem that they are so quick and sharp. When we meet foreigners, it makes us feel how quick and sharp Koreans are with their thinking. If Koreans, with such sharpness and intelligence, read the Bible, they would be the most spiritual people in the world. Honestly, Pastor Ock Soo Park doesn't know the Bible much. I only know very little. But the reason Pastor Ock Soo Park can stand here and preach is because others know even less. People do not read the Bible, so they do not know the world of the Bible.

The car industry develops day by day. When Korea first developed the Pony car and when it was exported to America, the Koreans living abroad thought, "Wow, a Korean car finally entered the American market." They hugged each other and cried. Even then, which was not too long ago, Korea was rock bottom. But now the reputation of Korean car companies is very good. When Korea first made cars, many people argued, saying, "It costs too much to build cars. Why don't we just purchase cars that are made abroad? What skill do we have to make our own cars?" But we can see how much this has developed today. Koreans are indeed very smart.

This is also true with electronics. Japan used to manufacture the world-best electronic products. Sony was the most admired electronic brand in the world. Samsung made a TV and exported it to Japan. If you go to an electronics shopping district in Japan, all the Japanese products would be out there on display and all the Samsung TVs would be sitting in the corner collecting dust and nobody would even look at them. That was just a few years ago. But now, Samsung has exceeded Sony and some people say that Sony will never be able to catch up to Samsung. Sony does not have any noticeable buildings in Korea, but there is a big Samsung building in the middle of Tokyo. When you exit the Narita airport and on the way to Tokyo, there is a big Samsung neon sign on a huge building, flashing at you. Not only has Samsung grown so much, but all of the electronic companies of Korea have been doing well. Nowadays, if you go to airports in other countries you can see that all home electronics have been taken over by either LG or Samsung. This is true even for cell phones. Cell phones made in Korea used to be huge, but now people all over the world enjoy using the Samsung Galaxy phones.

It is rare to find a country with highways as advanced as Korea. Most of the land in America is flat, so it's easier to build roads there. In Korea, however, there are many mountains and valleys, so it is not easy to build roads. Even so, the Korean people say, "We don't care if it's a mountain or a valley or whatever it is, let's go through the mountains and build bridges over the valleys."

My hometown is Gyeongbuk Seonsan and I often drive on the Joongbu Inland Expressway. This freeway runs through the Mungyeong Sejae, which is known for having rugged hills. They built roads in these kinds of areas and I often drive there. If I speed, it takes me a little less than two hours to get to my hometown.

They had an IQ test for people all over the world, Hong Kong scored the highest and Korea was second. Hong Kong is not a country but a city. So in terms of countries, it means that Koreans are the brightest.

Everyone, with that intelligence you have, if you read the Bible a little bit, you would become biblical leaders to the whole world.

I recently went to Kenya. Many people in Kenya thought, "What pastor from a Buddhist country would come here and hold a conference?" Because they are all Christians, they believe that they are on the cutting edge of Christianity and think of themselves as a country of faith. I recently held a one-week pastor's retreat in Kenya and five hundred Kenyan pastors attended. They were so amazed while listening to the Word. Of those, two hundred pastors decided to join our mission. They asked that we build a school in Kenya to teach them the Bible. So, we established the Mahanaim Bible College. We have about two hundred pastors there learning the Bible. Many pastors from Uganda also came when I recently went to Kenya. They said to me, "Pastor Park, Kenya is too far for us to a come here from

Uganda. There are many pastors in Uganda as well. Why did you establish this college only in Kenya? Please establish a college in Uganda as well."

Many pastors from Tanzania came to me and asked us to hold these kinds of Bible study meetings. Pastors from Rwanda requested these also. Right now there is a big wave of the Gospel in Africa and we are so short on manpower that we don't know what to do. Our mission does not have enough pastors. Next year, we are going to recruit pastors from other churches. We want to put them through a boot camp training and work together with them. There is so much work to do but not enough pastors to do the work.

When You Face Sin, Show the Sin Offering

Everyone, the Bible is so easy and fun. Let me ask you a question. What part of the Bible is so difficult? Genesis? Exodus? Leviticus? Numbers? Deuteronomy?

Even though I can't speak English, I can get by. January of this year, I had a difficult time because I didn't know any English. We were having a Global Camp in Thailand and I was the guest of honor at an evening banquet. There were ministers from Thailand, governors, and ambassadors from the UN. The place was filled with many dignitaries. They all spoke English fluently. I just wanted to be near someone who couldn't. But I was the only one who couldn't speak a word of English. I had much regret, thinking, "I should have learned English." Now, because I'm so old, even though learn one word, I forget another word.

Because I felt such a great shock in Thailand, I went on the Internet and listened to a lecture on learning English. The lecturer said that English is easy and told me not to think too much about it. He said that English is very easy. When I heard that, the first thing I said was, "It's easy for you. What? English? Easy? That makes no sense." That's what I felt in my heart. But that lecture was so easy.

"How do you say, 'I'?"

"I."

"How do you say, 'like'?"

"Like."

"Is that difficult? It's easy. All you have to do is say, 'like' and insert whatever you like to do: I like swimming."

His lecture was very easy. He said English was difficult because people expect to speak English as if they were reading a book. He said to memorize sentences so that they're on the tip of your lips. English is difficult because you only want to study a little bit, but be able to speak very well. But this teacher was telling us to become familiar with the words you already know so that you may freely be able to use them. As I listened to two of his 30-minute lectures, I thought, "He is such a great teacher. If he were a pastor, he would do a much better job than me."

Spiritual life is exactly like that. People try to know everything from Genesis through Revelation. That's why it's complicated and difficult. Everyone, we recently learned about the sin offering. Was it easy or difficult? It was easy. How many years did it take to learn this? Did we study for ten years? No. We just learned it in a few hours. In this way, if we learn step by step, spiritual life is so easy. If you learn about the sin offering this week, it will strengthen your whole life.

Actually, as we live life, it is very difficult to go through it without having anything to do with sin. Sin continually keeps crashing down on us. Isn't that right? Even though we try to avoid it, this thing called sin, keeps bumping and running into us. Everyone, no matter who it is, becomes bruised if he runs into sin. He feels guilty. His will becomes broken. In the newspaper, we see great and powerful people taking bribes and going to prison with handcuffs. You can see that their will is completely broken. Whether it be a minister or a congressman, this is true with any one of them. They can boast when their sin has not been revealed. But once they have their handcuffs on, they try to cover their faces with their clothes.

Without sin, they would live a very bright and joyful life. But sin has made your lives very dark and gloomy. It is sin that has made your lives heavy and painful. But everyone, it does not take much time to learn about the sin offering, nor does it cost a lot of money. Once you precisely learn about this, you can remain confident, even if sin charges at you. When the sin offering is put to a fight against sin, sin has no chance at all. No matter what the sin may be, once the sin offering is made, the sin just dies. You should live this kind of a life. You will see how exciting it is.

The Strange-Looking Brother

There was a certain brother in our church. I once went to the bathroom and there was a woman there. I didn't know what to do. I thought, "Oops! Did I just walk into the women's bathroom?" But it was a brother who had long, curly hair, and was wearing a colorful blouse. So I thought it was a woman. But when he turned around, I realized that it was a man. He came to our church after receiving salvation. The service starts at 10:30 in the morning and he would arrive at 11:30. So, I asked him, "Why are you always late for service?"

He said, "Pastor, I'm sorry. But I play the electric organ at a night business. I finish work at five in the morning. So I get just a little bit of sleep before I come. That's why I'm late."

There was nothing more I could say. I was just thankful enough that he would even come to begin with. One day, this brother came to me and asked, "Pastor, I want to go to Japan to study music."

I said, "Sure. Studying is good." But I was very worried about his spiritual life. I was always thinking, "I want to sit down with that brother and have fellowship with him."

But one day, this brother came to me and said, "Pastor, I'm going to Japan tomorrow."

I was shocked to hear that.

"Oh no! I can't just send this brother to Japan like this." I told him to sit down and asked him to give me his salvation testimony. As I listened to his testimony, it seemed that he was saved, or maybe not. So I opened the Bible and spoke to him about the Gospel. That day was a Sunday and I didn't have much time. I was sad that I did not get to speak to him more. This was a big mistake of mine. I should've talked to him a long when I had a chance. That brother moved to Japan. I thought, "Will that brother be able to live a spiritual life in Japan? No. I failed to lead him."

After some time, his mother came to me and said, "Pastor, my son is in Japan asking me to send him the *Secret of Forgiveness of Sin and Being Born Again* and some other books." I told her to send them immediately and to send many of them.

Then after a while, that brother called me and said, "Pastor, come visit me in Tokyo."

"Why?"

"I've been witnessing and about thirty people have been gathering. Pastor, please come and preach the Word to them."

I couldn't believe it. This strange-looking brother went to Tokyo where he didn't know anyone, and led thirty people or so to salvation? I got on the airplane and went to Tokyo. Indeed, there were thirty people gathered at a small apartment waiting for me.

Before I preached the Word, one sister came to the front and gave a testimony.

"I lived riotously, just like that Samaritan woman a long time ago. But I received salvation."

Then a brother came forward and gave a testimony. "Pastor, I lived like the Samaritan man."

This brother started witnessing at a bar where he worked, in Japan. When Korean college students go to study abroad in Japan, they often get part-time jobs. But if they worked all day long, they would get paid maybe about 8,000 yen. But if they worked at a bar, they can get paid 50,000 yen. That's why students, for the most part, choose to work in bars. That brother, as well, worked at a bar playing the electric organ. He saw that there were these female college students working at the bars. When the customers would ask them to drink, they would drink. These female students, who had gone to church previously, came to Japan to study, but ended up drinking and were so tormented living like this. Then they would grieve, singing, "Nearer my God to thee. Nearer to thee."

This brother was saved, but he did not know how to witness, nor did he know how to preach the Gospel. He saw these other part-time workers suffering. The students were studying in Japan but the cost of living was expensive, so they needed to get part-time jobs. Because they needed jobs, they would end up working at bars. When they worked at bars, they would end up drinking and committing sins. It broke this brother's heart to see them living in this kind of pain.

"I need to share the Gospel with them," he thought.

He knew how to receive the forgiveness of sins, but he did not know how to witness. That is why he called his mother and asked her to send him the *Secret of Forgiveness of Sins and Being Born Again*. He studied that book every day. Then, one day, he called one of the female college students over and asked her if she wanted to talk about the Bible. She was happy to. This brother opened the Bible on the table and kept the *Secret of Forgiveness of Sins and Being Born Again* under the table. He would talk to her for a long while and when he would get stuck, he would open up the book, find his place and speak again. That student listened to the Word and received salvation.

This brother was so amazed. He thought, "Wow, someone received salvation through my witnessing." Even he couldn't believe it. That female student changed so much after receiving salvation. She began to seek the Word and gave her testimony. She would also tell everyone that they needed to get their sins washed away. People would see this and see how much she changed in such a short amount of time. She was the one who used to always sing, "Nearer my God to thee," crying. But now she had completely changed.

In this way, one person got saved, another, and about thirty people had received salvation.

If You Received the Forgiveness of Sins You Would Be Glad to Stand Before Death

Everyone, once you have received the forgiveness of sins, life begins to appear very good. Today, early in the morning, I attended a funeral. Last night, I needed to send a script to a newspaper, and today was the deadline. I had put it off, but I could not any longer, so I wrote it all night long. After I finished, I wanted to get some sleep, but Pastor Sung Hoon Kim told me there was a funeral in the morning. I was so shocked. It surprised me because I had completely forgotten about it. I had to be there at 5:30 in the morning and it was already 5:05. I got in Pastor Sung Hoon Kim's car and went to the Asan Hospital. Fortunately, the roads were clear and we got there very quickly. When we arrived, there were many people sitting, waiting there for me. I was so embarrassed. I preached the Word. I spoke about death.

As people live in the world, some are great, well educated, and smart. But even such things last for a moment in their youth. When people pass the age of 60, they begin to fade away little by little. I'm sorry to say this of the elderly, but it is true. Once people turn 70, they begin to weaken significantly. It means they are getting closer and closer to death.

There is an old Korean poem that says,
"In one hand, a stick
In the other, thorns
You used to block the path of aging with the thorns
And block the grey hair with the stick.
But who knew the grey hairs would take a short cut
And be there before you."

Everyone, people grieve aging, right? The body does not function as well when it begins to age. I'm not that old, but nowadays I could sense my vision is getting worse and worse. That's why I ask people to not use the flash when they take pictures of me. When the camera flashes, I cannot see. As our bodies deteriorate like this, we get closer to the Jordan River of Death, which we will cross one day. When that time comes, we can see even the smartest, greatest, and most famous people tremble before death. It is so pitiful to see people grasping for life in those situations. Death is something we must all experience whether we want to or not. People try to outrun death. But once death catches up to us, it's over.

At the funeral today, I talked about the two paths to death: the eternal path of destruction and the eternal path of heaven. The person who clearly knows the secret of redemption, has received the forgiveness of sins, and is very happy when standing in front of death.

I've spoken about this often. About twenty years ago, when my grandmother passed away, I was hospitalized at the Hanyang University Hospital because of intestinal obstruction. I was hospitalized on Saturday night and was scheduled to receive surgery on Sunday early in the morning. But the surgery was postponed to Monday because there was no specialist at the hospital. It was about ten in the morning on Sunday; I could not go to church, and I was lying on the bed. I can remember, that was the first time I missed Sunday service after receiving salvation. I was lying on the bed and my wife looked down on me with a worried face. At that time, my daughter and son were in elementary school. They tape recorded, "Father, get well," and sent it to me. I listened to it. Before it became lunchtime, I looked at the worried face on my wife and I could see it becoming cloudy.

"Ah, I'm starting to lose it. I'd better snap out of it."

I could see my wife's face fading and getting cloudier. It felt as though I was falling off a cliff. I tried to snap out of it, but it became more and more cloudy. I thought, "Ah, I'm dying right now. Then before I die, let me square some things away." What I'd like to tell you is, though you may not actually stand in front of death, it is good to have your heart stand before death at least once. We have many complications and problems because we think of ourselves to be alive. But when you know that you're going to die, things become very simple. I thought that if I were to stand before death, there would be so many things I would have to settle and square away. But actually, when I thought of doing that, there really was nothing to settle and square away. Things became very simple. I first thought about my church. Because there are many pastors at my church, the church was not a problem. Then I thought about my family. I thought about how my loving wife and children would live after I die. My wife and I had nothing when we got married. But after getting married, God blessed our family so much. I felt that God would not just abandon my family just because I die. So that also was not a problem. Thirdly, I thought, "Then what would happen to my soul?" Everyone, when I considered my own soul in front of death, I felt, "My sins are all forgiven through the blood of Jesus." And I felt this spring of peace, rushing from my heart. I thought, "Soon, I will cross the river of death and enter the city filled with gold and jewels. The blood of Jesus has made me, white as snow even though I am evil and filthy. I will lack nothing to stand before God the Father." In my heart, I just wanted to go there quickly. I wanted to be together with the Lord at the Tree of Life, under its shade, walking by the riverside. I wanted to meet the saints who had gone before me.

Before this, when I thought about death, I thought, "Dying is going to be painful. It's going to be suffering, I'm going to be so scared." But when I actually stood before death, death was so much happiness. That's when I realized how our saints were able to pass. I had seen many saints close their eyes with peaceful faces and take their last breath. I felt, "This is what they must have felt in their hearts. What I feel right now." Everyone, my sins are forgiven! My sins are as white as snow! This fact had never brought so much happiness to my heart, as it had that time. From that time on, I was no longer afraid of death. Before, I thought I would be afraid and in pain when I thought about death. But after clearly learning what the sin offering was and realizing its meaning, that was not the case at all.

Everyone, you too, will all one day stand in front of God. That day is not pre-appointed. Some people pass away at an old age. And some impatient people pass away at a very young age. Anyhow, we will all one day stand before death. Even the great people, the smart people, and the rich people of the world tremble and fear when they stand before death. However, I cannot say, what a blessing it is that we can boldly cross the river of death because the blood of Jesus has washed all our sins away.

Now, God Deems Our Hearts as a Temple and Remains in Us

Everyone, Isn't it worth learning about the sin offering in the Bible? Aren't we so thankful that we can listen to this for one week and learn about it? Because we are weak and lacking people, we may make mistakes. We may commit sins. We may fall. We may fall in trial, and we may crumble. But if we realize what the sin offering is and receive the forgiveness of sins, it's ok even if we fall because we have Jesus falling with us and Jesus lifting us up. Even if there's a storm, we have Jesus to calm the storm. We are fine, even though we have problems because we have Jesus to solve them.

As I have lived for 45 years after becoming born again, I had many unspeakable difficulties before me. But not once have I failed. Every single time, the Lord led me with His grace. Just as I talked about yesterday evening, it's not because of my greatness or my diligence. I'm not just saying this. It's really true that I'm so lacking. It is not through my own righteousness that Jesus is together with me. It is not because of my goodness or truthfulness that Jesus is together with me. I'm nothing but a bundle of sin. Although I'm a bundle of sin, because the sin offering has been accomplished, Jesus lacks nothing and feels no discomfort to abide in me.

The Holy God dwelt at the temple of Jerusalem. But when sin entered the temple, He departed. That is why the temple of Jerusalem crumbled down. The temple that Solomon built all crumbled down. Now, God considers our heart to be the temple and abides there. But if you have sin in your heart, God cannot abide there. For God to abide in your heart, your heart must be holy, without flaw, and without blemish. But how clean did Jesus make us through His crucifixion on the cross? God has made us holy, righteous, and perfect enough for God to have no discomfort in abiding in us. That is so amazing. How could such a thing be done through the power of man? How could that be done through the effort or labor of man? That wouldn't make any sense at all. If you go to the wrong church, they say things contrary to the Bible. They say you have to repent of your sins and ask for your sins to be forgiven. In the future if you commit sins you will be shaken. Surely the devil will then condemn you, saying, "You may not be saved. You might go to hell," and try to shake you up. Then you will be shaken. But when this happens, listen to the sermon tapes from this conference. Take these sermon tapes and allow your family, your relatives, or your grandmothers, or grandfathers who are near death to hear the Word. If they listen to the Word, receive the forgiveness of sins and become born again, imagine how bold they would be in front of death!

A Misconception: You Must Be Good in Order to Go to Heaven

I've met so many people as I give spiritual counseling. When I'm done giving them the explanation about the sin offering, there are these two questions that are most frequently asked. The first question is: Jesus died two thousand years ago. We were not even born back then. Then how could He forgive the sins of us who live today? The second question is: Although Jesus was crucified and forgave us our sins, how can we be clean even when we still sin every day?

As I preach the Gospel to many people and personally give counseling about the forgiveness of sins, there are many people who rejoice and whose lives have been changed. There were also others who could not understand what I was telling them and were unable to believe it in their hearts. So they asked me various kinds of questions. Of them, these two questions are most frequently asked.

"Jesus died two thousand years ago which is before we ever sinned. Then how could the blood of Jesus who died two thousand years ago wash our sins today?"

"Although Jesus was crucified and forgave my sins, yet we still sin again.

Then how could we still be clean?"

They're saying, "Aren't we still sinners?" People ask these questions because they have not fully understood the Word, and precise faith has not come upon them yet. When you exchange just a few words with people, you can distinguish whether that person is born again or not. You also get to see what the problem is in that person's life of faith.

The most difficult thing getting in the way of us receiving salvation is the misconceptions we often have. Churches, for the most part, teach people to repent when they sin, saying, "God, I'm a sinner. Forgive me. I committed adultery, I lied, I committed theft. Forgive me." Then they teach you that you must be good in order to go to heaven. They teach you that you must keep the Ten Commandments, go to church on Sundays, tithe, not sin, and keep the law to be able to go to heaven. If you go to a church like that, then your whole life, you will never be able to have a spiritual life and you will only suffer. Why is that? If you must be good, as many would say, then according to which standard or to what extent must you be good? You must adhere to the standards in the Word of the Bible, or to the standards of Jesus. But, you could never reach those standards. No matter how hard you try, because you cannot reach it, ultimately you become disappointed and your spiritual life corrupts.

Even the pastors who preach, "Everyone, we must be faithful. We must love one another. We must serve God with all our might!" are unable to do that. There has never been a person in all of mankind who has perfectly kept the Word of God in the Bible. That's why, from the point when you listen to that kind of sermon and start to live that kind of spiritual life, it becomes painful, miserable, and tiring. Such a person can never live a true spiritual life.

Then, what must we do? We must know ourselves. We must know what kind of human beings we are. What we must clearly know, when we sin and when we say, "God I stole, forgive me. I committed adultery, forgive me," that saying these things is not true repentance.

If you get leprosy, your eyebrows begin to fall off, your face becomes deformed, and your fingers begin to fall off. Then everyone, is your eyebrow falling off leprosy? No, it's not. The leprosy is the leprosy germs. Keeping the eyebrows from falling off is not treating the leprosy. Trying to keep the fingers from falling off, or trying to keep the face from being deformed will not solve the problem. You must get to the root; you must destroy the leprosy germs. When you get malaria or typhoid, the hospitals will draw blood from you. Those of you who have not been through this probably don't know. They draw quite a large amount of blood, and doctors take that blood to study it. They first find and remove the germs from the blood, and cultivate those germs. They create germ cultures and put them into various test tubes, and then they try many different kinds of medication for them. Of those, if they feed the patient the medication that was most effective in killing the germs, that person will be healed. That is why we should not try to just get rid of the symptoms, such as the fever or cough, when we are fighting against a sickness. Rather, we must target the core of the germ or the virus. The disease will continue on unless those germs and viruses are destroyed.

When a person is sick, they first remove his blood, and measure the level of white blood cells in his blood. In normal people, they have about 5,000 to 10,000 white blood cells per milliliter of blood. White blood cells fight against diseases, therefore the amount of white blood cells increases very rapidly when there are germs in the body. If you suffer from a chronic illness, white blood cells that are not completely developed will pick up their guns and try to fight. In such a situation people say, "Ah, the white blood cells have come out with their diapers on." If the germs in the body are destroyed to a healthy state, the white blood cell count returns to normal. Then we can say that the person is healed.

To treat a disease, one must destroy the germs. By trying to destroy the symptoms of the disease, for an entire person's life can never treat the disease. The disease of sin is exactly like this. When your heart becomes sick with the disease of sin, hatred arises, the heart to steal arises, a lustful heart arises, and an evil heart arises. Those are the symptoms of sin. Symptoms. That is why if we do not treat the cause of sin in our hearts, but only address the symptoms that appear on the outside saying, "I should not steal, I should not commit adultery, I should not commit murder…," our problem of sin will never be taken care of our whole lives. As long as there is sin inside of you, no matter how hard you try, you will sin again and again. I'm sure all of you have experienced this as you have lived your spiritual life. You have tried to not sin, right? But the harder you try you will only sin more and more.

True repentance is not talking about the outwardly things you have done such as stealing. It is to confess that inside your heart you are nothing but a cluster of sin, and to turn away from your own heart. Apostle Paul said in Romans chapter 7, that with his inward man he pleases to do the law of God, but that there is another law in his members, warring against the law of his mind, bringing him into captivity of the law of sin. He says the things that he would, he does not, and that which he hates, he does. So who is this that is making me do evil, when I want to do good? He said that it is not himself, but the sin that remains in him. It means that there is a sin dwelling in you. This sin stirs up the lust in you, it stirs up the heart to steal, and it stirs up the heart of arrogance. It is this sin that must be taken care of. Everyone, if you read the Bible deeply then you can recognize these things.

"Ah, so this is the type of person I am. It is Satan who has entered my heart and is leading me this way. Ah, just as he put it into the heart of Judas Iscariot to betray Jesus, Satan is putting such hearts inside of me." That is what we come to recognize. Then the heart to trust in yourself comes crumbling down. You become able to deny yourself.

Jesus said, "Whosoever will follow me," and what did he say after that? "Shall deny himself." Because the Satan inside of you always leads you to the thoughts that are opposite of God, you cannot become free from sin. I denied myself upon realizing this. I did not trust in myself. I decided not to live following my thoughts. I could feel that after I denied myself, the heart to believe in God entered me and led me towards faith.

Satan Has Blinded the Hearts of Men

Everyone, faith does not form in you, when the Word of God and your own thoughts are all mixed within you, causing you to be confused. If you deny yourself, then things such as the problems of sin and the ambitions of your flesh become powerless within you. Even now, the evil heart arises in me, ambitions arise in me, the lustful heart arises in me, and the deceitful heart arises within me. But I know that these hearts did not come from me, to begin with, but from Satan. I also know that if I follow that heart, I will be destroyed. When I face a certain task, many thoughts come to me. Every time that happens, I say, "If I follow that thought, I'll be destroyed; I shouldn't do that." Therefore, I do not follow that heart. That's why those thoughts arise within me, but they quickly become powerless. Because I believe the Word of God, the dirty hearts of Satan that work in me become powerless. I can see that God is leading me.

Everyone, if you learn the sin offering, then the problem of sin will not be a problem anymore. A person who does not know how to swim would be afraid of swimming across a river. But if you're a good swimmer, you would not worry, no matter how deep the river is. No matter how bottomless the water is, it's not a problem. If you could just float on the water, swim, and move forward, then what problem would the depth of the river be? You would be free from the depth. But people who do not know how to swim worry about the depth of the river.

If you know the sin offering, you are free from any and all sin. That is why I love the Bible; that is why I seek it. I read the Bible every day, study it, and search it. Especially in Hebrews, it talks very precisely about the sin offering. It is not difficult at all to learn about the sin offering.

In 2 Corinthians chapter 4 verse 3, *But if our Gospel be hid, it is hid to them that are lost...* In the next verse it says, *In whom the God of this world hath blinded the minds of them which believe not, lest the light of the glorious Gospel of Christ who is the image of God should shine unto them...*

When my daughter was in the first grade in elementary school, she used to really like dolls. Whenever we would pass by the doll shop, she would always bug me, saying, "Daddy, that doll is so pretty." Once, I was with my daughter and we passed in front of the Mito Theater to go to church, and we came near a doll shop that was by the theater.

That moment I thought, "What if my daughter bugs me, asking me to buy her a doll?" Immediately, I came up with a plan.

"Eunsook."

"Yes, Dad?"

"You see that bus over there? And you see that person on the bus?"

"What is it?"

"That bus right over there!"

"What is that?"

I did that as we passed by the doll shop. I had deceived my daughter, but she had no idea that she was being deceived.

Whenever we want to come near God, the devil puts opposing thoughts within us. Even while we're listening to a sermon like this and even when we are in church, the devil is at work. The devil even worked upon one of the twelve disciples personally selected by Jesus. This devil even tempted Jesus; so then, who would he not tempt?

While you're sitting here listening to the Word, when I talk about how I went to a funeral this morning, the devil distracts you and makes you think, "Oh yeah! I remember my father's funeral...," and he makes you fall into those thoughts. The devil makes you think about that until the end of the sermon to keep you from hearing the Word. Even when we read the Bible, the Bible clearly says that Jesus washed our sins as white as snow. But when you read that verse, the devil comes to your heart and speaks to you again. He makes you think, "Although Jesus washed my sins as white as snow, I'm still a sinner because I still sin. I have so many sins!" There are many people who suffer like this.

God said to Noah that He would destroy the world with water. Noah shouted out to the people, "Everyone! God said that wickedness of man has filled the earth and that He will destroy the earth with water!"

Then the devil put many thoughts into the hearts of people. He told them, "No, there's going to be no punishment." People believed in that and did not prepare the ark. That is how the devil works.

In 2 Corinthians chapter 4 verse 4 it says, "The god of this world...." Who is the god of this world? It is talking about the prince of the power of the air, who is Satan. It is telling us that Satan blinds the hearts of those who do not believe. Let's read 2 Corinthians chapter 4 verses 3 and 4 once again,

But if our Gospel be hid, it is hid to them that are lost, In whom the God of this world hath blinded the minds of them which believe not lest the light of the glorious Gospel of Christ who is the image of God should shine unto them.

The devil has blinded the hearts of those who do not believe so that the light of the Gospel of the glory of Christ cannot shine upon them.

The sin offering is not difficult, and the forgiveness of sins is not difficult.

But every time we listen to the Gospel, the devil inserts thoughts inside of us.

"No, but I still have sin."

Satan places those kinds of thoughts inside of you. When I preach the Gospel, some say, "Pastor, I understand everything that you're saying. I know that Jesus died for my sins, and I know that He forgave my sins, but I just cannot believe it."

Every time they say that, I reply, "Do you know why you're saying that you do not believe? You're listening to the devil who is telling you, 'I cannot believe this,' and you're just repeating that." We are so simple minded; the devil toys with us. We will be dragged around continually by the devil if we do not know the Bible. Do you also not believe in the thoughts that arise within you? If you believe your thoughts, the devil leads you to a path that is different from God's.

The Bible says that, when you pray, God will answer. But the devil puts a thought in you: "What if I pray, but it does not get answered?" When that thought arises you just believe it right away. You think, "Yes, it would be nice to obey the Word of God, but what if this leads me to fail?" The devil continues to blind you and confuse your thoughts.

The sin offering is not difficult. It's so easy. When you listen to it, all of you can understand it. But the devil puts thoughts in you to mix up your thoughts with the Word of God so that you will be confused. When these things do not become squared away in your heart, you lose assurance. However, the Bible is so easy, and so much fun.

Obtained Eternal Redemption At Once

Today we read about the priest. When the biblical scholars calculated the year that Moses received the two tablets of stone on Mount Sinai, we don't know how accurate this is, but it was the year 1491 B.C. It means that the law came to this earth approximately 1,500 years before Jesus was born. What did the children of Israel do for those 1,500 years? The sons of Aaron, who were priests from the tribe of Levi, would give sin offerings for the sins of the people.

This week we only talked about the sin offering for a common man as described in Leviticus chapter 4. Leviticus chapter 4 verse 1 talks about the sin offering given when a priest sins, the sin offering given when the congregation sins, the sin offering given when a ruler sins, and the sin offering given when a common person sins. These are recorded all in order. For 1,500 years, the priests, every day at the altar, killed sheep and cows and sprinkled their blood. The smoke from the altar where the offerings were burnt every day rose up like clouds, and the blood of sheep flowed from the altar like a river. How long did these offerings continue? They continued until Jesus died on the cross. Until Jesus was crucified on the cross, they killed sheep and cows, and gave offerings to receive the forgiveness of sins.

However, even the priests who give the offerings commit sin. That is why the priests had to first give the sin offering for the sins they had committed. If a priest commits sins, he must bring a bullock to give as the sin offering. The priest must first kill the bullock to have the sins that he committed washed away. Then, he could give the offering for the sins of the common people. If so, should Jesus have given an offering for His own sins before dieing on the cross to forgive our sins? No, because Jesus had never sinned once. This is the primary difference between the priests of Aaron, and Jesus. The second difference is that the offerings given by the priests of the Old Testament were given daily. Because those offerings only washed away the sins that were committed at that time, an offering had to be given every time a sin was committed. That was why people would sin and give offerings every day.

In the Bible, it appears simple because it just writes that the people killed cows to give offerings. However, killing a cow to give an offering is no easy task. Is it easy to kill a cow? You have to completely skin it. You must cut it into pieces. You must remove its intestines and wash them in water. You must take its blood, so on and so forth. They had to give these kinds of offerings every day because they sinned every day.

Jesus did not give an offering every day. The offerings given by the priests of the Old Testament washed away the sin for that moment, but the offering that Jesus gave washed away our sins forever. If Jesus, like the priests of the Old Testament, could not wash away our sins forever, He must go to the cross and die every time we sin. If that were the case, because the people of this world sin every day, even going up to the cross many times a second would not be sufficient. Jesus does not have to do that because He has fulfilled the eternal redemption. He completed the sin offering, once and for all. That is why we do not need to give the sin offering. If Jesus, like the priests of the Old Testament, gave the offering, then we would need to be giving more sin offerings. But the effect of the offering that Jesus gave is eternal because Jesus obtained eternal redemption, once and for all. That is why His blood, which was shed 2,000 years ago, is powerful even today. Whether 1,000 or 10,000 years pass, His blood will continue to be eternal.

What? You Don't Have Sin? Don't You Sin?

Many people are not content with the cross of Jesus, and they think that their sins remain even though Jesus was crucified. There are many people who beg, "Please forgive my sins!"

Some people say, "Pastor Park! How dare you arrogantly say that you have no sin! Does that make any sense? Aren't you a human, too?" I have often been cursed at by people who I don't know, and also, I've been called a heretic.

When my kids were young, there was this man who would call my house every evening. My wife and I would often not be home because we would be away at conferences. My children would answer those phone calls, and they would tremble in fear. One evening, I was home and the phone rang. When my son answered the phone, he was stunned, and said, "Dad! Dad, it's him!" and I answered the phone.

"This is Pastor Ock Soo Park."

"Hey you punk! You punk, heretic!" he said and he cursed at me.

I said to him, "I don't know who you are. A heretic can only be cursed. Do you think I want to be a heretic? I don't want to be a heretic. If you could explain to me why you are calling me a heretic, then I will change. Tell me, why I am a heretic?"

"What? You don't have sin? Don't you sin? Aren't you a human being like everybody else? Don't you commit sins?"

"I commit lots of sins. Yes, I do sin."

"Then how can you say that you have no sin?"

"I had many sins, but they were washed as white as snow by the blood of Jesus. It is not that I never sinned. I did have many sins, but they were perfectly washed though the blood of Jesus."

Then his voice calmed down, and he said, "Pastor, I'm sorry," and hung up the phone.

Once, this person wrote me a letter: "Dear Ock Soo Park, the heretic...."

I'm sorry. Even though I receive many letters a day, I'm unable to reply very often. I can only reply to so many letters. But to this person, I wrote a reply:

"Dear honorable sir,

Until today, many people have called me a heretic, but you are the only person to actually write me a letter about it. I cannot express everything to you in a letter. I would like to speak to you on the phone."

I wrote my phone number in the letter and I got a phone call a couple of days later. He started to argue with me.

"You say that you have no sin."

"Yes, that's right. I say that I have no sin."

"Don't you commit sins?"

"How could I not sin? I've committed many sins."

"Then how can you say that you have no sin?"

"I was washed whiter than snow through the blood of the cross of Jesus."

Then that person became very quiet. He said, "Pastor, I'm sorry. It was my misunderstanding," and he hung up the phone. With only a few words they could understand, but their thoughts were unable to reach that point. It is because Satan has blinded them.

Once, a journalist from the Daegu Daily newspaper came to me asking for an interview. I sat down with him and spoke with him. The first thing he asked me was, "Pastor, I've never been to church. I don't believe in Jesus, but Pastor, how are you different from the other churches of today?"

I said, "Well, it's difficult to explain in a few words, but..."

"Yes, go ahead."

"Have you ever heard that Jesus was crucified for our sins?"

"Yes, I've heard of that before."

"I say that my sins are washed away because Jesus died on the cross for my sins, whereas the pastors of the churches today say that Jesus died on the cross but they're still sinners. That is the difference."

When I said that, this journalist didn't understand. He said, "What do you mean? If Jesus died for our sins, it means we should have no sins."

"That's right."

"But they still call themselves sinners?"

"Yes, they do."

"Is that true?"

"Go and ask them yourself."

"Do they really do that?"

"I said go ahead and ask them yourself."

He could not believe me. He could not believe that most of the churches today say that they're sinners even though Jesus died for our sins. So I told him to go ahead and ask them himself. He wrote a big good article about me in the newspaper.

The next day, many church-goers tirelessly called him on the phone and six pastors came to him and said, "Why did you write an article about a heretic church in your newspaper?" and threw fits. So he could not attend to his duties all day long. This journalist answered them, "I met Pastor Ock Soo Park myself, and I wrote what I felt about him. It is my right to write the article in this way."

A few years ago, at the Chosun Monthly Magazine, I was featured in the "Person of the Month" article. A reporter named Hyo Jin Oh interviewed me and wrote the article. Upon running the article, so many people complained on the magazine website, that they had to shut it down. In the Central Monthly Magazine, an article of my interview ran in 2002 and 2003. The reporter who wrote those articles received so many phone calls, that it was unbearable. People would argue with him saying, "Why did you write such an article?"

He would tell them, "Have you met Pastor Ock Soo Park? I've met him myself, and I wrote what I felt from that meeting."

"But that man is a heretic!"

"Whether he's a heretic or not, all I did was write my impression for my readers."

People, even without knowing what's going on, just say whatever they want. One sister who comes to our church said that her older sister called her crying, telling her to stop coming to our church. She said, "If you go to that church you'll be in big trouble. It will destroy our family. Stop going to that church!"

"Sister, I don't know much about this church. I've only been to it twice, but it's been good. Why do you say that going to this church will destroy us? What's wrong with this church?"

"I don't know, but that is what my pastor said."

"Sister, I really like this church. When you clearly find out what's wrong with this church, then come and tell me. Then, I'll stop going." Even to today, she has not heard from her sister.

Christianity in Korea has corrupted. It has swayed far from the truth. It has become evil. That is why I preach this Gospel of redemption. The offering that man gives is lacking and flawed, but the offering that Jesus gives is without blemish. The offering that Jesus gave, made us holy so that the Holy Spirit of God will lack nothing in remaining within us. We have been made holy. Not through our effort or diligence, but through Jesus Christ. That is why I preach this Gospel. I hope that all of us will be able to preach this Gospel.

CHAPTER 11
The Completed Offering

*Now where remission of these is,
there is no more offering for sin.* (Hebrews 10:18)

Hallelujah, I praise the Lord. It says that where there is remission of these, there is no more offering for sin. Loving folks, this is what grace is. It's not by us doing something well or by our efforts, but it's by receiving it freely. This is the true meaning of redemption, and this is the grace of God.

The Completed Offering

Hello everyone, it's nice to see you. This is the last session. I feel like we just began, but it's already over. As I spoke with you, I was so joyful to see that God revealed the Word to us, and that you all changed after the Word entered into your hearts. I truly thank and praise God, who has given such a lacking person like me this precious calling. This is our 11th session, and I want to tell you about the completed offering.

We'll read from Hebrews chapter 10 verse 18.

By the which will we are sanctified through the offering of the body of Jesus Christ once for all. And every priest standeth daily ministering and offering oftentimes the same sacrifices, which can never take away sins; But this man, after he had offered one sacrifice for sins for ever, sat down on the right hand of God; from henceforth expecting till his enemies be made his footstool. For by one offering he hath perfected for ever them that are sanctified. Whereof the Holy Ghost also is a witness to us: for after that he had said before, This is the covenant that I will make with them after those days, saith the Lord, I will put my laws into their hearts, and in their minds will I write them; And their sins and iniquities will I remember no more. Now where remission of these is, there is no more offering for sin. (Hebrews 10:10-18)

How am I Supposed to Discipline My Older Nephew?

As we shared the Word together about the sin offering this week, I had the heart that the life of living with the forgiveness of sins through the sin offering is such a blessed one. When I look at myself, I have no conditions whatsoever to do the work of the Gospel. Yet, my life is so peaceful, blessed, and thankful, because, through the forgiveness of sins that I've received from Jesus Christ, God was able to pass unto me all of the grace that He gave to Jesus.

My son's father-in-law, who used to live in Brazil, had stage four lung cancer and was on the verge of death. I invited him to Korea, and had him take an anti-cancer medicine called Ddobyul, which is developed by Unhwa Biotech. I saw him take this medication for about one week, and then I left for a witnessing trip to Africa. When I came back from Africa, the health of my son's father-in-law's was much better. While the other people in the hospital were dying day by day, he was improving day by day. Hence, the other people in the hospital room would ask, "Elder, what medication are you taking?"

About a month after my son's father-in-law had started taking Ddobyul, my son and his wife were dispatched to the United States as missionaries. As a final farewell, my son's in-laws, my wife and I, my son and his wife, and a few other people went to a restaurant together for a meal. That night, I was so deeply touched. I thought that we should be talking about my daughter-in-law's father's death, my son and his wife leaving for America, how it might be her last time with her father, that they would be weeping and crying, and doing things like that. But that day, I was so happy to see how we were all rejoicing.

Many problems came upon me. They were certainly difficult problems. However, after I realized that my sins were forgiven through the sin offering, and after I became one with Jesus, no matter what the problem was, I often saw it change into a blessing and into grace.

My older brother passed away in 1983. My older brother's first child was a daughter, and his second child was a son. I still cannot forget how happy my brother was to have a son, but that son caused many problems and troubles. I remember the Thanksgiving holiday of 1983. I was in my hometown at the time, and my older brother told me, "Why don't we get in your car, go remove the weeds, and clean our parents' tomb?" I drove with my older brother in the car, and we went to our parents' tomb. However, my older brother just sat there, while the rest of us cleaned the tomb.

My older brother lived in the countryside, while the rest of us lived in different areas of the country. So it was always my older brother who would clean the tombs. This time, he looked very ill, so I told my older brother, "You don't look so well. Why don't you come visit me in Daegu? I would like to take you to a hospital and get you examined." At the time, I was living in Daegu. However, my older brother said something shocking to me:

"Hey, why would I want to go to a hospital? I wish I had cancer. I've been wanting to die since long ago. But if I committed suicide, then the people who live in the Seonsan area would say, 'Pil Joo Park? I heard that guy committed suicide!' And I didn't want to hear that. That's why I didn't kill myself. I have no rest in this world. Even though I raised my kids…" My older brother had thrown his eldest son away. "I wish that I was in the last stage of cancer right now. I wish that I would die!" he said. Because my older brother's troublemaking son caused so many problems, my older brother knew all of the police officers, police commissioners, prosecutors, and judges.

A few days after the Thanksgiving holiday, my older brother came to Daegu. It was stage three liver cancer. Afterwards, my older brother struggled with his sickness for 40 days and finally passed away. After he passed away, I couldn't think of anything but my older brother's eldest son. "My older brother's eldest son, my eldest nephew, how am I supposed to discipline him?" Whenever I would go visit our hometown, I would see him fighting with his father and asking for money. "If he comes to me and throws a fit, how would I ever handle him?" I thought. That was what I was worried about the most.

That was October. In the spring of that following year, I came to Seoul, and my nephew, who was recently discharged from the army, came to see me. "Uncle, I'm discharged from the army!" he said. As soon as I saw his face, I started having a headache.

"Oh boy, how am I supposed to handle him?" I thought. Then I said, "Oh, great. Come on in." I took my nephew to the Eastern Gate market, and bought him some pants and a jacket. Then I sent him to his hometown. Before sending him off, I told him, "Young Joon, when you go back home, make sure you go to church."

"Sure, I'll go." My nephew was discharged in May of 1984, and we were having our retreat in July. With the retreat ahead of us, I remembered my nephew and gave him a phone call.

"Young Joon, we're having a retreat at the Pine Fields Retreat Center. Why don't you come?"

Then, he quickly answered, "Yeah sure. I'll be there, Uncle." My nephew came to the retreat. I was very busy when he came to see me and told me, "Uncle, I don't have a tent. Give me a tent. If I don't get one, I'm just going to go home." Later on, I heard that he had gotten into a fight, and had completely broken the mouth of one of the older guys in his village. When his father was around and such things happened, his father would settle everything. But now that his father had passed away and was not there to handle it for him, Young Joon had to pay all of the bills and was barely released from the police station. From then on, the friends of that older person had made a plan to kill my nephew. He was in great danger, but he had nowhere to run to. Right then, I had called him and told him to come to the retreat. Thinking this was his chance, he ran away to the retreat. My nephew attended that summer retreat and received salvation.

My nephew changed so much after receiving salvation. Now, I can't find any image of my old nephew in him at all. He has become a pastor and is leading a big church. He also built an alternative school, and is teaching faith to many young students. When I see my nephew, I'm so touched.

I don't have any power as I live my life. But after Jesus came into me, anything I faced was no longer my task. Rather, it was Jesus' work. No matter what difficulties came to me, God changed them into blessings and into joy. God was with me, and whether a hundred or a thousand hardships came, He changed all of them into blessings. I can't express in words, how thankful I am for all of that love. I'm thankful to the Lord because, now, you too have received the forgiveness of sins and salvation. And I'm thankful that the life of living inside of Christ Jesus has begun. I'm so thankful when I think about how Jesus, who worked inside of me, will live and work inside of you. This is what I often say in my church: "Everyone, what fun do you have in this world without becoming a pastor?"

Today, I also met with many people and had counseling about faith. Someone from Daejeon came to see me today, who was so worried about his loving son. I had about an hour of counseling with him. As I listened to how he was so worried about his son, I was able to confidently speak with him because, in my heart, I felt that Jesus can take care of his son. "Many kids like him have been changed and renewed. This is not a big problem. This is not hard. It's not anything for you to worry about. It is all taken care of through Jesus," I said. Everyone, we have no idea how much of a blessing it is for us to live together with that Jesus.

Holiness Is in the Blood of Jesus

Everyone, this is our last session. So, we're speaking about Hebrews chapter 10 verse 10. I will read on, little by little, from verse 10. We'll first read verse 10:

By the which will we are sanctified through the offering of the body of Jesus Christ once for all.

I have an older sister, who one day told me, "You don't give sermons like a pastor. You give sermons like an ordinary person. Most of the pastors disguise their voices."

And so I thought, "Should I? Am I supposed to do that?" So once, I went to a conference and tried it. But I couldn't even do it, because after doing it for about ten minutes, my normal voice came out without me even realizing it. Then, before the next sermon, I really made up my mind to speak in a falsetto. I spoke for a long while, but I could neither remember what I had said nor what I was supposed to say next. Then I began to break out in cold sweat; it was so difficult. Back then, I was too young to know, but now I realize that holiness is not in the voice. Holiness is not in the voice, but in the blood of Jesus Christ.

It does not say, "by the which will we *will* be sanctified through the offering of the body of Jesus Christ, or we *might* be sanctified, or we *think* we'll be sanctified, or *perhaps* we're sanctified." It says, "We *are* sanctified." It has already been achieved. I don't need to be holy. I had been trying to become holy. I don't need to try to become that, because I'm sanctified. Not by my works, my efforts, labor, or zeal. But the moment Jesus Christ gave his body, all of this was achieved.

If so, then how are we to believe? When I say that Jesus Christ finished all things, there are people who reply, "If Jesus Christ was crucified for our sins, then does that mean it's okay to do nothing? We don't need to work hard? We don't need to keep the law? We don't need to pray? And is it okay to just wait for good luck to role in?" In the Bible, holiness is not in our actions, but in the blood of Jesus Christ. We have been sanctified through the sin offering that was fulfilled through Jesus shedding His blood.

Now, It's All Over for Us. Look at That Tomb!

I often talk about this story. A father and a son were traveling across the desert when they became lost. Because they were lost in the middle of the desert, they were thirsty and tired. They were passing each hour with great pain. However, while the father had hope in his heart, there was no hope in the heart of the son. Although they were walking the same path, the heart of the father was very different from the heart of the son.

The son was complaining the whole time, "Father, why did you get us lost? Now we're going to die. I'm so thirsty. I can't move. I'm so tired. I can't walk anymore." He just sat there complaining, but the father was different.

"Son, why would we die? We're not going to die. Didn't you see the sun rise this morning? Right now, we're clearly heading east. You listen to what I have to tell you. I've been through this desert many times. And I've gotten lost many times. The wind blows throughout the desert all the time, and the paths are always changing. But, do you know what I did every time I got lost? I just kept on walking east. Now, we have almost reached the eastern end of this desert. If we walk a little further, we will reach the eastern side. There, we'll be able to drink water and eat food. Let's walk a little further."

"Father, you're lying to me. That was what you said yesterday. We walked all day long, but there was no oasis. Now, we're going to die." What saddened the father's heart was not the fact that they were lost in the desert, nor was it because they were thirsty. It was saddening to him that his son was in despair and thinking that he would die. Nonetheless, the father kept on speaking to give the hope that was in his heart into the son.

"When you walk through the desert as long as we have, you're bound to see a mirage. I've seen such a thing many times. I've crossed this desert more than twenty times. And I've even worked as a guide to walk across the desert. If you walk through the desert a little further, do you know where we will be? There will be a village. There will be coconut trees and water. And that is where we will soon arrive." Because there was hope in the father's heart, even though they were lost, the father was completely unaffected. All he needed to do was keep walking. If they kept on walking, as the father said, they would soon arrive at a village and be able to drink water and eat food.

However, because there was no hope in the son's heart, but only despair, he was so tired. "I can't walk. I can't take one step further." The father wanted to put hope in the son, but the son didn't accept it. In this manner, the father was barely getting his son to move forward. Then, all of a sudden, the son screamed. "Father, look over there!" The father looked where the son was pointing, and there was a tomb. The son just sat down. "Now, it's all over. Look at that tomb. The person in that tomb must've been lost, just like us. And he must've died of thirst. We will die just like him, right Father? When we die, who will tell Mother about our death? How is she going to raise my younger siblings? What are we going to do, Father?"

The father took the son by the hand, patted him on the back and said, "Now we've made it! Suppose that dead person, as you said, was lost in the desert and died of thirst. Then do you think he dug his own tomb, went inside, died, and then buried himself? There must've been somebody to bury him. Son, the fact that there is a tomb here means we're near a village where people live. Now we are near the village. Now we will be able to drink water. Now our suffering is over." The son heard that and was strengthened.

"That's right, Father. What you're saying is true. We have come near the village. Let's go quickly," he said. The father and son encouraged each other and continued to walk. Then, just as the father had said, they soon arrived at the village.

We Testify of Christ Who Was Crucified

In this story, the conversation between the father and son is very similar to the conversation between us and God. Although it was difficult for the father, he continued to speak with his son, to put the hope in his heart that they would soon arrive at the village. But the son had his own thoughts and did not accept the words of his father. "Father, you're lying right? We're going to die. I'm thirsty. I cannot walk anymore." The conversation we have with God is exactly the same as this.

God tells us, "You are clean. You are righteous. All of your sins have been forgiven through the blood of the cross. You are truly holy." This is what He says.

But we say, "No. I'm a sinner. Father God, forgive my sins." It means that God's heart and our hearts are different.

God says, "No. You were sinners, but your sins were washed through Jesus dying on the cross. It was finished at the cross. Sin is all taken care of. Now you don't have sins anymore. You are holy. You are righteous." That is what God is continually telling us in order to give the righteousness, the holiness, and the peace to us.

But we say, "No God. I have my sins. I'm a sinner." That is what people say. It is exactly like the exchange of words between the father and son.

Faith is the son coming to know, realize, and accept the father's heart. Faith is to accept the heart of the person telling you something. Distrust is to not accept those words.

Let's find the place in the Bible. 1 Corinthians chapter 6 verse 11.

And such were some of you: but ye are washed, but ye are sanctified, but ye are justified in the name of the Lord Jesus, and by the Spirit of our God.

It says, *and such were some of you*. It means that there were people who had committed sin, done evil, been dirty, filthy, lustful, and deceitful, as mentioned in the previous verse. But immediately after, it says, "but ye are washed. But ye are sanctified. But ye are justified in the name of the Lord Jesus, and by the Spirit of our God." This is the heart of God.

Faith is when God speaks to you, and you say, "Oh that's right," and accept the heart of God as it is. That's what faith is. You say, "God, are my sins washed away? God, am I righteous? I had no idea, but I guess I'm righteous. Then I believe." Are you made righteous? Amen. That's what faith is.

Faith is not riding on a cloud going up and down in the sky; it's not feeling your body heat up; it's not receiving some kind of a fire.

Many years ago, I was invited as a speaker to a large crusade in Kenya, Africa called "Move On." I wasn't the main speaker, but I gave a two-hour sermon there. The other pastors who spoke there called upon people who had AIDS or other sicknesses to come to the front. About 700 people then came to the front. When the pastors went in front of them and yelled out, "Pokea!" and hit them in the front of their foreheads, who fell backwards. They were saying that is how they received the Holy Spirit. It drove me nuts. I could not believe it. So, I asked the people who were in charge of the operations.

"This is a bit strange. Jesus raises people up. Why do you make people fall down? In the Bible, Jesus raised up all the people who had fallen down. Why do you make people who are standing, fall down?" The people who were in charge of running the conference asked me to come to the front to pray for the people who had come forward, so I went near them. I wanted to pray for one person, in particular, but he started to fall backwards. Afraid that he might get a concussion, I held him up. Everyone, you're laughing, but that was really what happened. Later, I found out that there was someone in the back to hold them up.

They say that falling backwards means you're receiving the Holy Spirit. They want to believe in those kinds of signs because they don't know the Bible. Receiving the fire. Speaking in tongues. Prophesying.

But this is what Paul said:

For the Jews require a sign, and the Greeks seek after wisdom; But we preach Christ crucified, unto the Jews a stumbling block, and unto the Greeks foolishness; (1 Corinthians 1:22-23)

The only thing we can boast of is the cross of our Lord, Jesus Christ. Our good works, our efforts, and receiving the fire; all of that is completely useless. If you receive a lot of fire, it may make you warm, and you may save on some heating expenses. But you cannot consider that to be your spiritual life. We believe in the blood of Jesus Christ.

Faith is not following your own thoughts. Faith is accepting the fact that our sins are washed through His crucifixion on the cross, and nothing more. The son overflowed with joy, strength, and thankfulness once he accepted the hope was in his father's heart. In the same way, we're saying that we should accept the Word of God by faith.

For God So Loved The World, That He Gave His Only Begotten Son

In Hebrews chapter 10 verse 10, it says, *By the which will we are sanctified through the offering of the body of Jesus Christ once for all.*

I don't know why people are unable to believe these words. Once, I went on a home visit, and I told the person, "We are sanctified."

"What, Pastor? How can a man dare say that he is holy? Who is holy? We're not holy."

So, I explained, "Why did God send Jesus to this earth? He gave all of Jesus to us." Suppose I didn't have a car, but an elder gave me a car. If that elder gives me a car and says, 'Pastor, here is your key. You may drive it all you want.' Then, that car becomes mine. But suppose while I'm driving that car, it becomes dark. And I say to myself, 'Oh, it's dark. Should I turn on the headlights? Oh no, I shouldn't. The elder didn't give me the headlights. So, I shouldn't turn them on.' It would be so foolish for me to think that. 'Oh no, there's a child in front of me. I need to step on the brakes, but the elder didn't give me the brakes. Would it be okay for me to use the brakes without asking the elder?' I would be so foolish to say such a thing. Once the elder passes the keys to me, he has given every part of the car to me. I can turn on the radio in the car, turn the heater on, turn the air conditioner on, I can sit in the chair, and I can lie down on the chair, too. All of that car is mine. When God gave Jesus Christ to us, He gave all of Jesus to us."

What does John chapter 3 verse 16 say?

For God so loved the world, that he gave his only begotten Son... What does it say? *That he gave his begotten Son.* Amen? *For God so loved the world, that he gave his only begotten Son.*

He gave Jesus to us. He gave His only begotten son to us. If so, then does the righteousness of Jesus become yours or does the righteousness of Jesus not become yours? It becomes yours. No matter when I die, I can go to heaven. It is because I have the righteousness of Jesus. Jesus was born into this world, lived for 33 years, and never sinned even once. That righteousness has been given to us.

When we go to heaven, it is not through our greatness or our good deeds. Rather, we go with the righteousness that Jesus has achieved in His 33 years. Since our righteousness is filthy and broken, we throw our own righteousness away, and go forward with the righteousness of Jesus. Isn't there a hymn that talks about this?

When He shall come with trumpet sound,
O, may I then in Him be found.
Dressed in His righteousness alone,
Faultless to stand before the throne.
On Christ the solid Rock I stand
All other ground is sinking sand

It means that we stand on the righteousness of Jesus, who is the solid rock.

Everyone, look here. Here, we have two cups. There's a white cup, and there's a blue cup that is a little blemished. Let's call this white cup the righteousness of Jesus. Let's call this blemished, blue cup our righteousness, which is dirty and full of sin. Whether it's broken or not, let's just kick this blue cup away with our foot. God has given us this white cup, the righteousness of Jesus. With this, we are able to go to heaven. The angels in heaven will see this and say, "Hey, see Ock Soo Park over there? He has righteousness that is righteous and clean." It is because I threw away my righteousness, and brought forth the righteousness of Jesus.

Everyone, do not try to cleanse your own righteousness which has already been defiled with the sins of the world, evilness, adultery, and theft. Rather, call your righteousness filthy rags and throw it out. Go forward only with the righteousness of Jesus. Jesus' righteousness is my righteousness. Because I take the righteousness of Jesus and go to heaven, Jesus has taken my sins and died on the cross. We have exchanged each other's righteousness.

Everyone, going to heaven is not through our righteousness. It is taking forth the righteousness of Jesus Christ, who is the son of the living God. Then, we can respectfully enter in. The angels in heaven see this and say, "Hey Pastor Ock Soo Park, your righteousness is so clean. There is not one blemish. You have no sin. You are holy." Why? It is because I brought forth the righteousness of Jesus. On the other hand, because it was Jesus who took our sins, they would see Him and say, "Look, why does He have so many sins? He's dirty. He's filthy. He needs to be crucified on the cross." This is what they would say.

Everyone, you cannot go to heaven through your good deeds. You have committed evil, and you have many dirty sins. You must pass all of that over onto Jesus, and bring forth the holy righteousness of Jesus.

What does 1 Corinthians chapter 6 verse 11 say here?

And such were some of you: but ye are washed, but ye are sanctified, but ye are justified in the name of the Lord Jesus, and by the Spirit of our God.

God sees us and says, "You are washed. You are justified. You are sanctified." Why? It is because we come forward with the righteousness of Jesus.

Everything Is in the Blood of Christ

You need to have a ticket to ride an airplane. That is why there is so much information written on an airplane ticket. It has the name of the airline. If it's Korean Air, it says, "Korean Air." If it's Asiana, it says, "Asiana." If it's Delta, it says, "Delta." The information is recorded there as code. Then it has the flight number: Flight 001, flight 002, flight 011. Then it has the time: What month, what date, what time for departure. It also has your seat class: First class, second class, third class. Also written there is how much luggage you can bring: 30 kilograms, 40 kilograms, 50 kilograms. It also has the time period: The valid dates of that ticket, whether it's six months or one year. All of that is written on the airplane ticket, and the price is determined according to that information.

The airplane ticket is just like a receipt. Whether it is a first-class or a second-class ticket, it shows you all the cost necessary to take you to America has been paid. If I, at the designated time, show my ticket at the counter of that airline, then they must give me a seat. That is the responsibility of the airline. They also have to load as much cargo as is designated on that ticket. And during the flight, if I become thirsty, they have to give me something to drink. If I become hungry, they have to give me something to eat. They have to provide me all of the services for my comfort. All of that is included in my ticket.

There was a certain person who had purchased a ship ticket to go from England to the United States. However, because he did not have enough money for food, he went hungry during the whole trip. Later on, he found out that the ticket already included meals in the cost.

Everyone, everything is already inside of the blood that Jesus Christ shed on the cross. Washing away our sins is included in it. It also includes making us righteous. It also includes making us holy. Once you show your ticket, the airline will designate a seat for you, load your baggage, and give you food. In the same way, if we believe in the blood of Jesus, we gain all things. So, the only thing we have to do is believe in the blood of Christ.

Everyone, do they only let you on the plane if you wear nice clothes? Do they only let you on if you've had cosmetic surgery? Do you have to be handsome with a porcelain face to be let on a plane? No. Even if you're not so handsome, even if you're short, even if you wear shabby clothes, if you have a ticket, they let you on. Everything is included on the ticket. So, if I dress nicely and put foundation on my face, will they let me on the plane? They will not. They don't care about any of that; they only look for the ticket. The airline employees do not look to see whether that person is tall or short, or whether that person is good looking or not. They only look to see whether he has the ticket or not. A seat is given, food is given, and services are provided according to that ticket.

In the same way, when you go to heaven, God does not look at whether you are good or evil, or any of that. He only looks at one thing. He looks to see whether you have faith in your heart to believe in the blood of Jesus or not. Do you believe that your sins were forgiven on the cross or not? Do you still think you have sins or not? Do you believe that your sins were washed at the cross or not? That is the faith that God looks at. Within that faith, all conditions for us to go to heaven are met. That is why spiritual life is so easy.

The condition for us to go to heaven is not something that we must strive to meet. Jesus already met all of those conditions. Because we could not do it, Jesus did it. Yet, because we couldn't believe that and tried to do it ourselves, we say it is difficult.

The Sound of Bells Echoing When the High Priest Sprinkles the Blood on the Mercy Seat

Everyone, do you know what the tenth day of the seventh month is in Israel? It is the Day of Atonement. What sin is forgiven on the Day of Atonement? The sins that the children of Israel committed for one year are forgiven. All year long, the high priest Aaron enters into the holy place of God to work, but he does not enter into the most holy place. However, on the Day of Atonement, he enters into the most holy place. There, between the holy place and the most holy place is a veil. On the Day of Atonement, Aaron performs his duties at the holy place. Before entering the most holy place, he examines himself: whether the crown on his head is properly worn, whether the plates on his chest are properly set, whether he is wearing the ephod properly, and finally, whether he is holding the blood in his hand. He does this because Aaron himself is human and he, too, may commit crimes and do something wrong. If you open the veil and enter into the most holy place with sin, you are immediately put to death. Here, Aaron becomes extremely tense and nervous. Even Aaron's sons, Nadab and Abihu, died for giving offerings the wrong way. That's why Aaron takes a deep breath and examines himself before entering into the most holy place.

The garment that the priest wears is called the robe. At the end of the sleeves of the robe are bells made of pure gold. The sleeves of the robe are made long so that the priest can cover his eyes when he sees something unclean, and on the long sleeves are these bells. The high priest may die as he enters into the most holy place. The people outside incline their ears to the sound of the bells that come from the garment of the high priest. The sound of "ring-a-ling" echo from the clothes of the high priest Aaron.

"Ah, he must be changing the bread on the bread table right now. Right now, he is setting up the lamp on the candlestick. Right now he is lighting the incense." Each time he would move, the bells would make the "ring-a-ling" sound. They would hear the sound and that's how they could tell what he was doing.

Now, Aaron stands before the most holy place. If the people outside do not hear any more sound from the bells, they can tell that the high priest is standing before the most holy place. The high priest then settles himself down and examines himself. Finally, he checks to see if he has the blood in his hand.

Let's read Hebrews chapter 9 verse 7:

But into the second went the high priest alone once every year, not without blood, which he offered for himself, and for the errors of the people.

He enters into the most holy place, once a year, but it says that he does not enter without what? It says that he does not enter without blood. Why does he take the blood? As he takes the blood in his hands, he says, "God, I'm human. How could I be perfect? I'm lacking. But this calf died and shed its blood, didn't it? This blood was shed as the offering for all of my sins. This blood is proof that all of my sins were taken care of. May you look at this blood and permit me to enter into the most holy place." That's what he is doing here.

Everyone, if the high priest did not take the blood on the Day of Atonement when entering into the most holy place, but rather took with him a one-million-dollar check, what would happen? He would die. How about if he had taken a ten-million-dollar check, instead? He would die. Even if he takes a diamond as big as a fist and says, "God, please look upon this diamond and accept me," and opens the veil to enter in, then at that moment, "boom," he will fall over and die. How about if he brought over pretty roses? Yes, that too, is useless. If you bring forth the good that you have done; if you bring forth how you cared for the orphans and the widows; if you bring forth how you cared for the pitiful people, what would happen? You would still die. Everyone, how about if you brought the fact that you sold your house to build a chapel? You would die; you cannot enter without the blood.

Even though we may have myriads of sins that we've committed, our flaws, and our wrongdoings, it is the blood that forgives all of our sins. It is the blood that we must take. Now, the high priest opens the veil to the most holy place. People listen to the bells from the outside and begin to talk to one another saying, "That sounds like the opening of the veil." Then from the most holy place, they can hear the "ring-a-ling."

Where in the most holy place does the high priest go? He goes before the ark of the covenant. The mercy seat is on top of the ark. He dips his finger into the blood that he brought and sprinkles it upon the mercy seat. The moment the blood is sprinkled onto the mercy seat, the sin is forgiven. However, the sound that the bells make when the blood is sprinkled onto the mercy seat is different from the usual sound. Usually, the bells just make a "ring-a-ling" sound, but when the blood is being sprinkled onto the mercy seat, it is on the tip of the finger, and therefore makes a "ring-a-ling-a-ling-a-ling," sound—a much wilder ringing sound. When that sound is heard from the outside, they say, "It is done! The sin offering is finished. Our sins are washed clean!" Therefore, the sound of the bells is the Gospel.

Once the bells ring, sounding, "ring-a-ling-a-ling-a-ling," it means that our sins are all forgiven. The people cannot see what the high priest is doing inside of the tabernacle. All they can do is listen for the sound of the bells. When they just hear the ring-a-ling of the bells, and at the end, when they hear the wild, "ring-a-ling-a-ling-a-ling," they come to realize, "Ah, the blood has been sprinkled onto the mercy seat." Because the blood has been sprinkled onto the mercy seat, they can say, "Now my sins have been taken care of. My sins are all washed away. I'm so joyful."

Everyone, do you know what you're all doing right now? Just as the Israelites outside of the tabernacle are inclining their ears to the sound of the bells of the high priest, who has entered into the holy place, you are now inclining your ears to the Word that is being preached right now. What are you listening for? You are listening for the Word of the Bible that says your sins have been washed clean. This is what the Gospel is. "Ah, my sins are all washed. Amen! Hallelujah!" That's what true faith is.

Everyone, faith is not a tale, like the *Arabian Nights*, where you can walk around the skies and jump from cloud to cloud. Having a divine experience, falling over, or foaming at the mouth, isn't faith. How can your body trembling and shaking be receiving the Holy Spirit? Because the Holy Spirit is the spirit of Jesus, one should become like Jesus when he receives the Holy Spirit. But when did Jesus shake and tremble? I guess nowadays, the Holy Spirit that people receive is a bit strange. And I heard that at prayer houses, people are taught how to speak in tongues. "Alleluia, Alleluia, Alleluia…" And as they do that, if they start saying something strange, they call that receiving the Holy Spirit.

All you have to do is simply accept in your hearts that your sins have been forgiven. Amen? All you need to do is listen to the sound of the Gospel. We have not entered into the most holy place. We cannot see what the high priest Aaron did. The only thing we can hear is the sound of those bells.

People heard the wild sound that the bells made when the high priest Aaron sprinkled the blood onto the mercy seat, and said, "Ah, the blood has been sprinkled. My sins must be forgiven because the blood has been sprinkled onto the mercy seat." That's how they were able to believe. Amen? Is it difficult to believe this?

Pastor, How Can You Call that Sin? I'm the One Who Has Many Sins!

Once, I had a conference in Los Angeles. After the conference, all the people had gone home. As I was exiting the conference hall in the back, I saw a certain lady sitting and leaning against the wall, appearing very weak. I was going to just pass her by, but I decided to speak to her. "Hello. How are you?" I asked. That lady lifted her head, looked at me and, since I was the main speaker, answered me.

"Yes, Pastor?"

I went close to her and asked, "Are you satisfied with your spiritual life?"

"Pastor, I'm exhausted. I have reached my limits," she replied. I really love to hear those kinds of words because I have so much to say to such a person. Why would you get exhausted when you live spiritual life? You get exhausted when you do it. If God did it, would you get exhausted? It's tiring if you do it. If the Lord does it, why would it be so tiring? It's tiring because you try to take care of your sins, but it's so easy when the Lord takes care of them.

Right now, our mission is very short on pastors. We have many churches and there are many countries where missionaries need to be sent to, including places in Africa. There are so many places asking us to send missionaries. At present, we have established the Mahanaim Bible College in Africa and are doing many things there. However, we are so short on people. That's why, in the future, we are planning on recruiting pastors. We want to put them through a short training period and work together with them.

In the churches throughout Korea, there are so many pastors, so this is the work we are planning to do. The pastors will rejoice so much to be here because, until now, things have been very difficult and tiring for them as they have been trying to live their spiritual lives. They have to go on home visits. They have to do early morning service. They have to go out witnessing. But here, it's so easy. There is no work for us to do; God does it all.

One time, I met the chairman of a company. He was an elder; and I went to go witness to him. So, first, I made an appointment to meet him. Before our meeting, I asked his daughter-in-law things that I should know before meeting him. She said, "Pastor, recently another pastor visited my father-in-law and told him that he was a sinner. My father-in-law was infuriated and said, 'Pastor, did you ever see me sin? What sin do I have that you call me a sinner?' And he became all upset." She told me that.

After hearing that, as I went to go meet this chairman, I thought, "I'm going over to tell him about the forgiveness of sins, but you have to be sinner to be able to hear the words about the forgiveness of sins. But if he does not see that he is a sinner, what am I going to talk to him about?" Thinking that, I didn't know how to go about this. When I arrived at his company, I gave him my testimony. "I've been going to church since I was very young. But I committed many sins."

"Wait a minute. What sin did you commit, Pastor?" he asked.

"When I was young, I stole apples from my neighbors' houses. I also stole their peanuts, and the persimmons they would lay out to dry. I would steal and eat them, and steal other things, too. I committed many of those kinds of sins."

He looked at me and started yelling, "Pastor, how do you call that sin? I'm the one who has many sins!" I was completely shocked.

"I was a platoon leader during the Korean War. We were battling against the Chinese communist soldiers. I killed many of the Chinese communist soldiers, but through my mistakes, many of my men died as well." This elderly man had been suffering for decades from the guilt that, through his mistakes, many of his subordinates died while he served as their platoon leader during the Korean War.

I become energized when I hear these kinds of things because it makes me want to talk about the sin offering. Don't you think so? Why don't you try this as well? When I see someone who is crying because of sin, I think in my heart, "I want to tell them about this. And I want to tell them about the sin offering from the Old Testament, the words of the Gospel from the book of Isaiah…." All of you will feel that way, too. That day, he received the forgiveness of sins and rejoiced so much. Let me ask you: Is it Pastor Ock Soo Park who did this work? The Lord did it!

Recently, I met a demon-possessed person. He lived doing whatever the demon inside of him told him to do. He said that he did not have any discomforts and was fine with that. So I told him, "Sir, when spies recruit people, they first spend time trying to win that person over and get him on their side. During that period of time, they allow him to do whatever he wants. At that time, it's easy and comfortable. When that is over, the training begins. Afterwards, he is put to use. That's when the problems start. Satan, as well, treats us very well when he is recruiting us." He was so shocked. That day, he heard the Gospel and received salvation. It was not I who was doing this, but God. That's why witnessing is so exciting.

Everyone, what fun do you have in the world without becoming a pastor? You work all day and night and search for joy by visiting Mt. Seorak? I heard that people from Seoul drive for five or six hours with heavy traffic on the freeway, just to go to a mountain, use an outdoor burner, roast their meat, and then come back down from the mountain. That's it. But I cannot say how joyful I am to be a pastor and preach the Gospel to another person and see that person receive salvation. Even before I go to heaven, that alone is a reward enough. I'm so happy. I'm so joyful.

There Is No More Offering for Sin

Loving folks, Hebrews chapter 10 verse 10 tells us,

By the which will we are sanctified through the offering of the body of Jesus Christ once for all.

Everyone, are you holy? Raise your hand if you're holy. Hallelujah, Amen!

A long time ago, when I used to attend a Presbyterian church, I said that I was holy because I received the forgiveness of sins. One friend replied to me like this, "That punk Ock Soo Park. He cracks me up. I know him. He says that he has no sin?"

He and I used to commit sins together. He knew that we had gone around sinning together, but he did not know how I had been sanctified. That was why he could only say what he did.

Everyone, there is a time to sin and a time for forgiveness. Also, there's a time to do evil and a time to have those evil things washed. If they are washed, it is the same as having never done them. I'm not saying that I did not sin, but what I'm saying is that I am washed, through the blood of Christ, even whiter than the snow. These are not my words, but this is something the Bible testifies of. The Word of God testifies this:

And every priest standeth daily ministering and offering oftentimes the same sacrifices, which can never take away sins: (Hebrews 10:11)

These are words about the offerings given during the Old Testament. The sons of Aaron, of the tribe of Levi, gave offerings every day in the Old Testament. It was because the people sinned every day. That is why, with this offering, sin cannot be washed away forever.

Verse 12:

But this man, after he had offered one sacrifice for sins forever, sat down on the right hand of God;

The offering that Jesus gave is different from the offering that man gives. The offering that the priest gave in the Old Testament washed away their sins for that moment, but the one offering of Jesus lacks nothing to wash all of our sins away forever. No more offering is necessary. One offering completely finished it.

From henceforth expecting till his enemies be made his footstool. For by one offering he hath perfected for ever them that are sanctified. (Hebrews 10:13-14)

What just happened? It says that He has perfected forever.

For by one offering he hath perfected for ever them that are sanctified.

It means that the Lord has perfected you. If it says that He has done it, has He done it? Amen? Everyone, are you perfect? You are perfect! Not because you did not sin, but because the Lord has perfected you. Believe it.

I'm sorry to say this, but if God makes all of you into pigs, then all of you will become pigs. If He makes all of you into cows, then all of you will become cows. You will not be here, but you will go around saying, "Moo!" God made you human, so you are human. Likewise, if God makes us clean, then we become clean. If God makes us righteous, then we become righteous. If Good makes us holy, then we become holy. Faith is not looking at yourself, but rather looking up to God. Hallelujah, I praise the Lord!

Whereof the Holy Ghost also is a witness to us: for after that he had said before, This is the covenant that I will make with them after those days, saith the Lord, I will put my laws into their hearts, and in their minds will I write them; And their sins and iniquities will I remember no more. (Hebrews 10:15-17)

Hallelujah! Does God remember your sins? Just as data is erased from a computer, God has wiped out your sins from His memory. They have been blotted out by the blood of Jesus.

Now where remission of these is, there is no more offering for sin. (Hebrews 10:18)

Hallelujah, praise the Lord! For these sins are forgiven. It says that, *Where remission of these is, there is no more offering for sin.* Loving folks, that's what grace is. It's not by us doing something well or trying hard. It is something we have gained freely. This is the true meaning of redemption. This is the grace of God.

Everyone, my whole life all I did was terrible things, but now I have been made holy. It's not because I did good or was kind, but because Jesus washed me with His blood. Because Jesus made me good, the perfect goodness is now achieved in me. I hope that you will believe that God has achieved this for you also.

Church Directory (North America)

EAST COAST

Good News New York Church
718-878-4246
300 Nassau Rd., Huntington, NY 11743

Good News Manhattan Church
212-695-1294
268 West 44th St. 5th Floor, New York, NY 10036

Good News Bronx Church
646-339-6432
685 Morris Park Avenue 2nd floor, NY 10462

Good News Brooklyn NY Church
917-526-7498
765 43rd St. 1st FL, Brooklyn, NY 11232

Good News Flushing Chinese Church
631-535-1169
134-24 Cherry Ave., Flushing, NY 11355

Good News Atlanta Church
404-966-6352
11000 Rogers Circle, Johns Creek, GA 30097

Good News Atlanta Spanish Church
678-387-9271
2635 Fairlane Drive, 2nd FL, Doraville, GA 30340

Good News Philadelphia Church
215-379-0501
305 Township Line Road, Elkins Park, PA 19027

Good News Chicago Church
847-329-0237
4825 W. Jarlath St., Lincolnwood, IL 60712

Good News Washington Church
703-309-7132
5044 Portsmouth Rd., Fairfax, VA 22032

Good News Memphis Church
901-206-7891
4162 Owen Rd., Memphis, TN 38122

Good News Minneapolis Church
612-354-3909
3000 West Broadway Ave., Minneapolis, MN 55411

Good News Orlando Church
407-456-0470
1120 Arden St., Longwood, FL 32750

Good News New Jersey Church
201-406-4677
1075 Queen Anne Road, Teaneck, NJ 07666

Good News Detroit Church
248-971-4151
1181 Harding Ave., Rochester Hills, MI 48307

Good News Indianapolis Church
317-919-5640
383 S. Emerson Ave., Indianapolis, IN 46219

Good News Miami Church
786-247-2308
331 NW 65th Way, Hollywood, FL 33024

Good News New Orleans Church
504-432-6000
3205 Cherry St., New Orleans, LA 70118

Good News Jacksonville Church
904-800-7890
3850 Beach Blvd., Jacksonville, FL 32207

Good News Boston Church
617-943-9739
4 Church St. #8, Malden, MA 02148

Good News Charlotte Church
704-500-6063
8731 Green Ivy Lane, Charlotte, NC 28217

Good News Fort Wayne Church
260-797-3412
3316 S. Calhoun St., Fort Wayne, IN 46807

Good News Maryland Chinese Church
301-250-1138
85 Orchard Dr., Gaithersburg, MD 20878

Good News Nashville Spanish Church
615-927-8980
120 Arbor Knoll Blvd., Antioch, TN 37013

WEST COAST

Good News Central Church
213-386-0097
3500 W. 1st St., Los Angeles, CA 90004

Church Directory (North America)

Good News Tacoma Church
253-582-3599
10103 South Tacoma Way, Lakewood, WA 98499

Good News Albuquerque Church
505-301-7167
3001 Cuervo Dr., N.E. Albuquerque, NM 87110

Good News Dallas First Church
972-272-4724
4502 Lawler Rd., Garland, TX 75042

Good News San Jose Church
408-893-2267
1548 Curtner Ave., San Jose, CA 95125

Good News Las Vegas Church
702-248-0572
2880 Red Rock St., Las Vegas, NV 89146

Good News Salt Lake Church
801-656-5299
353 Park Creeke LN #B, Salt Lake City, UT 84115

Good News O.C. Baptist Church
714-226-0595
3330 W. Lincoln Ave., Anaheim, CA 92801

Good News Anchorage Church
907-258-9987
1020 W. Fireweed Lane, Anchorage, AK 99503

Good News El Paso Church
915-478-3576
8001 Magnetic Street, El Paso, TX 79904

Good News Portland Church
971-300-1127
6225 S.W. Dale Ave., Beaverton, OR 97008

Good News San Antonio Church
210-315-0346
405 Walton Ave., San Antonio, TX 78225

Good News San Diego Church
619-559-6287
4920 Ocean View Blvd. #3, San Diego, CA 92113

Good News Denver Church
720-308-3442
9825 E. Girard Ave. #3W-233, Denver, CO 80231

Good News Kansas Church
816-210-0351
1301 E 100th TER, Kansas City, MO 64131

Good News Hawaii Church
808-679-2800
1219 Keeaumoku St., Suite 400, Honolulu, HI 96814

Good News Houston Church
713-498-1980
6534 Rolla St., Houston, TX 77055

Good News Phoenix Church
480-273-2199
9001 West ELM St. #5, Phoenix, AZ 85037

Good News Sacramento Church
916-996-4655
7136 Fair Oaks Blvd., Carmichael, CA 95608

Good News Oklahoma Church
405-535-9553
5316 Huddleston Drive, Oklahoma City, OK 73135

CANADA & CARIBBEAN

Good News Vancouver Church
1-778-881-5508
9930 Lyndhurst St., Burnaby, BC V3J 1E9, Canada

Good News Ottawa Church
1-647-770-3379
275 Rue Laramée, Gatineau, QC J8Y 3A1, Canada

Good News Toronto Church
1-416-321-2004
70 Mcgriskin Rd., Toronto, ON M1S 4S5, Canada

Good News Jamaica Church
1-876-318-0189
63b Deanery Road, Kingston 3, Jamaica W.I.

Good News Dominican Republic Church
1-809-350-1429
Calle 26 #2, Valle Verde 1, Santiago, La Republica Dominicana

Good News Haiti Church
509-70-8253-2511
Rue Jeremie #7 bis Delmas 33, Port-au-Prince, Haiti

EXPERIENCE A HEART BREAKTHROUGH

Introducing a *groundbreaking* book that identifies and resolves the issues that affect our *hearts*

Navigating the Heart: Who is Dragging You?

BY PASTOR OCK SOO PARK

Navigating the Heart: Who is Dragging You? is a groundbreaking publication in self-development that lights the path toward peace and reconciliation by organizing the core issues of the heart.

With over 50 years international experience in spiritual counseling and assessment, Pastor Ock Soo Park utilizes real-life case studies to formulate insights into the importance of humility, opening up, and connecting to the hearts of others.

Navigating the Heart: Who is Dragging You? will not only free you from negative thoughts, but give you the foundation for a truly beautiful life.

NOW AVAILABLE AT
AMAZON.COM
or at your local Good News Church

Paperback and eBook download available
Search our title at TatePublishing.com/bookstore